A - E
LB

Palgrave Studies in Languages at War

Series Editors
Hilary Footitt
Department of Modern Languages and
European Studies
University of Reading
Reading, UK

Michael Kelly
Department of Modern Languages
University of Southampton
Southampton, Hampshire, UK

Languages play a crucial role in war, conflict and peacemaking: in intelligence gathering and evaluation, pre-deployment preparations, operations on the ground, regime-change, and supporting refugees and displaced persons. In the politics of war, languages have a dual impact: a public policy dimension, setting frameworks and expectations; and the lived experience of those 'on the ground', working with and meeting speakers of other languages.

This series intends to bring together books which deal with the role of languages in situations of conflict, including war, civil war, occupation, peace-keeping, peace-enforcement and humanitarian action in war zones. It will offer an interdisciplinary approach, drawing on applied linguistics, sociolinguistics, translation studies, intercultural communication, history, politics, international relations and cultural studies. Books in the series will explore specific conflict situations across a range of times and places, and specific language-related roles and activities, examining three contexts: languages and the military, meeting the other in war and peacemaking, and interpreting/translating in war.

More information about this series at
http://www.palgrave.com/gp/series/14615

Amanda Laugesen • Richard Gehrmann
Editors

Communication, Interpreting and Language in Wartime

Historical and Contemporary Perspectives

Editors
Amanda Laugesen
Australian National Dictionary Centre
Australian National University
Canberra, ACT, Australia

Richard Gehrmann
School of Humanities and Communication
University of Southern Queensland
Toowoomba, QLD, Australia

Palgrave Studies in Languages at War
ISBN 978-3-030-27036-0   ISBN 978-3-030-27037-7   (eBook)
https://doi.org/10.1007/978-3-030-27037-7

© The Editor(s) (if applicable) and The Author(s) 2020
This work is subject to copyright. All rights are solely and exclusively licensed by the Publisher, whether the whole or part of the material is concerned, specifically the rights of translation, reprinting, reuse of illustrations, recitation, broadcasting, reproduction on microfilms or in any other physical way, and transmission or information storage and retrieval, electronic adaptation, computer software, or by similar or dissimilar methodology now known or hereafter developed.
The use of general descriptive names, registered names, trademarks, service marks, etc. in this publication does not imply, even in the absence of a specific statement, that such names are exempt from the relevant protective laws and regulations and therefore free for general use.
The publisher, the authors and the editors are safe to assume that the advice and information in this book are believed to be true and accurate at the date of publication. Neither the publisher nor the authors or the editors give a warranty, express or implied, with respect to the material contained herein or for any errors or omissions that may have been made. The publisher remains neutral with regard to jurisdictional claims in published maps and institutional affiliations.

Cover illustration: guvendemir/ Getty Images

This Palgrave Macmillan imprint is published by the registered company Springer Nature Switzerland AG.
The registered company address is: Gewerbestrasse 11, 6330 Cham, Switzerland

Acknowledgements

This volume is a product of the symposium *Language in Times of War and Conflict*, held at the Australian National University in November 2017. We would like to thank all of the participants and attendees for their support. Also, we would also like to acknowledge and thank the College of Arts and Social Sciences, which provided a small grant to support the symposium. Julia Robinson provided valuable support for the smooth running of the symposium.

We are grateful to Cathy Scott, Alice Green, and the Palgrave Studies in Languages in War series editors for their support of this volume, as well as the anonymous reviewers.

Phoebe Garrett of the Australian National Dictionary Centre assisted us in the preparation of the manuscript and we would particularly like to give her our thanks. Her help has been invaluable.

Contents

Section I Introduction 1

Introduction: Understanding Communication, Interpreting, and Language in Wartime 3
Amanda Laugesen and Richard Gehrmann

Section II Experiences of Cross-Cultural Communication in Wartime 23

Cross-Cultural Communication and the Experiences of Australian Soldiers During the First World War 25
Amanda Laugesen

Unfamiliar Allies: Australian Cross-Cultural Communication in Afghanistan and Iraq During the War on Terror 45
Richard Gehrmann

Section III Strategies of Communication and Language Teaching 71

The Implications of War for the Teaching of Japanese Language in Australian Universities, 1917–1945 73
Jennifer Joan Baldwin

Effectiveness of Intensive Courses in Teaching War Zone Languages 89
Yavar Dehghani

The Challenge of Strategic Communication in Multinational Military Operations: Approaches by the United States and Germany in the ISAF 109
Jasmin Gabel

Section IV Experiences of Interpreters in Wartime and After 129

'Rediscovering Homeland': Russian Interpreters in the Wehrmacht, 1941–1943 131
Oleg Beyda

Interpreters at Australia's War-Crimes Trials, 1945–1951: From 'Ready-Mades' to 'Happenchancers' 153
Georgina Fitzpatrick

Interpreting the 'Language of War' in War-Crimes Trials 171
Ludmila Stern

Working with Australian Defence Force Interpreters in Timor
1999 and Aceh 2005: Reflections Drawn from Personal
Experience 207
Matt Grant

Risk Perception and Its Management: Lessons from Iraqi
Linguistic Mediators for the Australian Defence Force in the
Iraq War (2003–2009) 223
Ali Albakaa

Section V   Conclusion 253

Conclusion: Cross-Cultural Communication and Language in
Wartime: Reflections and Future Directions 255
Richard Gehrmann and Amanda Laugesen

Index 267

Notes on Contributors

Ali Albakaa is a former interpreter and translator in Iraq armed conflict. He is a PhD candidate in Linguistics and Applied Linguistics at the School of Languages, Literatures, Cultures, and Linguistics at Monash University. He has worked as a contracted interpreter with the Australian Defence Force (ADF) during the Second Gulf War in Iraq in 2003, as well as other foreign military agencies on the ground in Iraq. He is an accredited and practising interpreter (Arabic-English) in Australia. His fields of interest are military linguistic mediation studies in armed conflict, applied linguistics, systemic functional grammar, political conversation analysis, creative writing, and politics and social media analytics.

Jennifer Joan Baldwin is a researcher at the University of Melbourne in the School of Historical and Philosophical Studies and Languages and Linguistics and the Melbourne Graduate School of Education. After extensive experience in tertiary admissions and careers counselling, she completed a Masters of Applied Linguistics at Monash University and a PhD at the University of Melbourne. Her book *Languages Other than English in Australian Higher Education* was published in February 2019. She is researching the beginnings of Italian language teaching and the legacy of a University of Melbourne alumna and benefactor. She is particularly interested in the history of Australian tertiary education.

Oleg Beyda completed his PhD in History at the University of New South Wales, Canberra, in 2019. Beyda's thesis concerned White Russian émigrés who fought in the Wehrmacht on the German-Soviet front. His recent publications include two chapters on French and Soviet collaboration with the German side in D. Stahel (ed.), *Joining Hitler's Crusade: European Nations and the Invasion of the Soviet Union, 1941*, and the annotated memoirs of an émigré who served in the Spanish 'Blue Division', *Un ruso blanco en la División Azul. Memorias de Vladimir I. Kovalevski (1941)* (2019).

Yavar Dehghani is a language manager, self-published author, linguist, and lecturer in Iranian languages, including Persian (Farsi & Dari) and Pashto, and Turkic languages, including Azeri and Turkish. His PhD thesis was on comparative grammar of English, Persian, and Turkish Yavar at LaTrobe University in Melbourne. Yavar has been a lecturer in Persian Linguistics, Persian as a Second Language, and English as a Second Language for several years in universities. He has written books on grammar, phrasebooks, and dictionaries (see www.yadehghani.com). Yavar is Head of Foreign Languages (European, Middle Eastern, Chinese, Korean, and Japanese languages) at the Defence School of Languages in Melbourne.

Georgina Fitzpatrick is an associate at the School of Historical and Philosophical Studies, University of Melbourne, working on aspects of historical war-crimes trials. She was the lead author (with Tim McCormack and Narrelle Morris) of *Australia's War Crimes Trials, 1945–51* (2016), which was shortlisted for the Premier of NSW's History Awards 2017 in the Australian History category. She has been a research fellow (historian) based firstly at the Australian War Memorial (2009–2011) and then at the Asia-Pacific Centre for Military Law (2012), partners with Defence Legal in an Australian Research Council (ARC) Linkage project entitled '*Australia's Post-World War II Crimes Trials of the Japanese: A Systematic and Comprehensive Law Reports Series*'.

Jasmin Gabel received her MA in Intercultural Communication from the Adam-Mickiewicz University Poznan and her MA in Language,

Culture, and Communication from the European University Viadrina Frankfurt (Oder). Jasmin has also been actively involved with the Berlin-based grass-roots think-tank Polis 180 e.V., which focuses on foreign and security politics. She co-authored a policy paper on the relationship between Germany, Turkey, and the United States within the NATO mission "Inherent Resolve."

Richard Gehrmann is a senior lecturer at the University of Southern Queensland, where he teaches History and International Relations. With Jessica Gildersleeve, he is the editor of *Memory and the Wars on Terror: Australian and British Perspectives* (2017). His recent work on war and society has been published in *Peace Review, Popular Entertainment Studies,* and *Australian Journal of Jewish Studies* and in the edited collections *Rendering the Unspeakable Past: Legacies of Violence in Modern Australia* (2016), *Trauma and Public Memory* (2015), and *Fashion and War in Popular Culture* (2014). He served in Iraq in 2006–07 and in Afghanistan in 2008–09 as an Australian Army Reservist, and is researching Australian experiences of the wars in Iraq and Afghanistan.

Matt Grant served as a public relations officer with the Australian Army between 1996 and 2006. He was deployed to Timor-Leste, Bougainville, Indonesia, Iraq, and Afghanistan during this period as a Military Camera Team leader and as the senior public affairs officer responsible for whole of government communications. A former newspaper and television journalist who has held senior communication positions in both government and commercial sectors, he is Lecturer in Public Relations at the University of Southern Queensland.

Amanda Laugesen is an associate professor and director of the Australian National Dictionary Centre at the Australian National University. She is a historian and lexicographer, and has written widely in the areas of book and publishing history, the social and cultural history of war, and the history of Australian English. She is the author of a number of books, including most recently *Furphies and Whizz-bangs: Anzac Slang from the Great War* (2015) and *Taking Books to the World: American Publishers and the Cultural Cold War* (2017). She is also manager and chief editor of the Australian National Dictionary project.

Ludmila Stern is Professor of Interpreting at University of New South Wales, Sydney, and the founder of the Master of Interpreting and Translation, for which she was awarded the Dean's and the Vice-Chancellor's Excellence Awards. Her research covers interpreting in war-crimes trials in domestic and international courts. Her projects include *From the Nuremberg Trials to the International Criminal Court. Interpreting in War Crimes Prosecutions* and *Communication Between Judicial Officers and Court Interpreters: Implications for Access to Justice*. Her historical research examines Western intellectuals' involvement with the Stalinist USSR in the interwar period.

List of Tables

The Challenge of Strategic Communication in Multinational Military Operations: Approaches by the United States and Germany in the ISAF

Table 1	Topical categories of press releases	120
Table 2	Thematic frames in press releases	121
Table 3	Position frames in press releases	122
Table 4	All frames used in press releases	123

Section I

Introduction

Section I

Introduction: Understanding Communication, Interpreting, and Language in Wartime

Amanda Laugesen and Richard Gehrmann

Wars inevitably bring together speakers of different languages, and successful communication can be vital to the effective prosecution of war. Yet the linguistic and communicative dimensions of war remain understudied, especially with respect to particular wars and particular national narratives of war. Scholars such as Hilary Footitt and Julian Walker have asserted that wars are multi-lingual environments, and must be understood as such.[1] As Footitt elsewhere argues, languages 'are surely an intrinsic part of th[e] materiality and embodiment of war.'[2]

Inspired by such work, in late 2017, a symposium was held at the Australian National University on the theme of 'Language in times of war

A. Laugesen (✉)
Australian National Dictionary Centre, Australian National University, Canberra, ACT, Australia
e-mail: amanda.laugesen@anu.edu.au

R. Gehrmann
School of Humanities and Communication, University of Southern Queensland, Toowoomba, QLD, Australia
e-mail: Richard.Gehrmann@usq.edu.au

and conflict.' It brought together a number of scholars to address the topic through a range of different disciplinary and methodological perspectives. This collection and its companion volume *Expressions of War in Australia and the Pacific: Language, Trauma, Memory and Official Discourse* are primarily based on work from the symposium, and they continue the valuable scholarship developed through the "Palgrave Studies in Languages at War" series.[3]

In particular, this volume aims to expand our knowledge of aspects of translation and communication in conflicts past and present around the globe. It seeks to illuminate the story of interpreting in wartime, adding to our expanding knowledge about the work and experiences of translators, as well as the policy and issues surrounding translation, in both conflict zones and war-crimes trials. In recent years, there has been increased scholarly interest in the role of language intermediaries, interpreters, and translators in war. Footitt and Tobia note the importance of addressing issues such as how processes of language mediation contribute to the construction of discourses that permit and support war; the role of translators themselves; and the question of the invisibility of translators.[4] They also call attention to the need for consideration of issues such as the class and gender of translators, and a consideration of how attitudes might have shaped acts of language mediation.[5] Mona Baker further adds that translation and interpreting must be considered a fundamental part of the institution of war.[6] These practices are essential in both the articulating and the resisting of the narratives that underpin violent conflict.[7]

We also seek to illuminate the complex nature of cross-cultural communication in war zones. Wars can be understood as relational spaces. They are cosmopolitan zones of contact between people. Werner and Zimmermann suggest the value of an approach they call *histoire croisée*.[8] At the heart of this is the notion of intersection.[9] They argue the importance of analysing the 'manner in which individuals actually connect themselves to the world, the specific construction of the world, and the elements of context produced by this particular activity in each particular case.'[10] Ideas of intersection and contact are useful for scholars of language and war, as language and communication provide a useful prism for considering the nature of cross-cultural communication and encounter in the context of conflict.

War and Its Language Demands

Wars require language resources. Over the course of the twentieth century, military forces became increasingly aware of the need for preparations for war to include the support of linguists, and for language and cultural training to be undertaken. Trained military interpreters are essential, but once war breaks out, demands can change. Professionals often have to be supplemented by locally hired linguistic mediators, and once on the ground, immediate challenges can lead to a range of language and communication strategies needing to be put in place. A history of translation and interpreting in wartime needs both to grapple with the broader logistical requirements for language skills and to examine individual case studies that foreground the actual experiences of interpreters and interpreting on the ground. Individual stories in particular can help to highlight the many different experiences and issues that are raised in this history.

A brief account of the careers of five interpreters helps to demonstrate the intersection of the three themes of this book: communication, interpreting, and language in wartime. Their stories provide a tangible sense of those who have used language skills in war to a variety of purposes and ends. Their varied backgrounds, motivations, experiences, and understandings of their place in the military system shaped what was often a very diverse capacity to use their language skills to advance the cause of military authorities and the state, as well as sometimes their own interests. Military linguists might be an integral part of the machine of war, but they are also individuals with their own human concerns, and their actions can be shaped in diverse ways as they experience the impact of war. They serve to illustrate the human face of language in war across time.

Collecting Qualifications and Competencies on a Paid Holiday: The Professional Interpreter

In the case of British General Sir John Marshall-Cornwall (1887–1985), the decision to qualify as an interpreter was based partly on his natural competence but also on the benefits he could accrue by studying languages and acquiring interpreter qualifications. Marshall-Cornwall learned French and German at school and received the prize for gaining first place in German at the Royal Military Academy at Woolwich, a clear demonstration of his interest in languages. His parents had retired from colonial India to Edinburgh, where he was subsequently stationed with the British army, but the military culture of his era mandated that it was inappropriate for an officer to spend his two months' annual leave at his garrison location. He began the practice of living abroad for two months every year from 1908 to 1914, studying a language of the country he was visiting and formally qualifying as an interpreter in that language, all the while having his annual holiday subsidised by a succession of War Office language grants.

Marshall-Cornwall's facility for languages saw him progress rapidly down the pathway of becoming a professional collector of military interpreter qualifications, initially qualifying in German and French in 1908 and 1909. In an army where a subaltern's pay rate had not increased since the Napoleonic wars one hundred years earlier, the language grant of £50 for German and £25 for French was most welcome. A chance meeting with a Norwegian officer while skiing in Germany resulted in an invitation to visit Norway and his annual acquisition of language interpreter qualifications continued from Norwegian to Swedish and then Dutch. Unlike his less studious and wealthier contemporaries he continued to spend his holidays studying in-country and soon qualified in Italian and Spanish.[11] This linguistic polyglot was only obliged to pause his language acquisition because of the disruption of the First World War, where his language ability resulted in a professionally fruitful wartime military-intelligence career that included questioning of prisoners of war, translation of documents, and analysis of the disposition of German forces on the Western Front.[12]

Following the war, Marshall-Cornwall began studying Turkish and Modern Greek when he was posted to Turkey. The decision to study Turkish gave him the added luxury of six months on official language leave in Istanbul, plus the £125 language allowance, giving him a pleasant working holiday for a language that by this stage he was fluent in.[13] A subsequent posting to China led to the acquisition of basic

Chinese-language qualifications and an ever-helpful £50 language grant, with his linguistic interpreter qualifications culminating with colloquial Arabic, acquired during a period of duty in Egypt.[14] Throughout the Second World War he held positions as a negotiator with the Turkish government and as a military commander, completing his military career with MI6 and the Special Operations Executive.[15] His eleven interpreter qualifications and obvious ability to use his holidays constructively provide examples of how official structures conducive to language learning have been used to the linguist's advantage, both for enjoyable vacations and professional advancement.

Non-native Native Speaker Shaping Events

In contrast to the hard-working Marshall-Cornwall, Major General Sir Edward Spears (1886–1974) had a natural advantage in becoming a British military interpreter. Born in Paris to a British family of long-term residents, his early childhood in France left him with a natural fluency and a slight French accent when he spoke English. Spears joined the British army, and his unorthodox upbringing shaped his career as an unorthodox army officer. He became an accredited French-language interpreter and, by the age of twenty, further demonstrated his military language capabilities by translating a French military account of the recent Russo-Japanese war into English.[16] At a time when Britain and France were undertaking secret planning in the event of a possible war with Germany, he joined a team of British officers working with the French military in Paris.

This close association with the French military and his facility in what was essentially his native language led him to become a liaison officer at the start of the First World War. In this position he managed to achieve far more significance than expected of an officer of his particular rank, and as a low-ranking officer, he undertook negotiations between Sir John French, the British commander, and his French army counterparts. This experience was to be the basis of his post-war book *Liaison 1914* and also demonstrates the significance and authority that an interpreter can have. In this instance, a comparatively junior officer was in a position to interpret for his superiors and at times guide them. Spears was a lifelong Francophile, to the point where some of his English contemporaries were suspicious of his loyalty. Elected to Parliament during the interwar period, his Francophile views led to him being referred to as 'the member for Paris.'

Spears rejoined the army during the Second World War and again used his language skills to mediate between the British and the French, this time as a senior-ranking Major General with significant political links to the ruling Conservative party, speaking not as a subordinate but as an equal. His fluency in French and his senior position meant Spears could play an active leadership role in trying to prevent the French government from surrendering in 1940, an attempt that was ultimately unsuccessful. As a known French linguist and senior army officer, he worked with Charles de Gaulle's Free French movement in its efforts to shift the allegiance of French colonial governors away from the pro-German Vichy government. Ultimately appointed as British Commissioner for Lebanon and Syria, he was an influential figure in these formerly French territories from 1942 to 1945.[17] In Spears's story, we see an example of a military linguist, with a deep-seated admiration for a country other than his own, playing an important role in shaping policy at a high level both as a junior officer in his youth and as a senior officer in middle age.

Amateur as Kind Interrogator

Widely regarded as one of the most successful Second World War interrogators, Lance Corporal Hanns Scharff (1907–1992) falls into the category of an amateur who was in the right place at the right time and succeeded because of his skills and powers of observation. Born in Germany, Scharff spent a decade working in South Africa, where he married a native English speaker and developed a thorough understanding of English language and culture. It was only by accident that the outbreak of war found him visiting his family in Germany, and he was conscripted into the army. Despite his English-language skills, he was trained as an infantry soldier and was in the process of being sent to serve on the Russian Front when his wife managed to convince a general that her husband had skills that could be employed in a more constructive fashion. He was transferred to an interrogation centre in an administrative capacity, where he made use of his time observing the work of other interrogators to try and determine what was successful or not successful. He was eventually sent on a Luftwaffe interpreter-training course and employed as an interrogator.

It became apparent early on that Allied airmen who were captured expected harsh treatment, so Scharff disarmed them by treating them with kindness. After a series of formal interviews, his confidence-building measures included days of seemingly pointless pleasant conversations, on occasion involving walks through the woods or apparently social chats in other innocuous locations. In his memoir he gives an example of his interrogation technique, explaining how he had to determine from his captives why Allied fighter pilots were shooting with white tracer bullets, what specific orders they had to attack ground targets, and under what circumstances they released their long-range spare fuel tanks. Relaxed conversations, use of American idiom, subtle flattery, jocular comparisons between Germany and the USA, and disarming expressions would lead to a casual introduction of the key question, and collection of the answer, which had to be remembered and included in a subsequent report of the interrogation that the hapless pilot did not even realise was still taking place.[18]

Scharff was an untrained interrogator who looked at the successes and mistakes of other interrogators and by trial and error came up with his own approach.[19] This technique was based on taking the perspective of the source themselves, and is still used and studied today.[20] The experiences of Second World War interrogator interpreters such as Scharff were to have profound consequences in military intelligence practices. At the conclusion of the war he was employed by the American Counter Intelligence Corps, subsequently immigrating to the USA where he gave presentations to the military on his interrogation techniques.[21] During the Cold War and beyond, American interrogation training drew on Scharff's experience of 'kind' interrogation of hundreds of aircrew.

Cultural Knowledge That Saves Lives

Australian Warrant Officer Arthur Page (1922–2011) was born in Japan to the Greek-Russian Pappadopoulos family and learnt Japanese as a child, courtesy of his Japanese nanny. He learned what he was later to refer to as perfect grammar school English at the English Mission School in Kobe. Many of his classmates were of mixed Japanese and European ancestry, and with the coming of the Second World War, his former school mates joined a variety of armies with two brothers actually serving in the British and Japanese army, respectively, one of whom was to later arrive at Page's interrogation centre as a prisoner.[22] Increasing anti-foreign sentiment caused his family to leave Japan in one of the last neutral ships to sail before the war, arriving in Australia in July 1941.

Arthur Page and his father thought their language skills would be of use to the Australian military and tried to enlist, but were refused because of their foreign background. It was only after Japan entered the war that both were conscripted for military service, with Arthur being sent to the infantry, specifically to a unit for foreigners 'that can't speak the Kings English.'[23] His 'foreign' identity kept him from using his skills until the Japanese bombing attack on his station on the West Australian coast when he correctly identified the aircraft type by the sound of its engine.[24] His explanation of why he had a familiarity with Japanese aircraft led to the realisation that he had critically valuable Japanese language skills and he soon found himself transferred to the Intelligence Corps.

Page and his father were both assigned where they could use their linguistic skills, in Page's case initially translating Japanese broadcasts before he was sent to the interrogation centre at Indooroopilly in suburban Brisbane, where he was classified as a Grade A interrogator.[25] His linguist career initially involved translation and then interrogation, a task he found easier than the translation of documents. Having learnt Japanese from his nanny and exposure to everyday life in Japan, his knowledge of written Japanese was limited. Page explains that the interrogation of Japanese prisoners involves both knowledge of language and knowledge of culture. Japanese military culture indoctrinated troops with the concept that Japanese soldiers could never surrender. Those who were captured had never expected it, and so found themselves nervous and distressed in what was for them an unimaginable situation. Furthermore, having a perception of Japan as a unique culture, they were usually dumbfounded when questioned by a Japanese-language speaker, at which stage they would nearly always relapse into open dialogue.[26] His subsequent military career saw Page attached to the US military during their liberation of the Philippines and interpreting at war-crimes trials, but it was his work with Australians at the conclusion of the war that led to his most demanding wartime experiences.

Following the surrender of the Japanese government, a key requirement was to ensure that subordinate Japanese commanders throughout Southeast Asia also surrendered, and this was a task that demanded high-level interpreter skills. Page found himself occupying a key role in not one but two surrenders on the island of Borneo. Firstly, he was flown to Balikpapan to assist commander of the Seventh Division Major-General Milford to accept the surrender of his Japanese counterparts. Milford was determined to avoid further loss of life and wanted 'someone with the knowledge of the Japanese temperament—and language, of course— someone able to cope with summing up the Japanese psyche as the conversation goes on.'[27] Page found himself in a series of meetings with the Japanese throughout which he was instrumental in explaining to his superiors that they could initially convince the Japanese to consider a temporary suspension of hostilities in order to move them down the path towards surrender.[28]

An even more challenging experience for Page was the surrender ceremony that took place in Banjarmasin, also in Borneo. This was an event where his knowledge of Japanese culture was far more significant than his linguistic skills. Prior to the surrender ceremony, he tried to explain concepts of syntax and vocabulary that would be significant to the Australian commander, Colonel Robson, as well as key aspects of shame and Japanese culture. Robson refused to pay attention to his interpreter, and during the surrender ceremony demanded the Japanese Commander General Uno place his sword on the ground. Uno refused, the Colonel aggressively repeated his demand, tension increased, and as seconds passed, the stalemate intensified with an increasingly stressed and shamed Japanese general almost pushed to breaking point. In Japanese militarist culture, surrender itself was highly shameful but to place the sword on the ground rather than in the hands of an enemy was a symbol of absolute dishonour. Page could see that General Uno's sense of military virtue and samurai honour could well lead him to draw his sword and commit suicide—after first beheading the Australian Colonel and Page, his interpreter. In the ensuing long, drawn-out seconds, Page quickly managed to think of an appropriate Japanese concept that would clear the general from any sense of disgrace regarding his own personal honour, using phrases to convince him that laying down his sword related to the symbolic defeat of the nation and surrender of the Emperor, rather than of Uno. By placing the emphasis on the Emperor rather than on Uno, Page managed to resolve what could have been a disaster. While his understanding of the cross-cultural issue of shame and his knowledge of the exact language to use to mitigate the possible crisis were critical, as a low-ranked Warrant Officer interpreter, Page found himself ignored following the ceremony and not even thanked.[29] This particular story illustrates two other aspects of the role of communicating and interpreting in wartime, that of the need to understand culture, and that interpreters' superiors need to work with them, rather than viewing a linguist as nothing more than a language machine.

Understanding Culture and Interpreting the Unfamiliar

A final story of the military linguist in war takes us to the contemporary, in considering the experience of Sergeant Kayla Williams (1976–). Her pathway to the US Army came through a series of experiences that included unemployment, attending college before dropping out, drugs and alternative culture, low-level jobs, and finally graduation with a degree in English literature. Williams enlisted in 2000 to challenge herself and to challenge the perception others had of her. Her previous exposure to language came through an Arab Muslim boyfriend. This relationship taught her both words and phrases, and more importantly, also gave her a rich understanding of the cultural constructs implicit in Arab society and of Arab attitudes towards Western society.[30] Her very high score in the US Army language tests had her classified as a Category Four language student, capable of learning the more difficult language of Arabic at the Defense Language Institute, which she described as 'a college campus for soldiers.'[31] Williams undertook crypto-linguist training and qualified as a signals intelligence specialist and was deployed to the Middle East for the 2003 invasion of Iraq.

While her specialty was primarily as a signals intelligence analyst, her wartime language experiences in Iraq included working as a document translator, as an interpreter, and on one occasion as an assistant to military interrogators. Williams initially thought she was being asked to assist with the interrogation of female suspects but then found that she was to be used for her status as an Arabic-speaking blonde American female, as part of an interrogation ploy involving humiliation of male Iraqi prisoners. This is an aspect of language and war which incorporates elements of cultural knowledge and cross-cultural communication, in this case, used against prisoners. She was disturbed when the interrogation session went beyond the Geneva Conventions, seeing it as both illegal and counterproductive, and refused to take part in further interrogation sessions.[32]

There were more positive aspects to her work as a military linguist, and some very successful interactions with local people where Williams was able to contribute with her Arabic-language skills, but cross-cultural considerations were always present. A unit she was attached to in Baghdad found a soccer field full of unexploded artillery shells, and she spoke with the local people who wanted the Americans to clean up the site to make it safer for the children who persisted in playing in the area. Several days later an accidental explosion in this area led to her translating for wounded and dying Iraqis, one of whom even while bleeding through his shattered legs was embarrassed and concerned that a female could see his exposed genitals. The complex situation included her American superiors being hypervigilant about the possibility of a secondary explosion and other soldiers trying to treat the injured, while relatives of a dead man were expecting the Americans to do something for his family. Having involved themselves in the crisis, under Islamic law they had now become implicated. This is a telling illustration of the complex situations wartime linguists can experience on the ground. Williams found the situation distressing, feeling she was helping some people but not as much as she could have.[33] Those who have language ability in war can find themselves feeling torn between commitment to their own side and those whose language they are translating.

On occasion, relationships with her fellow Americans were problematic for Williams. Cross-cultural communication can be difficult for highly stressed or culturally confused soldiers deployed to an environment where the language of the country is unfamiliar, the people of the country are unfamiliar, and their customs are unfamiliar. In such situations it is possible to blank out sights and sounds that should be understood. One of the more bizarre experiences of her deployment was when Williams was attached to a military team searching an Iraqi Catholic monastery. Arriving at the monastery, the infantry team with her was confronted by a smiling Iraqi monk who explained in English they had nothing to hide. The officer in charge of the mission paused, looked at Williams, and asked her to interpret what had been said, at which point she explained the monk was speaking in English. In a bizarre cross-cultural exchange, the officer (who Williams now presumed could not understand the monk because he *looked* foreign) spent a period of time questioning the monk through the interpreter, despite the fact that the Iraqi monk and Williams were speaking English to each other. This confused the monk and amused the lieutenants' subordinates, but the more Williams insisted that English was being spoken and she didn't need to interpret, the more the officer demanded she continue with this bizarre non-translation exercise. Despite efforts to convince him otherwise, the officer remained convinced that Arabic was being spoken. As the monk began to simplify and slow down his English as if talking to a child, the exchange continued until the search was concluded.[34] This again reminds us of the challenge for highly skilled linguists who because of their low rank are unable to rectify situations of avoidable linguistic confusion.

Historical and Contemporary Perspectives on Interpreting and Communication in War

The stories outlined above reveal the complex and fascinating stories that can be told when placing the interpreter and their work at the centre of study. By uncovering these stories, and the broader context and policy environment that shapes such stories, we can come to a better understanding of the role of interpreters and the challenges of translation and communication in relation to war.

Our chapters offer perspectives that include those drawn from personal experience, as well as those drawn from oral history interviews and the traces left in archives, diaries, and letters. This collection aims to make an original contribution through its inclusion of accounts informed by personal experiences of language in the context of war. Several of the chapters are written by authors who have combined their past experiences as practitioners with an academic approach to address issues of language in war and disaster zones, as well as in war-crimes trials. Such accounts placed within and alongside academic reflections help to enrich and deepen our understanding of language and communication in war.

Several chapters investigate and uncover the stories and experiences of language mediators in the context of conflict. Amanda Laugesen in her chapter identifies several interpreters in the First Australian Imperial Force (AIF) during the First World War. We know very little about those who worked (formally or informally) as language mediators in the First World War, but their stories are slowly being identified. Oleg Beyda's chapter looks at the complicated situation that emigré Russians who worked as interpreters for the Germans in the Second World War found themselves in. He examines, through the accounts they left of their experiences, their motivations for doing such work and considers the way they performed those roles in very difficult circumstances. His chapter brings an important new perspective to the complicated history of the Eastern Front.

The experiences of language mediators in more recent conflicts are examined by Matt Grant and Ali Albakaa, both of whom have personal experiences in war and disaster zones. Grant undertook deployments with the Australian Defence Force (ADF) to both East Timor and Indonesia after the 2004 tsunami. His personal reflections offer insight into the evolution of ADF experiences with language professionals, as well as providing insight into the challenges of communication when on the ground in a conflict or disaster zone. Albakaa, who worked as a local interpreter with the ADF in the Second Iraq War before going on to investigate the experiences and policies around language mediation in the ADF, contributes a powerful chapter that draws on his own experiences in a conflict zone. Using oral history interviews with many Iraqi interpreters, as well as ADF personnel, Albakaa's chapter also aims to draw practical lessons from these experiences. He suggests the importance of establishing clear guidelines and policies to help guide the actions and protect the welfare of local language mediators in conflict situations.

Interpreting in the context of war-crimes trials is also taken up by two of the chapters in this volume. Georgina Fitzpatrick's chapter uncovers the stories of those Australians who served as interpreters during the Japanese war-crimes trials at the end of the Second World War. Drawing on oral history interviews, as well as the extensive archives created by the trials, she demonstrates how necessity led to a wide variety of people being drawn into interpreting work, and she points to some of the challenges they faced. Ludmila Stern's chapter examines the various issues faced by interpreters—drawing in part from her own experiences—and by the legal system in dealing with communication difficulties during war-crimes trials since the Second World War. Her chapter conveys the extreme complexity of interpreting in such trials, where multiple languages might be spoken and where cultural understanding (and translation that conveys cultural and linguistic nuances) can play a critical role. Like Albakaa, Stern's chapter offers important lessons that can be used to address these issues in future trials.

Language teaching is another topic taken up in this volume. Such teaching is a critical part of preparing for war. Jennifer Joan Baldwin's chapter uncovers the history of Japanese language teaching in Australia through the period from the First World War through to the Second World War. Not only does she show what factors led to the establishment of such teaching as part of broader cultural and military policy, she also uncovers the stories and experiences of Japanese-language teachers in Australia. Yavar Dehghani, himself a teacher of languages to the ADF, draws on this work to demonstrate some of the ways in which language skills are currently taught for deployment, including a consideration of some of the cultural preparation that is necessary for such deployment.

A number of chapters in this volume illuminate issues of language and communication in twenty-first-century wars. For Australia, Afghanistan has been, Kevin Foster argues, the worst reported and least understood conflict in Australian history.[35] We still await its history, and this is perhaps even truer of other conflicts and peacekeeping missions that Australians have been involved in.[36] In particular, such conflicts and involvements have not had a great impact on popular knowledge and understanding. But aspects of language and communication can begin to give us some insights into the nature of Australian involvement and experience of these wars, especially beyond the official histories.

Kevin Foster's work in this area reveals that there was little public debate (and even awareness) around the Australian wars in Iraq and Afghanistan.[37] Other scholars have examined the way that public language around the 'war on terror' was used to help manufacture consent for military actions. Richard Jackson, for example, uses Critical Discourse Analysis as a methodology for examining the language that legitimised twenty-first-century conflicts within the war on terror.[38] Jasmin Gabel's chapter uses the methodology of frame analysis to consider the various ways national governments within a broader coalition force sought to frame and communicate their national participation within war, providing insight into how such a methodology can illuminate the difficulties of developing a consensual narrative around going to war.

Language(s) also plays a central role in shaping identity. This issue is taken up in two chapters that deal explicitly with cross-cultural communication. In Laugesen's chapter, encounters with, and experiences of, foreign languages served to reinforce and even shape Australian soldiers' identities during the First World War. In Richard Gehrmann's chapter, an analysis of how Australians interacted with other allied armies in the Second Iraq War—in this case, the Americans and the Dutch, provides insight into cultural differences and communication challenges. Other chapters, such as those discussed that look at the stories of interpreters and language teachers, also engage with elements of cross-cultural communication. As they demonstrate, cross-cultural communication (and miscommunication) is an integral element of the experience of war.

Methodologies and sources vary considerably in this book. As Footitt and Tobia have argued, while language and translation can be understood as integral to the policies, practices, and experiences of war, there is a challenge insofar as they sometimes remain invisible in the archives.[39] Other sources of information, especially for more recent conflicts, can include oral history, memoir, and biography. While self-reflective research has been a contested field, memoirs of war can also be subjected to quantitative assessment as the work of Woodward and Jenkings shows,[40] and can also be analysed to discern how soldiers and veterans come to understand and frame their own experiences.[41] The five chapters in this volume that draw from personal experiences in recent conflicts offer both valuable primary-source accounts of these conflicts and critical perspectives on various aspects of language and communication within a military and conflict context.

We organise the volume into three Sections, apart from the introduction and conclusion: experiences of cross-cultural communication in wartime; strategies of communication and language teaching; and experiences of interpreters in wartime and after. Each of these Sections draws together chapters from different wars and aims to juxtapose chapters based on different methodologies, disciplinary perspectives, and approaches.

The first Section takes up the idea of cross-cultural communication, as discussed above, demonstrating how issues of language and cross-cultural communication can be seen as critical aspects of most, if not all, modern conflicts. As Gehrmann makes clear, even in an Anglophone situation, cross-cultural differences can be of significance in shaping the relationship between different national forces. The second Section brings together chapters on communication and language teaching. Following from the discussion of the challenges of cross-cultural communication, we see some of these issues played out in both language teaching and communication strategies. The third Section focuses on the figure of the interpreter in both war zone and war-crimes trial. Drawing on personal experiences as well as the archival record, and covering a broad sweep of modern conflicts, we can see the importance of studying the experiences and treatment of language mediators, and again tracing some of the challenges of cross-cultural communication through these stories.

Conclusion

This book on communication, interpreting, and language in wartime aims to provide a multi-disciplinary approach to the subject of translation and cross-cultural communication in times of war and conflict. It examines historical and contemporary experiences of interpreters in war and war-crimes trials, as well as considering policy issues in communication and interpreting. Furthermore, it also foregrounds the importance of cross-cultural communication and communication difficulties in war-related contexts. Not only does this offer us insight into the experience of those who have used language in war, it offers important broader perspectives into both the history of war and contemporary military policy.

It is salutary to evaluate the lived experience of those who have been engaged with language in war, whether as teachers, policymakers, interpreters, or the end-users of interpreting, and this collection aims to provide an important contribution to the ongoing project of understanding language in times of war and conflict.

Notes

1. Hilary Footitt (2016), 'War and Culture Studies in 2016: Putting "Translation" in the Transnational?', *Journal of War and Culture Studies*, 9:3, pp. 209–21, here p. 218; Julian Walker (2017), *Words and the First World War: Language, Memory, Vocabulary* (London: Bloomsbury), p. 28.
2. Hilary Footitt (2010), 'Languages at War: Cultural Preparations for the Liberation of Western Europe', *Journal of War and Culture Studies*, 3:1, pp. 109–121, here p. 111.
3. They include Christophe Declerq and Julian Walker (eds) (2016), *Languages and the First World War: Representation and Memory* (Houndmills: Palgrave Macmillan); Julian Walker and Christophe Declerq (eds) (2016), *Languages and the First World War: Communicating in a Transnational War* (Houndmills: Palgrave Macmillan); Hilary Footitt and Michael Kelly (eds) (2012), *Languages and the Military: Alliances, Occupation and Peace Building* (Houndmills: Palgrave Macmillan); and (2012) *Languages at War: Policies and Practices of Language Contacts in Conflict* (Houndmills: Palgrave Macmillan).
4. Hilary Footitt and Simona Tobia (2013), *WarTalk: Foreign Languages and the British War Effort in Europe, 1940–47* (Houndmills: Palgrave Macmillan), p. 2.
5. Footitt and Tobia, *WarTalk: Foreign Languages and the British War Effort in Europe, 1940–47*, p. 10.

6. Mona Baker (2006), *Translation and Conflict: A Narrative Account* (London: Routledge), pp. 1–2.
7. Mona Baker, *Translation and Conflict: A Narrative Account*, p. 2.
8. Michael Werner and Bénédicte Zimmermann (2006), 'Beyond Comparison: *Histoire Croisée* and the Challenge of Reflexivity', *History and Theory*, 45, pp. 30–50.
9. Werner and Zimmermann, 'Beyond Comparison: *Histoire Croisée* and the Challenge of Reflexivity', p. 37.
10. Werner and Zimmermann, 'Beyond Comparison: *Histoire Croisée* and the Challenge of Reflexivity', p. 47.
11. James Marshall-Cornwall (1984), *Wars and Rumours of Wars, A Memoir* (London: Leo Cooper, Secker and Warburg), pp. 7–12.
12. For more on the diverse cohort he became part of, see Jim Beach (2008), '"Intelligent Civilians in Uniform": The British Expeditionary Force's Intelligence Corps Officers, 1914–1918', *War & Society*, 27:1, pp. 1–22.
13. Marshall-Cornwall, *Wars and Rumours of Wars, A Memoir*, p. 65.
14. Marshall-Cornwall, *Wars and Rumours of Wars, A Memoir*, pp. 74, 114.
15. Marshall-Cornwall, *Wars and Rumours of Wars, A Memoir*, pp. 202–208.
16. Max Egremont (1997), *Under Two Flags: The Life of Major General Sir Edward Spears* (London: Phoenix), p. 8.
17. Egremont, *Under Two Flags: The Life of Major General Sir Edward Spears*.
18. Raymond Toliver (1997), *The Interrogator: The Story of Hanns Scharff, Luftwaffe's Master Interrogator* (Altglen: Schiffer Publishing), pp. 102–09.
19. Pär Anders Granhag, Steven M. Kleinman, and Simon Oleszkiewicz (2016), 'The Scharff Technique: On How to Effectively Elicit Intelligence from Human Sources', *International Journal of Intelligence and Counter Intelligence*, 29:1, pp. 132–50.
20. Lennart May and Pär Anders Granhag (2016), 'Techniques for Eliciting Human Intelligence: Examining Possible Order Effects of the Scharff Tactics', *Psychiatry, Psychology and Law*, 23:2, pp. 275–87.
21. Toliver, *The Interrogator: The Story of Hanns Scharff, Luftwaffe's Master Interrogator*, pp. 304–05.
22. Arthur Page (2008), *Between Victor and Vanquished: An Australian Interrogator in the War against Japan* (Loftus: Australian Military History Publications), p. 32, 65–66.
23. Page, *Between Victor and Vanquished*, p. 1.

24. Page, *Between Victor and Vanquished*, p. 51.
25. Page, *Between Victor and Vanquished*, p. 87. For more on the operation of this centre see Colin Funch (2003), *Linguists in Uniform: The Japanese Experience* (Clayton: Japanese Studies Centre, Monash University), pp. 98–111.
26. Page, *Between Victor and Vanquished*, p. 167.
27. Page, *Between Victor and Vanquished*, p. 409.
28. Page, *Between Victor and Vanquished*, pp. 409–20.
29. Page, *Between Victor and Vanquished*, pp. 423–35.
30. Kayla Williams (2005), *Love My Rifle More than You: Young and Female in the US Army* (New York: W. W. Norton), pp. 33–37.
31. Williams, *Love My Rifle More than You*, p. 47.
32. Williams, *Love My Rifle More than You*, pp. 246–52.
33. Williams, *Love My Rifle More than You*, pp. 130–38.
34. Williams, *Love My Rifle More than You*, pp. 114–21.
35. Kevin Foster (2013), *Don't Mention the War: The Australian Defence Force, the Media and the Afghan Conflict* (Clayton: Monash University Publishing), p. xvii.
36. Official histories of peacekeeping have been written, but there are few other accounts. See the six volume *Official History of Australian Peacekeeping, Humanitarian and Post-Cold War Operations* published by Cambridge University Press. The official history of Australia's war in Afghanistan is currently being written.
37. Kevin Foster (ed.) (2011), *The Information Battlefield: Representing Australians at War* (Melbourne: Australian Scholarly Publishing); Kevin Foster (ed) (2009), *What Are We Doing in Afghanistan? The Military and the Media at War* (Melbourne: Australian Scholarly Publishing); Foster, *Don't Mention the War*.
38. Richard Jackson (2005), *Writing the War on Terrorism: Language, Politics and Counter-terrorism* (Manchester: Manchester University Press), p. 1. Another study of the public language around the war on terror is John Dower (2010), *Cultures of War: Pearl Harbor/Hiroshima/9–11/Iraq* (New York: W. W. Norton), which looks at how historical discourses and tropes were mobilised after 9/11.
39. Footitt and Tobia, *WarTalk: Foreign Languages and the British War Effort in Europe, 1940–47*, p. 5.

40. Rachel Woodward and K. Neil Jenkings (2012), '"This Place Isn't Worth the Left Boot of One of Our Boys": Geopolitics, Militarism and Memoirs of the Afghanistan War', *Political Geography*, 31:8, pp. 495–508.
41. For example, see Frances Houghton (2019), *The Veterans' Tale: British Military Memoirs of the Second World War* (Cambridge: Cambridge University Press).

Section II

Experiences of Cross-Cultural Communication in Wartime

Section II

Cross-Cultural Communication and the Experiences of Australian Soldiers During the First World War

Amanda Laugesen

Sergeant Cyril Lawrence, a New Zealander serving in the Australian Imperial Force (AIF), wrote in a letter home to his sister in June 1916 that he was about to enjoy a period of leave in England. In the boats heading from France to England, he wrote, were men from 'almost every unit in France.' 'Golly, the lingo,' he observed, 'Welshmen trying to talk to Scots, Maoris to Ghurkas and so on.'[1] Lawrence's observations remind us of the multilingual nature of the First World War.

War brings together people, both civilian and military, of different nationalities. How they communicate with each other can be of critical importance in the successful prosecution of war, but communication is also an integral element of the experience of war for individuals. As Julian Walker writes in his book *Words and the First World War*, 'Multilingualism during the war provided the potential for bonds between people, the opportunity to learn, and the environment for chaos.'[2] Hilary

---

A. Laugesen (✉)
Australian National Dictionary Centre, Australian National University, Canberra, ACT, Australia
e-mail: amanda.laugesen@anu.edu.au

Footitt additionally observes that 'any war will create its own languages landscape.'[3]

This chapter examines the question of how Australian soldiers experienced cross-cultural communication in the First World War and also looks at how their depictions of such communication reflected their own sense of identity and their cultural understandings. It therefore seeks to contribute to the reconstruction of the 'languages landscape' of the First World War, while also investigating how soldiers experienced and made sense of that landscape. It further aims to engage with work currently being done around 'experiential cosmopolitanism,' work that looks at cosmopolitanism as lived reality and explores moments of encounter between people, including in conflict zones.[4]

Recent scholarship has begun to consider the importance of language and communication in the context of war.[5] The First World War has received some attention within this growing area of research. For example, Krista Cowman's work on how British soldiers learned and used 'trench French' on the Western Front provides an important perspective on questions of language in this theatre of war.[6] And the experiences of interpreters and language mediators, although remaining largely invisible in the context of the First World War, have begun to be reconstructed, however partially.[7] Recent histories of the First World War have also begun to incorporate experiences of language and communication into larger accounts of aspects of the war, notably Craig Gibson's study of the complex relationships between British soldiers and French civilians.[8]

Yet few histories of the Australian experience of the First World War have been concerned with the challenges of communication and language, or what they might reveal about the experience of war. In the Australian First World War context, little attention has been paid to date as to how Australian soldiers might have experienced moments of cross-cultural communication. This chapter therefore seeks to address this gap in what we know of the experiences of Australian soldiers, and in particular to pay attention to how Australian soldiers sought to depict and make sense of such encounters.

Language Learning

As Julian Walker points out, the First World War was a war fought in a multilingual environment.[9] Yet it is impossible to estimate how many soldiers spoke a second language. Craig Gibson estimates that no more than 1% of the British Expeditionary Force (BEF) was conversant in French, although exact numbers are difficult to estimate.[10] Similar numbers for the First AIF do not exist. One figure we do have is the number of French-Australian AIF members. This number was fairly small, less than 150 soldiers, and we can only assume that these men spoke French.[11] More Australian soldiers spoke German, as in 1914 Germans were the largest non-British immigrant group in Australia.[12] Sir John Monash, who would go on to be one of the most renowned Australian military commanders of the war, spoke, read, and wrote German.[13] Overall, however, numbers of Australians who spoke a second language at the beginning of the war can be estimated as being small.

A lack of language skills posed a challenge for soldiers who wished to communicate with locals once they were abroad, as one soldier quickly realised on his arrival in Egypt. Harry Cadwallader excitedly wrote home from Egypt to tell his family that he had just seen his first Charlie Chaplin film. However, with all the intertitles being presented in French, he was unable to understand much. He observed in his letter home that: 'I wish I had paid more attention to language when at school.'[14] Cadwallader's experience of being confronted with a language he did not understand was typical of the experiences of many, and so language learning became something that some soldiers actively pursued.

Language learning took various forms during the war, but much of it took place in incidental ways.[15] One important means of gaining a few rudimentary words and phrases that could have some functional value was through the use of dictionaries, guides, and phrasebooks. We can trace some of the ways such print material connected with soldiers: for example, the British Expeditionary Force distributed 1000 copies of pocket-sized English-French dictionaries among units at the Western Front in Spring of 1915, and Australian officers en route to the Western Front in summer 1916 were all given French primers.[16] The personal effects listings of Australian soldiers who were killed during the war also reveal that dictionaries (along with New Testaments, prayer books, and other devotional texts) were sometimes in their personal possession.[17]

Soldiers near the front could spend time in YMCA, Red Cross, and Salvation Army huts and tents. Such venues offered important spaces for soldiers to read, write, listen to music, and engage in other pursuits separate from war and military life. These organisations also offered language classes to soldiers.[18] Sapper Edward L. Moore wrote in his diary in January 1915 that while in Egypt he was learning 'a bit of French at the YMCA.'[19] In April 1916, a month after his arrival in France, he noted in his diary that 'I am beginning to pick up a few words of French now but I think it would take a few years for me to learn.'[20] Reg Telfer also wrote in his diary that he spent some time taking French classes at the YMCA in 1917.[21] But language learning could be laborious, as Gunner W. J. Duffell observed in a letter home: 'I am trying to pick up some French but it is slow work & not easy.'[22]

Percy Smythe's story provides insight into how soldiers undertook language learning in a variety of ways and as an ongoing process. The first mention Percy made in his diary about studying French was on his way to the Middle East in August 1915.[23] Textbooks and dictionaries were essential to his learning process: in April 1916 he noted that he had 'bought a little textbook on French for the purpose of studying the language.'[24] A few days later, he went into Hazebrouck, and while there bought a French-English dictionary.[25] In June, he purchased yet another book to help teach himself French, and a week later he wrote that he was trying to obtain French newspapers in order 'to get the latest news.'[26]

As might be expected, Percy's language skills improved as time went on. In July 1916, he was billeted in a house in Saint-Omer where he was able to talk to the family in French; Percy noted in his diary that: 'It is much easier to understand French spoken by a girl than by a man, as they seem to speak more distinctly.'[27] A few days later, he spoke to a French soldier 'and his girl'; the latter, he wrote in his diary, 'knew about as much English as I knew of French, and between us we managed to carry on the conversation all right.'[28] Percy was under no illusions about his French skills, although he clearly was keen to try and communicate as best he could. In October, Percy wrote in his diary (after having fought at the

Somme only months before) that he 'could not sleep' and so had gone up to the local village, where he had, in his own words, 'jabbered pigeon-French to a couple of froggies who looked in at our billets.'[29] Percy bought another French textbook in February 1917 while on leave in London.[30] He then wrote his diary entries in French for a period in April 1917, although by June he had returned to writing in English. In October 1917 he noted listening to 'several of our boys … who could speak French well,' observing that 'its about as easy as learning to read morse from a telegraph instrument. Am improving, however.'[31]

Percy Smythe's story is insightful of the continuing process by which someone who was keen to learn and speak French managed to acquire something of the language. It suggests the importance of access to books and dictionaries, as well as the necessity for everyday interaction with native speakers, although difficulties in communication and comprehension continued to be a source of frustration. After the Armistice, Percy continued his language learning, turning to German. In November 1918, he noted in his diary that he had bought a copy of Hugo's *German Simplified* 'to learn a smattering of German for when we go up to the Rhine.'[32] How his acquisition of German went is not revealed in his diaries. Percy headed home to Australia in August 1919.

Soldiers' magazines, produced by the soldiers on the front, also provided some basic instruction in language, although these magazines tended more often than not to make their language guides more humorous than educational (see below). However, there were some exceptions to this. In an October 1918 edition of the Middle Eastern soldier magazine for Australians and New Zealanders serving in Egypt and Palestine, *The Kia Ora Coo-ee*, an article entitled 'Arabic made easy' was included. An editor's note explained that this article had been written by the author of an Arabic dictionary and was being published in response to requests from readers 'that Arabic words and phrases that appear frequently in the Magazine should be translated for the benefit of Home readers.'[33] This suggests that while the soldier-readers of the *Kia Ora Coo-ee* could understand some Arabic, those at home (to whom these publications were often sent) could not. Here language instruction was not just something that was about practical value for soldiers; it was also something that could be used as a means for soldiers to find common cultural ground with those at home. Language also fed into the development of a degree of cosmopolitanism brought into Australian culture through the influence of the war (and more particularly through the letters, newspaper reports, and war-related publications that circulated during the war years).

The article in *The Kia Ora Coo-ee* also provides insight into the views that some soldiers had towards foreign languages, especially one as unfamiliar to them as Arabic. The introduction to the article stated that Australians and New Zealanders found Arabic to be 'as strange to them as Chinese.' Yet the article acknowledged that few knew how to properly pronounce the words, and so gave clear instructions on how they should sound, as well as providing clear information as to the pragmatics of speaking Arabic.[34] Guides such as these were by necessity brief, but nevertheless sought to make a foreign language more understandable for those who wanted more instruction, and not just make language a source of soldier humour.

Overall, language skills had very real benefits for soldiers. As we saw with Percy Smythe, interaction with the local population and with French soldiers could be more effective with some basic language skills. For prisoners of war, language skills could also be of great benefit. In letters written to Mary Chomley, an Australian woman who worked with the Red Cross in London during the war, Australian prisoners of war in Europe requested various books from the organisation to make their time in captivity more tolerable, and their requests included language texts. Private C. R. Armstrong, a POW in what was then East Prussia, requested French, German, and Russian dictionaries, commenting in his letter to Chomley that he wished 'to learn a little of these three language And I think the present time will be the best to learn Because I am daily in touch with the people who speak the languages which I mention.'[35] Two other Australian POWs, Private J. T. Wright and Private A. L. R. Hanton, both requested German grammars.[36] Wright, who also requested a German dictionary in his letter, wrote to Chomley that he had 'some slight smattering of German, and would like to perfect it.'[37] Presumably these languages could be useful for conversing with captors (and locals, if a soldier was able to escape), but language study also had an essential value in staving off boredom and keeping the mind alive.[38]

Language Mediators

As discussed earlier, the First AIF included soldiers from European backgrounds, including French-Australians and German-Australians. Most of these men would have brought their language background into the AIF. Many German-Australians enlisted in the AIF, not least to assert their loyalty to Australia (anti-German sentiment in Australia was very strong), and German language skills could be extremely useful on active service. A number of German-Australians acted as interpreters in the interrogations of German POWs.[39]

There is limited evidence relating to the experiences of AIF language mediators during the First World War. But there were numerous individual language mediators who played a role within units, and we catch occasional glimpses of these men. Cyril Lawrence noted that his company included a fluent French-speaking interpreter he described as a 'Russian count.'[40] In Bert Smythe's company, a former schoolteacher acted as interpreter.[41] C. E. W. Bean, war correspondent at Gallipoli and later official historian of the First AIF, also comments in passing in his diary on the presence of a divisional interpreter at Gallipoli. He describes the interpreter speaking to some Turkish prisoners of war and helping them obtain some food and water.[42]

Albert E. Coates, who went on to become a notable Australian medical doctor and Second World War POW in the Pacific, had a passion and skill for languages. Born into poverty, Coates left school at age eleven, but thanks to a mentor was able to matriculate through night-school study, with languages being one of his areas of study. He enlisted in the AIF in 1914 and became a medical orderly, first being sent to Gallipoli and then France. While in Egypt, he continued with his French studies as well as learning Arabic.[43] For Coates, studying language was a way to occupy himself, but he also realised the practical value of language skills. He wrote in his diary in 1915 that: 'The Arabic is very useful for conversing with the natives, asking for what you want, etc., and they have a great deal more respect for one who speaks a little of their own tongue.'[44]

In March 1916, Coates was transferred to the Western Front and his battalion fought at the Somme. His language skills saw him attached to an intelligence unit from February 1917.[45] Coates spent time on the Western Front improving his French and German, studying with fellow soldiers, and taking any opportunity he could get to read French- and German-language publications.[46] As a member of the intelligence section, he played an important role during the war in interrogating German prisoners and translating German documents.[47]

French-Australians who served in the AIF also became interpreters. The Comte Gontran de Tournouer, who after the war wrote articles, verse, and cartoons for the Returned Sailors and Soldiers Imperial League of Australia (RSSILA) periodical *The Queensland Digger*, worked as an interpreter during the war. He arrived in Australia in 1903, and matriculated from the University of Queensland, as well as studying at the Sorbonne. De Tournouer then built up pastoral and sugar interests in Queensland. He enlisted in the AIF in 1914, and was appointed Assistant Censor and Interpreter to the Anzac Mounted Division, serving in the Middle East. According to *The Queensland Digger*, his censoring and interpreting work made use of his skills in eight different languages.[48]

Another French-Australian who served as an interpreter in the First World War was Jacques Playoust. Playoust was born in France, but grew up in Australia. When war broke out, he joined the French army, fighting at Verdun and the Somme.[49] He was attached to the 13th Australian Field Artillery Brigade, 5th Australian Division, from January 1918. Playoust had knowledge of both French and German, making him a particularly valuable language mediator.[50] His knowledge of signals was also very useful for the brigade.[51] In October 1918, Playoust saved the lives of French civilians while under heavy shellfire.[52] He was subsequently awarded the Distinguished Conduct Medal.[53] One of his roles as interpreter was 'informing the senior staff of the condition of the liberated villages.'[54]

Playoust was popular with his Australian comrades, who called him 'Turps.'[55] But his popularity appears to have been largely based on his 'Australianness.' His biographers note that the Australian soldiers were keen to get a rise out of their French interpreter, playing tricks on him, including at one point making a horse bolt with him on it. 'Fortunately Jacques was an experienced horseman,' writes his family biographer Jacqueline Dwyer, 'and not only brought it under control, but returned to hurl a string of good Aussie oaths at the soldiers. This certainly won their respect and formed the basis of future friendships.'[56]

Encountering the 'Other' Through Language and the Construction of Australian Identity

Australian soldiers encountered speakers of other languages as soon as they reached countries beyond the shores of Australia. For some of them, the experience of encountering the people of other countries was one of culture shock, and speakers of other languages could elicit responses as varied as horror, disgust, or excitement. Soldiers' accounts of language encounters provide insight into how Australians viewed the (to them) 'exotic other,' as well as how language came to play a role in the construction of Australian identity.

Egypt was undoubtedly confronting to Australians. T. E. Drane, who came from the small Australian town of Forbes, New South Wales, visited the markets in Cairo soon after his arrival. 'There were French Arabs, Turks, Indians, Dagoes,' he wrote in his diary, 'every nation under the sun represented here.'[57] He and his mates then went to a French bar, where he observed that the people speaking French sounded 'just like a lot of monkeys in a zoo.'[58] Racism clearly shaped the attitudes of many Australian soldiers towards those they encountered abroad, especially in the Middle East.[59] AIF soldier John Baensch, for example, called Egyptians 'niggers,' and while he learnt some Arabic in order to communicate with them, he described their language as 'blabber.'[60] This way of describing the sound of foreign languages is not unusual. For Jim McConnell, the Germans ('Fritz') 'yabbered,'[61] and as we saw above, Percy Smythe called his own speaking of French 'blabbering.'

When Australian soldiers went on leave to England, they often expressed relief at returning to the cultural security of an English-speaking environment. Arthur Davison, on leave in England in June 1916, wrote home to say that '[you h]ave no idea what it felt like after arriving at Folkestone, after thirteen months practically in foreign countries, to see English on the stations and hear it spoken. It was next best to going home.'⁶² Alfred Morison Stewart, who was wounded on the Western Front and sent to England to recuperate, wrote in his diary: 'It is indeed a treat to be back to real civilization, seeing everybody English, instead of foreigners.'⁶³ And Stanley Thomas Tuck similarly expressed that on going to England with a 'blighty' wound, he welcomed being somewhere 'clean, tidy, and sweet smelling, *and* a Christian language.' He went on to observe, 'It's wonderful to hear a civvy speak intelligibly.'⁶⁴

After the war, an incident of miscommunication could be turned into a source of humour. In an edition of *The Reveille*, a magazine for the RSSILA (New South Wales branch), 'F O'M.,' who had served with the 9th Field Ambulance in France, described his efforts to try and buy a frying pan to make some eggs and potatoes:

> Frying pan was one of the words not in our French vocabulary, so we tried to explain our wants to the shopkeeper by signs, while emphasizing our liking for ouefs and pommedeterres. Still puzzled, the woman shook her head. My mate then had a brain wave. Grabbing a piece of paper, he drew a picture of a frying pan. 'Oui,' said madam, nodding and smiling, and she buzzed out of the shop and returned 20 minutes later with two nicely-cooked omelettes.⁶⁵

Another account of 'diggers' French' written by a French-Australian after the war for a returned-servicemen magazine, also turned Australian soldiers' limited facility with the language into a source of humour. A long anecdote about an Australian soldier trying to tell a French woman about some cows in her garden had the Australian saying 'There, you compre le lait beaucoup promenade your lettuce. No jolly bon for you?' which the author wrote could be translated as 'you understand the milk much walk your lettuce.' This was, he observed, a 'heroic version' of saying 'Polly, your cows are in the garden.'⁶⁶ It is not always easy to understand the humour of these kinds of stories one hundred years on, but the fact of miscommunication was an important and common source of nostalgic humour in magazines such as these. This no doubt reflected very real experiences soldiers had during the war of trying to communicate effectively.

As is clear from these brief descriptions of encounters with the 'other,' communication and language played a critical role in the construction of Australian identity for soldiers. The First World War is often cited as a critical moment in the development of Australian nationalism. The sacrifice that Australia made in sending so many of its men to fight and die, especially at Gallipoli in 1915, became the basis for the forging of a sense of Australian nationalism. Typically, slang has been seen as one of the ways Australian soldiers asserted their sense of national identity,[67] but the use of language in the evolution of Australian identity can be expanded to thinking about foreign languages, as well as the assertion of an 'Australian language' against other varieties of English.

If many Australian soldiers would have identified as British, and seen Britain as 'home,' the experience of war created some interesting complexities to this sense of identification as Australian nationalism evolved. Australian soldiers quickly sought to portray themselves as superior to British troops, and their own cultural productions, such as soldier magazines, often included jokes and humorous anecdotes that poked fun at the British. An example of this is the following humorous piece published in the soldier periodical *Honk*, which illustrates the way language was deployed in a deliberate and self-conscious way to reinforce Australian identity within soldier culture, against British identity:

> Two English privates were sitting in an estaminet t'other evening conversing loudly in French. A couple of Australians at an adjoining table decided that they were not going to allow themselves to be out-swanked. So one, who came from NSW, remarked excitedly to his companion: 'Wagga Wagga Walgett Woolloomooloo wee waa Wallerawang Woolgoolga yarramalang.' 'Woollongabba,' replied his comrade who came from Queensland, 'Cunnamulla toowoomba toowong thorgomindah indooroopilly camooweal goondinwindi.' 'Bondi coogee maroubra,' said the other with great determination. It made the Englishmen slew round and take notice. 'Excuse me,' said one, 'but what language is that you're speaking?' 'Oh, that's our Australian language,' he was told. 'We learnt English before we came away, but we always prefer to speak our own language among ourselves.[68]

This anecdote makes deliberate use of Indigenous Australian (Aboriginal) place names to construct the soldiers' fictional language. This kind of use of Aboriginal languages was not unique to soldier culture, and drew on a longer Australian cultural-nationalist tradition and appropriation of Indigenous culture promoted by Australian popular magazines such as *The Bulletin* (which was widely read by soldiers). But what this kind of anecdote (which formed part of a broader culture that mocked the British soldiers) clearly did was to demonstrate that Australians were seeking to promote their identity as something quite separate from other nations. Such representations of the British were underpinned by real attitudes that individual Australian soldiers held towards the British. Instead of discovering that the British were just like Australians (or New Zealanders), they found that they were decidedly different. Various aspects of the British soldier, including their accent, came in for criticism. For example, Cyril Lawrence, who we met earlier, described the British accent as 'peculiar' and 'aggravating.'[69]

Language of course also distinguished Australians from their enemy. This was obvious insofar as different languages were spoken, but it was also implied that even Germans who could speak English failed to grasp the distinctiveness of Australian English. An Australian newspaper related an apocryphal story about the way in which Australian slang had revealed a German spy in the Australian soldiers' midst at Gallipoli. A suspicious Australian officer asked the 'traitor,' 'Is that fair dinkum?' to which the traitor innocently replied, 'Yes, that's my name.' He was immediately killed. The article was headlined 'German Treachery Discovered by Use of Slang.'[70] Here again we see the mythologising of Australian English during the war, and the way this process shaped attitudes towards the 'other.'

Borrowings from Other Languages

Many words were borrowed from other languages into English during the war, and these borrowings attest to the nature of communication between speakers of different languages during the war, as well as the ways Australians made use of languages such as French and Arabic.

Australian soldiers also adopted words used in the British Army from before the war, a number of which had their origins in British imperial rule in places such as India.

While in Egypt and the Middle East, Australian soldiers borrowed a number of words from Arabic, including the terms *aiwa, feloosh, igri, imshi,* and *saeeda. Aiwa,* meaning 'yes,' was a rendering of the Arabic *aywah. Feloosh* (from the Arabic *fulūs*) was in general use to refer to 'money.' *Igri* (also *igaree,* from the Arabic *ijri*) used as an exclamation, 'hurry up,' was in widespread use, along with *imshi* 'go away' and *maleesh* 'never mind.' The adoption of terms such as these suggest the importance of orders and imperatives in communication with local people. Some of these Arabic words were already in British English, through the British army's presence in Egypt. They include *baksheesh* 'free of charge; something for nothing' (and sometimes rendered as *buckshee*), *bukra* (from Arabic *bukratan,* 'tomorrow'), and *mafeesh* 'finished, done with.'

Australian soldiers also borrowed numerous words from French, words often shared among the Anglophone troops in France. Some were a crude rendering of the pronunciation of French words, such as *compree* (from the French *compris* 'understand?'), and some were Anglicisations of French words or phrases, such as *sanfairyann* (from *ça ne fait rien,* 'it does not matter') and *napoo* (from *il n'y en a plus,* 'finished, gone'). Some of these words were very much in popular use during the war: slang lexicographers and First World War veterans John Brophy and Eric Partridge in their *Songs and Slang of the British Soldier: 1914–1918* noted *compree* as being 'in constant use' during the war. They also glossed the popular *napoo* with the comment: 'the word came to be used for all the destructions, obliterations and disappointments of war.'[71]

Australian soldiers clearly adopted these words into their everyday vocabulary as evidenced in letters home and in their diaries. William Slater, who served in France as a stretcher bearer, noted at one point in his diary in 1917 that his 'chances are napoo.' Jim McConnell in a letter home described himself rushing 'toot sweet' into a cellar when he heard a shell coming. Private Hubert Demasson wrote home to his son in 1917 and mentioned the expression *très bon,* translating it into vernacular Australian: '"Tray Bon" as the Frenchies say, that means very good or what you would say you young scamp "Bonzer." "No bon" means no good, a lot of the men are able to speak a good lot of French.'[72] The use of foreign-language borrowings in the language of the Australian soldiers meant that such words also were communicated to those at home. Although few borrowed words remained in Australian English beyond the war years, some words lingered. The word *napoo*, for example, continued in Australian English usage through the interwar period, only dropping out of usage around the time of the Second World War.

Borrowings were also often highlighted in humorous glossaries during the war. While such glossaries often included a relatively accurate definition of how a word was used, there was usually some element of humour that often spoke to the wartime experience, or the construction of a soldier's (national) identity. One such glossary, included in a 1917 edition of the soldier periodical *The Kookaburra*, reveals some of the multiple meanings conveyed in these glossaries. For the entry *alley, toot sweet* (*allez tout suite*), a regular definition was provided—'In regimental parlance "at the double"'—but so was a humorous one: 'In the language of the Anzac "spring off your tail you Roo."' This second definition both aimed to convey humour, but also asserted a strong sense of 'Australianness.' Another entry, *tray bong* (*très bon*) was glossed as 'Not as supposed by some blokes to be a bonbon costing a tray. It's the expression you use when consuming strawberries and cream at the front—in your dreams.'[73] This gloss captured something of a typical lament of the soldier periodical—a lack of tasty food.

In the case of both Arabic and French borrowings, such borrowings indicated a basic desire to communicate with local populations, often to achieve basic transactions such as purchasing something. But little about these borrowings indicates more than a superficial engagement across cultures and languages. Indeed, the mutilation of words and phrases from other languages was more often used as a celebration of the wit of the Australian soldier, as we see with the humorous glossaries discussed above, and in discussions of such language after the war. In 1922, a newspaper article commenting on the slang of the Australian soldiers noted that the phrase *come a tallez plonk* was used much in the same way as the Australian expression *come a gutser*, and was described by the author of the article as both 'ingenious' and a mark of the soldiers' 'gay disrespect' for the French language.[74] Comte de Tournouer similarly observed in his discussion of 'digger's French' after the war that the Australians had 'quickly adapted themselves to the "pidgin" or trench French of the back areas.' Most French words, he observed, underwent a process of being 'diggerised.' For example, he claimed that *tout de suite* evolved to *toot sweet* and then to *chooks feet*. *Bonsoir* became *Bonzer war* and *comment allez vous?* evolved beyond the well-attested anglicisation *come and tally plonk* to the diggerised *come on tell el Kebir*.[75]

Conclusion

These brief investigations of cross-cultural communication and experiences of language during the First World War have helped to bring into focus some aspects of the 'languages landscape' of the war. Language learning and attempts to communicate in foreign languages were an important aspect of Australian soldiers' experiences of the war, but they were also strongly impacted on and shaped by the challenges of learning languages, the sense of racial superiority that some Australians had towards non-English speakers, and the increasing celebration of Australian English and Australian slang as integral to Australian national identity. Language mediators are also increasingly being investigated as an important group within the story of the First World War. Some of their stories have been told here, but much more work needs to be done on tracing their stories and bringing their work and experiences into focus. Language and cross-cultural communication need to be more central features of the story of Australians at war, and this chapter offers a contribution towards making this happen.

Notes

1. Cyril Lawrence, letter, 21 June, 1916, in Peter Yule (ed.) (1987), *Sergeant Lawrence Goes to France* (Melbourne: Melbourne University Press), p. 1.
2. Julian Walker (2017), *Words and the First World War: Language, Memory, Vocabulary* (London: Bloomsbury), p. 44.

3. Hilary Footitt (2012), 'Introduction', in Hilary Footitt and Michael Kelly (eds), *Languages and the Military: Alliances, Occupation and Peace Building* (Houndmills: Palgrave Macmillan), pp. 1–11, here p. 4.
4. Santanu Das (2018), 'Entangled Emotions: Race, Encounters and Anti-colonial Cosmopolitanism', in Santanu Das and Kate McLoughlin (eds), *The First World War: Literature, Culture, Modernity* (Oxford: Oxford University Press), pp. 240–61, here pp. 242–43.
5. Notably a number of works in the Palgrave Studies in Languages at War series, such as Hilary Footitt and Michael Kelly (2012), *Languages at War: Policies and Practices of Language Contacts in Conflict*, Hilary Footitt and Simona Tobia (2013), *'Wartalk': Foreign and the British War Effort in Europe, 1940–47*, and Julian Walker and Christophe Declerq (eds) (2016), *Languages and the First World War: Communicating in a Transnational War*.
6. Krista Cowman (2016), 'The … "parlez" Is Not Going Very Well "avec moi": Learning and Using "Trench French" on the Western Front', in Walker and Declerq (eds), *Languages and the First World War: Communicating in a Transnational War* (Houndmills: Palgrave), pp. 25–43, here p. 25.
7. Sandrijn Van Den Noortgate (2016), 'Caught in the Crossfire: Interpreters During the First World War', in Walker and Declerq (eds), *Languages and the First World War: Communicating in a Transnational War* (Houndmills: Palgrave), pp. 98–112, here p. 100.
8. Craig Gibson (2014), *Behind the Front: British Soldiers and French Civilians, 1914–1918* (Cambridge: Cambridge University Press).
9. Julian Walker, *Words and the First World War*, p. 28.
10. Craig Gibson, *Behind the Front*, p. 147.
11. Pauline Georgelin is currently completing a thesis looking at the experiences of French-Australians during the First World War, 'For Noble and Valiant France': French-Australian identities during the First World War' (University of Melbourne).
12. John F. Williams (2003), *German Anzacs and the First World War* (Sydney: UNSW Press), p. xv.
13. John F. Williams, *German Anzacs and the First World War*, p. 5.
14. Harry Cadwallader, Letter, 15 Feb 1916, 'Letters from the Great War 1914–1918: Private Henry (Harry) Thomas Cadwallader No 4160, 7th Battalion', AWM PR01199.
15. Julian Walker, *Words and the First World War*, p. 31.

16. Craig Gibson, *Behind the Front*, p. 149.
17. See AWM 250, Personal Effects Cards. For a longer discussion of this, see Amanda Laugesen (2012), *Boredom Is the Enemy: The Intellectual and Imaginative Lives of Australian Soldiers in the Great War and Beyond* (Abingdon: Ashgate), pp. 39–40.
18. Chaplain Lieutenant-Colonel James A. Gault (1920?), *Padre Gault's Stunt Book* (London: Epworth Press), p. 162.
19. Edward L. Moore, Diary entry, 22 January 1915, in *Gallipoli to the Somme: The WWI Diaries of Sapper Edward L. Moore* (Harkway, Vic.: Self-published).
20. Moore, Diary entry, 7 April 1916, in *Gallipoli to the Somme*.
21. Reg Telfer (1996), *Dad's War Diaries 1915–1919* (N.P.: Self-published, Claire Taplin), 15 August 1917.
22. Duffell, letter, 3 April 1916, in Gilbert Mant (ed.) (1992), *Soldier Boy: The Letters of Gunner W.J. Duffell, 1915–18* (Kenthurst: Kangaroo Press), p. 34.
23. Smythe, diary entry, 16 August 1915, *Anzac History World War I Letters from the Trenches, Smythe Family Letters*, http://www.smythe.id.au/letters/
24. Smythe, diary entry, 2 April 1916, *Anzac History World War I Letters from the Trenches, Smythe Family Letters*.
25. Smythe, diary entry, 8 April 1916, *Anzac History World War I Letters from the Trenches, Smythe Family Letters*.
26. Smythe, diary entry, 7 June, 13 June 1916, *Anzac History World War I Letters from the Trenches, Smythe Family Letters*.
27. Smythe, diary entry, 11 July 1916, *Anzac History World War I Letters from the Trenches, Smythe Family Letters*.
28. Smythe, diary entry, 15 July 1916, *Anzac History World War I Letters from the Trenches, Smythe Family Letters*.
29. Smythe, diary entry, 24 October 1916, *Anzac History World War I Letters from the Trenches, Smythe Family Letters*.
30. Smythe, diary entry, 5 February 1917, *Anzac History World War I Letters from the Trenches, Smythe Family Letters*.
31. Smythe, diary entry, 23 October 1917, *Anzac History World War I Letters from the Trenches, Smythe Family Letters*.
32. Smythe, diary entry, 23 November 1918, *Anzac History World War I Letters from the Trenches, Smythe Family Letters*.
33. *The Kia Ora Coo-ee* 2:4 (15 October 1918), p. 13.

34. *The Kia Ora Coo-ee* 2:4 (15 October 1918), p. 13.
35. AWM, 1DRL/615, Letter from 1129 Private C. R. Armstrong, Lager No. 255, 409 Heilsburg, East Prussia, 2 October 1918, Box 1, Folder 2, Chomley Papers.
36. AWM, 1DRL/615, Letter from Private J. T. Wright, n.d., Box 1, Folder 6, and Letter from Private A. L. R. Hanton, 30 January 1918, Box 1, Folder 3, Chomley Papers.
37. AWM, 1DRL/615, Letter from Private J. T. Wright, n.d., Box 1, Folder 6, Chomley Papers.
38. Laugesen, *Boredom is the Enemy*.
39. John F. Williams, *German Anzacs and the First World War*, p. 66.
40. Cyril Lawrence, diary entry, 2 April 1916, in Peter Yule (ed.), *Sergeant Lawrence Goes to France*, p. 1.
41. Smythe, letter, 14 January 1915, *Anzac History World War I Letters from the Trenches, Smythe Family Letters*.
42. Bean, diary entry 8 August 1915, in Kevin Fewster (ed.) (2007), *Bean's Gallipoli: The Diaries of Australia's Official War Correspondent* (Crows Nest, NSW: Allen and Unwin), p. 189.
43. Albert E. Coates, diary entry, 19 October 1915, in Winifred Gherardin and Walter Gherardin (eds) (1995), *The Volunteer: The Diaries and Letters of A.E. Coates No. 23 – 7th Battalion, 1st AIF, First World War 1914–18* (Burwood, Vic.: W. Graphics), p. 83.
44. Albert E. Coates, diary entry, 19 October 1915, in *The Volunteer*, p. 83.
45. Rowan Webb (1993), 'Coates, Sir Albert Ernest (1895–1977)', *Australian Dictionary of Biography* (National Centre of Biography, Australian National University) http://adb.anu.edu.au/biography/coates-sir-albert-ernest-9772/text17269, published first in hardcopy 1993, accessed online 2 May 2019.
46. Albert E. Coates, diary entry 9 April 1916, letter 7 June 1917, in *The Volunteer*.
47. Albert Coates and Newman Rosenthal (1977), *The Albert Coates Story: The Will That Found the Way* (Melbourne: Hyland House), p. 22.
48. *The Queensland Digger* 3:3 (1 August 1927), pp. 5–6.
49. Jacqueline Dwyer (ed.) (1985), *Wartime Diaries and Letters of Jacques Playoust or 'Seven Aussie Poilus' 1914–18* (Sydney: Self-published), p. 2.
50. Jacqueline Dwyer (2017), *Flanders in Australia: A Personal History of Wool and War* (Melbourne: Australian Scholarly Publishing), p. 193.

51. Eric Berti (2015), 'Jacques Playoust (1883–1947): Poilu and Pillar of the Sydney French Community', in Eric Berti and Ivan Balko (eds), *French Lives in Australia*, (Melbourne: Australian Scholarly Publishing), pp. 294–318, here p. 304.
52. Jacqueline Dwyer, *Flanders in Australia*, p. 228.
53. See AWM record.
54. Eric Berti, 'Jacques Playoust (1883–1947): Poilu and Pillar of the Sydney French Community', p. 308.
55. Jacqueline Dwyer, *Flanders in Australia*, p. 194.
56. Jacqueline Dwyer (ed.), *Wartime Diaries and Letters of Jacques Playoust or 'Seven Aussie Poilus' 1914–18*, p. 85.
57. Drane, diary entry, 15 December 1914, Complete Anzac Gallipoli War Diary by T.E. Drane http://bushroots.com/wp/2009/06/extracts-from-anzac-gallipoli-war-diary-by-tedrane/
58. Drane, diary entry, 15 December 1914, Complete Anzac Gallipoli War Diary.
59. Joan Beaumont (2013), *Broken Nation: Australians in the Great War* (Crows Nest: Allen and Unwin), p. 60.
60. John Baensch, diary entry, 25 November 1915, in (1993), *War Diary 1915–1916* (Geelong: Geelong Historical Society), p. 20.
61. McConnell, letter, 10 February 1918, in Dorothy Gilding (ed.) (2012), *Letters from the Front* (Sydney: Horizon Publishing Group), p. 109.
62. Davison, letter, 18 June 1916, in Daphne Elliott (ed.) (2013), *Arthur James Russell Davison: From Private to Captain in the 17th Battalion 1915–1918* (Adelaide: DPA Publishing), p. 99.
63. Stewart, diary entry, 12 August 1916, in Margaret Wilmington (1995), *Alfred Robert Morison Stewart: Diaries of an Unsung Hero* (Luddenham, NSW: Self-published), p. 141.
64. Tuck, diary entry, 9 September 1918, in Gertrude Kirby (ed.) (1989), *The War Diaries of Stanley Thomas Tuck 1917 and 1918* (Geelong, Vic.: Self-published).
65. *The Reveille*, 2:5 (January 31, 1929), p. 18.
66. *The Queensland Digger* (1 June 1927), p. 27.
67. Amanda Laugesen (2015), *Furphies and Whizz-bangs: Anzac Slang from the Great War* (South Melbourne: Oxford University Press).
68. Item from *Honk*, 29 August 1915, reprinted in David Kent (1999), *From Trench and Troopship: The Experience of the Australian Imperial Force 1914–1919* (Alexandria: Hale and Iremonger), p. 152.

69. Lawrence, diary entry, 24 March 1916, in Peter Yule (ed.), *Sergeant Lawrence Goes to France*, p. 1.
70. *Bendigonian*, 9 September 1915, p. 9.
71. John Brophy and Eric Partridge, *Songs and Slang of the British Soldier: 1914–1918* (London: Scholartis Press, 1930).
72. Demasson, letter, 19 March 1917, in Rachael Christensen (ed.) (1988), *To All My Dear People: The Diary and Letters of Hubert P. Demasson 1916–1917* (Fremantle: Fremantle Arts Centre Press), p. 141.
73. *The Kookaburra*, 2 (July 1917), p. 5.
74. *Daily News* (Perth), (22 April 1922) p. 11.
75. *The Queensland Digger*, (1 June 1927), p. 25.

Unfamiliar Allies: Australian Cross-Cultural Communication in Afghanistan and Iraq During the War on Terror

Richard Gehrmann

Former Australian soldier Shane Bryant quickly found transition to war in Afghanistan as a contractor had its cross-cultural challenges. 'The other dog handlers and I were travelling on what the Americans call Space-A – space available transport. I was starting to learn a whole new language and Space-A, translated, meant low priority. Uniformed American personnel got top billing, arranged by rank, and coalition soldiers and airmen were next. At the bottom of the heap were the civilian contractors like me.'[1]

Australian military[2] language, like any other, has adopted lexical components over time as Australians have engaged in cross-cultural communication with a wide variety of military partners.[3] Adoption of various expressions can arise because of exposure over time, a practical desire to use commonly understood terms to simplify communication, or it can relate to a value placed on specialist language. Before the First World War, British military language and style were valued. The phrase

---

R. Gehrmann (✉)
School of Humanities and Communication, University of Southern Queensland, Toowoomba, QLD, Australia
e-mail: richard.gehrmann@usq.edu.au

© The Author(s) 2020
A. Laugesen, R. Gehrmann (Eds.), *Communication, Interpreting and Language in Wartime*, Palgrave Studies in Languages at War,
https://doi.org/10.1007/978-3-030-27037-7_3

all Sir Garnet, a shortening of 'it's all Sir Garnet' meaning everything is all right, was a tribute to a very competent, late-Victorian British General Sir Garnet Wolsey, but it is now almost unknown.[4] Some terms from Australia's long military association with British India have endured: every day sick Australian soldiers arrive at a military medical centre to see the medic or the doctor and are given a *chit* (Indian army slang for a small piece of paper) excusing them from duty or stating what medical restrictions they have. *Dhobi* is a term for 'washing', while a *puggaree* (decorative cloth band) still adorns the Australian Army slouch hat. Other terms still in use reflect Australian military deployments to Malaysia, Indonesia, Vietnam, the Solomon Islands, and Bougainville. In his Afghanistan war memoir, Nathan Mullins notes the use of *makan* (Indonesian Malaysian term for 'eating'), *vui tui* (small plastic leaflet book, from the Vietnamese for small photo album), and *em tasol* (South Pacific pidgin for 'that's all, everything is finished').[5] The survival of such terms is tribute to the enduring significance of cross-cultural communication in military environments.

The wars in Afghanistan and Iraq provided opportunities for further linguistic and cross-cultural exchange. At least 34,500 Australians in total were to serve in Afghanistan (2001–14) and nearly 17,000 in Iraq (2003–10), although far smaller numbers at any one time rotated through these deployments. In both wars, Australian military commitments to an area collectively known as the Middle East Area of Operations (MEAO)[6] were relatively small scale, and Australians were almost always deployed as subordinate elements of larger coalition formations where they were compelled by circumstances to interact with different military cultures.

The past decade has seen a growth in the examination of warfare from the perspectives of language and communication, notably in the work of Footitt and Kelly.[7] This chapter contributes to this scholarship on language, while also building on earlier scholarship addressing the way individual memoirs reveal the experience of war, such as the contributions of Woodward and Jenkings.[8] It examines accounts of Australians who participated in two recent conflicts to trace instances of cross-cultural communication. There is a rich vein of scholarship examining the memoirs of participants in recent conflicts,[9] but research on the Australian experience is still in its infancy. During the war on terror Australians served with Iraqis, Afghans, Italians, Canadians, and Singaporeans among others, but this chapter will explore the social history of Australian military communication with their US and Dutch allies. This research is based on selected personal accounts[10] that reveal how participants understood and experienced cross-cultural communication in war, and positions these accounts beside news reports, as well as the author's personal experiences in Iraq and Afghanistan in 2006–07 and 2008–09, respectively.

The deployment to the MEAO meant Australians had to address two specific issues of communication, interpreting, and translation in war, one relating to the locations of the wars and the other to the allies they worked with. Firstly, a common feature in both deployments was that the local populations spoke languages (primarily Arabic or Pashtun) that most Australians were unfamiliar with. This lack of familiarity complicated Australian interaction with their allies in the Iraqi and Afghan security forces, the sometimes neutral civilian population, and also their insurgent enemies. Such unfamiliarity meant use of interpreters was essential and even with such mediation, linguistic interaction with local nationals could be obscured by differences. Cultural differences between Australians, Iraqis, and Afghans provided further communication challenges. Secondly, a common feature of both deployments was that the stated mission language was English, the majority language of the United States and a widely spoken second language of the Netherlands (NLD), and this might have been supposed to have eliminated communication difficulties. But despite linguistic commonalities between Australia and the United States, there were some challenges of communication, interpretation, and language and even greater differences emerged between Australians and the Dutch.

The experience of Australian communication with allies in the two theatres of war varied to a tremendous degree. For younger or junior-ranking Australians who might never have travelled overseas, never worked with people from another country, and who lacked exposure to different cultural practices, deployment with the US or Dutch military could provide a significant culture shock. For those meeting Americans for the first time, this culture shock might perhaps have been partially alleviated by the ubiquitous presence of American popular culture in the Australian mass media. But the fictive media version of the United States differed from the reality.[11] Other more experienced Australians had well-developed prior understanding of their future coalition partners. Before serving as a senior commander at the US headquarters in Iraq in 2004–05, Major General Jim Molan had practical exposure to working with the Americans on joint military exercises, giving him a real understanding of American military culture.[12] Unlike the accounts of other soldiers, his memoir rarely dwells on matters of cross-cultural communication.

Trying to Communicate with the Locals in an Unfamiliar World: Language Mediators

While the focus of this chapter is on linguistic and cross-cultural communication with Australia's Western coalition allies, this needs to be considered in the context of the degree of isolation and social distance that could be felt by those engaged in linguistic and cross-cultural communication with Afghans and Iraqis. Tone and intensity could aid in communication but spoken words might be unintelligible, as infantryman James Prascevic discovered when he walked into potential danger from sniper fire in Baghdad—'I was yelled at by an Iraqi soldier and although it was in his language, I knew that he was telling me off.'[13] Operating in a linguistically and culturally unfamiliar environment, the Australian Defence Force worked to reduce problems by deploying military members who had native fluency through their own migrant heritage, by training troops without native language background in the challenging languages required for the Middle East deployments, and by employing contract interpreters. Unfortunately, despite a large and diverse immigration programme, Australia did not have a vast supply of military-grade Iraqi (language), Iraqi Arabic, and Afghan language speakers. The Australian military was unable to recruit many migrants with native fluency in these languages,[14] a factor in part explained by structural and language issues[15] and a natural reluctance of those who have migrated from war-torn countries to join the military or have their children join the military.

The Australian Defence Force School of Languages at Point Cook supported military deployments by conducting year-long courses, three-month courses, and month-long courses in a range of languages,[16] and some Australians were given specific language training in Arabic and in the Afghan languages Pashtun and Dari. Previous Australian deployments to Bougainville, East Timor, and the Solomon Islands required instruction in Indonesian/Tetum (Timorese) and variants of Pidgin English, and trainees could gain a degree of competence in these languages in a limited study time. Very basic communication could be achieved in a very short timeframe, as infantryman Paul de Gelder found out when his completion of a two-week basic Tetum course and the fact that nobody else could speak Tetum resulted in him becoming his platoon's translator.[17]

The languages required for Iraq and Afghanistan were more difficult to learn, and in the case of Arabic training for the Iraq deployment, one of the complications was that there are extensive variants of Arabic throughout the Arab world. In both wars there was a reliance on contract interpreters, although the Australian Defence Force was engaged in competition for international trained interpreters with the United States, the primary end user for interpreters. These (mostly male) interpreters ranged from native-born speakers who were American citizens to local nationals who were often university-educated young men taking considerable risks by operating unarmed in a war zone. These urban-centric tertiary-educated interpreters also had to deal with the challenge of living and working in what for them were harsh conditions in rural areas and the significant risks of combat. Despite their unarmed status, there were instances of interpreters using weapons. For example, in January 2009, one interpreter working with Australians training the Afghan National Army (ANA) was caught in an ambush and responded to the crisis by using a weapon captured from insurgents to fire at the opposing Afghan insurgents, before using his language skills 'to motivate the ANA in the rear squad,'[18] forms of 'cross-cultural communication' which were highly appreciated by the Australian soldiers he was working with. But there are limits to what interpreters could do to bridge gaps. Given that Australians were in war zones where they experienced a high degree of social distance and isolation from the unfamiliar local people, it would be anticipated that Australians would gravitate towards US or Dutch soldiers whose culture on the surface appeared to be so much more familiar.

Working with Americans in Iraq and Afghanistan

Australian military engagement in the MEAO covered specific phases and locations. A small Australian force entered Afghanistan to drive out the Taliban in 2001, and following this, small numbers of Australian troops were located at Kabul's Kandahar airfield, and eventually 1500 were deployed in 2006 at Tarin Kowt in the southern province of Uruzgan. In 2003, a small number of Australians participated in the invasion of Iraq, and in the subsequent reconstruction phase, a small number of Australians were posted to staff, logistics, and air traffic control positions in the capital city of Baghdad, in the Green Zone of central Baghdad, and at Baghdad International Airport (BIAP). A security detachment (SECDET) was maintained to protect the Australian Embassy in Baghdad, and further troops were sent to train the new Iraqi army. Between 2005 and 2009, Australia had a 500-strong task force in the southern provinces of Al Muthanna and Dhi Qar. With the exception of the Dutch-run Uruzgan province, Australians were principally located near Americans.

Australia and the United States are English-speaking, Anglo-dominated, multicultural nations sharing many common cultural links, both through historical experience and through more recent globalisation, so it might be presumed that wartime cross-cultural communication problems would be rare. As allies through the ANZUS (Australia New Zealand United States) treaty and other military pacts, Australians conducted routine military exercises with Americans, and personnel from both nations served on reciprocal exchanges. Australians had previously fought alongside Americans in the Second World War and in Vietnam, and have a history of cooperation. However, the American Iraq and Afghanistan war commitment to a whole-of-nation struggle engaging large numbers of regulars, reservists, National Guard, and civilians was significantly different to the small-scale Australian deployments. Indeed, when Jim Molan first arrived in Iraq in 2004, he noted that while the entire coalition of predominantly US troops numbered 175,000, he was one of only 311 Australians in Iraq.[19] Challenges emerged both from the management of American expectations and from everyday Australian interactions in an ultra-patriotic American military culture. As a subordinate partner, Australians understood American military language and communication processes, frequently adopting lexical aspects of the American military, and despite some differences, cross-cultural communication problems were generally overcome.

The United States was fighting a high-intensity war in which year-long repeat deployments were common. David Savage, an Afghanistan-based defence civilian working on aid projects (who was to subsequently be wheelchair-bound with significant brain and spinal injuries following a child-suicide-bombing attack) recalled the experience of one of his security detachment, a twenty-three-year-old American. This soldier was on his fourth deployment to the Middle East, having previously served on two tours to Iraq and one to Afghanistan, a not uncommon story that reflected the very high deployment rate that was just part of the American war experience.[20] While the number of Australians deploying on multiple occasions increased over time, unlike their American allies, few undertook repeated twelve-month tours of duty.

Australian troops arriving in the MEAO had to adjust their expectations of Americans. For many in the Australian military, the Australian heroic representation of the Vietnam War experience[21] had created a perception that Australians had a much greater warfighting ability than the Americans. Jim Molan recalled, 'Since I had joined the army, almost every story I had heard from my superiors and every account I had read concentrated on the deficiencies of our powerful friend. I believed that US soldiers were certainly brave but far from competent … We spoke of how the US lost the Vietnam War, not how "we" lost the Vietnam War.'[22] The experience of being on the sidelines in Iraq[23] and of performing a less significant role in Afghanistan than Commonwealth allies Canada or Britain meant this perception of Australian superiority required some modification.[24]

American Culture and Uses of Language

Troops arriving in the MEAO had already received briefings on Iraqi or Afghan culture during their pre-deployment training in Australia. On arrival in staging locations in the Arabian Gulf such as Kuwait or the United Arab Emirates Al Minhad base, they could also be given further briefs on cross-cultural adjustment—in this case on adjusting to Americans, as allies they would be working and living with.

These briefs were designed to reduce tension between Australian and US troops, and to increase mutual understanding. Topics included the risk of causing offence by disparaging very distinct American values and religiosity. Shane Bryant worked as a contractor with the US military in Afghanistan, and viewed Americans positively but observed cultural differences. He recalled: 'They were generally friendly and polite, and I had already picked up that many were overtly religious compared to Australian soldiers. It wasn't unusual to see guys saying grace before they ate.'[25] Australians were warned about American attitudes of hierarchy and respect, and their high degree of ultra-patriotic loyalty in comparison to Australia's more casual and iconoclastic culture. Another topic to be avoided was the low American pay and allowances in comparison to the high Australian service allowance, although infantryman James Prascevic noted that some 'did say that it would be great to be on the sort of money we were but for them it was all about representing their country. Whenever I asked the question, "why did you join up?" most of the time the answer was "9/11." They were so proud of their country and the fact that they could represent it overseas.'[26] Regardless of whether they voted Republican or Democrat, the US President was their commander-in-chief and was accorded significantly more respect than Australian Prime Ministers were, and public Australian speech with Americans had to be adjusted accordingly. The American propensity to wear unusually short haircuts, so-called 'high and tight' haircuts, and to spend hours in the gym weight lifting also distinguished them from Australians. A number of Australians were embedded in predominantly American coalition headquarters, and the requirements to understand American cultural norms posed a daily challenge for them, a cross-cultural challenge that was far less pressing for their fellow Australians based in the large all-Australian deployments in Al Muthanna and Dhi Qar in southern Iraq.

Respectful language and the use of profanity was a further cultural difference. While in private everyday speech military conversations between ordinary American soldiers could range from polite to explicitly coarse,[27] in public or official interactions, the American military exhibited a high degree of political correctness in relation to appropriate language use and unacceptable behaviour. This was taken to what Australians could see as extreme lengths. All troops in the Middle East were lectured on the requirement to drink enough water, and a basic test individuals could perform on themselves was to check that they had clear rather than dark yellow urine two times per day. The American public-advisory slogan was a circumspect 'be clear twice a day' while the very direct Australian version was 'piss clear twice a day.' Political correctness and circumspection was also reflected in the language that could be used in public gatherings. Award-winning stand-up comedian Tom Gleeson has described his experiences undertaking a concert tour to the Middle East in 2006,[28] where he performed his highly amusing musical parody of British artist James Blunt's song 'You're beautiful' to mixed Australian and American audiences. Having comprehensively trashed the character, life, and music of Blunt, Gleeson concluded this segment of his performance with the words 'James Blunt, rhymes with c[un]t.' Americans would visibly recoil in horror, complaints would be made, Gleeson's public relations minders would tell him not to do it—and of course he did it again in the next performance!

American military culture regulated aspects of the interaction between males and females. While both militaries had rules prohibiting inappropriate sexual contact or fraternisation, Australians were accustomed to a more relaxed level of everyday interaction between males and females, and found American restrictions unusual. When transiting through US staging bases in Middle Eastern countries for short periods, Australians were accommodated on stretchers in large hangar-sized temporary sleeping tents. As guests, Australians were obliged to adhere to American requirements that dictated males and females sleep in separate tents, despite the fact that the male sleeping tent might be crammed full to overflow and the female tent might only be occupied by half a dozen soldiers. In such circumstances, Australians in transit would have been comfortable sleeping in the same location regardless of gender. This is not to imply that US rules of public behaviour protected Australian[29] and American women[30] from unwelcome sexual attention. There was a difference between the prescribed rules and the actual realities of everyday life, especially in an environment where women were a minority. Some female Americans experienced sexual assaults by male soldiers. Signals officer Sarah Watson commented that the gender imbalance and her obviously foreign status made her stand out: 'It did add an unwanted pressure. I got hit on quite a bit by the Americans in the mess. They were just blatant.'[31]

Cross-cultural differences also included ethnic diversity and public affirmation of such diversity. The vast US armed forces that deployed to Iraq and Afghanistan were far more ethnically diverse than the much smaller Australian military, with significant numbers of Americans from minority communities, including African-Americans, Hispanic-Americans, and Asian-Americans. This diversity was reflected in public celebratory aspects of US military culture. For example, in Baghdad Australians eating at the DFAC (Dining Facility or mess hall) occasionally encountered posters, singers, musicians, and food celebrating the diversity of America for events such as National Hispanic American Month or Korean American Day. Such public displays of national multiculturalism surprised many Australians who had presumed the United States to be far more monocultural. There are no similar Australian celebrations, despite Australia's ethnic diversity.

Australians on a US base would usually have their meals in an American-run DFAC. They would be offered a varied array of typically American food where high-fat and high-sugar options appear to dominate, but there was enough choice to ensure that the food was still acceptable to Australian tastes. However, even just going to eat was a daily experience of linguistic and cross-cultural engagement. Troops entering the DFAC had to produce their ID card and often submit to being greeted by the armed soldiers on guard with the distinctively American 'Hooah' call, a call Americans would reply to with the same word as an antiphonal response. Australians would usually only respond with that term if they were deliberately making fun of the DFAC guards, or they could alternatively respond with a purposefully clichéd 'g'day mate,' which over time could lead to the DFAC guard being subtly 'retrained' to use this greeting for Australians.

Borrowing of US Military Language

As well as cross-cultural adjustment, more formal acculturation of Australians towards the American language of war came with the wholesale adoption of a range of US military terminology by Australians serving in the Middle East. This occurred both because of the functional or practical requirements to match the dominant military partner and use a common pattern of spoken and written military behaviour, but also because use of such language was a marker of veteran expertise and legitimacy. By using American Middle East military terms, individual Australians demonstrated status and experience of having served in *the sandpit* or *the sandbox*, rather than a benign and therefore lower-status peacekeeping mission such as East Timor or the Solomon Islands.

Functional or practical terms were official acronyms and expressions that simplified communication. The author's recollection of terms included *TIC* ('tick,' troops in contact), *TOC* ('tock,' tactical operations centre), *DFAC* ('Deefack,' mess hall), *MSR* (main supply route), *CSH* ('Cash,' combat surgical hospital), IED (improvised explosive device), 5 and 25s (search pattern) for IEDs, and *YPOC* ('Whypock,' yellow palm oil container possibly re-used and filled with explosives for an IED). Different people were referred to as *LN* or local national (a citizen of Iraq or Afghanistan), *TCN* (third country national and usually a contractor from the Global South), and *terp* (interpreter). The name for the enemy in each country varied over time. The acronym *AIF* (anti-Iraqi forces) was problematic for military Australians accustomed to associating these letters with the venerated Australian Imperial Force of the First World War, so it was a welcome change when the term *INS* (insurgents) became standard.

T walls were the thick concrete blast walls commonly used to protect troops in Iraq from rocket attack or small-arms fire, whereas in Afghanistan *HESCO gabions* (wire mesh containers filled with gravel) were common.

A prisoner was a *PUC* ('puck,' person under control). Nouns could of course also have their verb form, as the following exchange would indicate: 'Did they bring a PUC in with them?'—'yes—actually they pucked two guys in the last raid.' In US headquarters, operations staff officers were referred to as battle captains and battle majors. This was a practice followed by Australians in the national headquarters or who were embedded in coalition headquarters, despite the fact that there was a clear disjuncture between actual fighting in a battle with a weapon, and the role of a staff officer performing an equally significant, but far less heroic, task of fighting the war with PowerPoint.

Of course, unofficial US military slang terms were also adopted. *Battle rattle* referred to complete military equipment, including body armour, and a *pogue* was a derogatory term used by infantry to refer to everyone else. *FOB* ('fob') was an official term that stood for Forward Operating Base which was a large secure military base occupied by Fobbits, those whose jobs did not take them into areas of risk *outside the wire*, which meant the only risk they faced was *IDF* (indirect fire), usually from rocket or mortars. The *Green Zone* in Baghdad was the slightly safer area around the embassies and national headquarters in central Baghdad, which one would reach by travelling along Route Irish from Camp Victory, the main US base located at Baghdad International Airport (BIAP) on the edge of the city. Confusingly, in Afghanistan, the Green Zone was not safe but was the potentially very dangerous cultivated and inhabited area located along a river valley. While many Australians knew a few Arabic (*shukran,* thank you) or Pashtun/Dari (*tashakor,* thank you) phrases, the greatest source of loan words was the most dominant power in the MEAO, the US military.

Working with the Dutch in Afghanistan

Although some Australians were based in Kandahar and Kabul, the majority of Australians in Afghanistan worked with the Dutch at Camp Holland in the southern Uruzgan province under the auspices of NATO, as part of the International Security Assistance Force (ISAF). Despite being fellow members of the Western alliance, the Dutch were a relatively unfamiliar ally with no recent history of shared military cooperation with Australia. While a small number of Australians had fought with the Dutch against the Japanese, Second World War military cooperation with the Dutch was minimal and the post-war Australian military occupation of Indonesia did not improve Australian-Dutch relations. For soldiers serving together in the twenty-first century, the lack of past military cooperation exacerbated existing cultural differences.

The Netherlands was a more open and progressive social culture than Australia, and this was reflected in aspects of their military communication and practice. During the years of military cooperation in Uruzgan province between 2006 and 2010, it became apparent that Dutch liberal social values and consensus, and the Dutch discussion-based military culture, differed from that of Australia. Even Dutch food was different, as was their propensity to wear spandex tights while exercising. Despite military cooperation in war and the high levels of English spoken by Dutch soldiers who were far more linguistically talented than their Australian counterparts, a degree of distance remained between the Dutch and Australian military, and Dutch military terminology did not become part of the Australian military lexicon.

Small numbers of Australian Special Forces deployed to Afghanistan in 2001–02 and again in 2005, but large-scale regular army deployments only began in 2006. The primary Australian commitment in Afghanistan was the contingent serving as part of Task Force Uruzgan from 2006,[32] which marked perhaps the first long-term[33] Australian deployment in which Australians served under non-English-speaking operational command. While service under American command had seen the adoption of American military terminology, Australian troops in Afghanistan only adopted Dutch terminology on rare occasions. The Task Force was Dutch-led, but over time comprised elements from a variety of countries including Australia, France, Norway, Singapore, Slovakia, Britain, the United States, and also Afghanistan. Visiting journalist Chris Masters observed that in the Dutch-run mess, 'Each national force tends to keep to their respective tables; neither openly warring nor enthusiastically bonding, the Task Force Uruzgan allies assume a posture of armed neutrality.'[34]

Dutch Culture and Uses of Language

The Dutch were proud of their relaxed military culture, which even included casual parade behaviour on 'formal' parades, and their casual military style was apparent in their physical appearance and dress. The rituals of standing to attention and at ease were far more easy-going than those of the Australian military. A comparative study of military culture has revealed the Dutch military have been perceived as being independent, sociable, flexible and informal, loose and impertinent, but also as comradely and competent.[35] Like some of their other European counterparts that Australians shared a military base with (Italians in southern Iraq, French and Slovakians in Afghanistan), the Dutch had a more relaxed attitude to haircuts and shaving. In military circles, there was a significant degree of prestige in the beards Special Forces soldiers grew, but European beards were often more fashionable and tailored. In the words of Australian Major Rachel Brennan: 'You'd see them around the gym or eating in the mess hall. They'd have long hair. Some of them had mohawks. They'd get around in their lycra get-up. Just different. We thought they were a bit more loose than how we ran things. They'd come around in normal vehicles and not armoured vehicles. They had a different approach to things.'[36]

Dutch national characteristics of consensus and discussion were also part of Dutch military culture. This became readily apparent to Australians (such as the author of this chapter) who regularly worked with the Dutch. Getting to know the Dutch well on a daily basis over eight months provided a different perspective on their unique approach to military issues, their genuine commitment, and their very quirky sense of humour. But events that Australians expected to be formal military meetings could be marked by a high level of open discussion, informal critique, and ambivalent responses, which to some Australians appeared to be unprofessional, leading to cross-cultural misunderstanding and stress.[37] This is somewhat paradoxical because it has been argued that the Australian military prides itself on a culture of egalitarianism and informality, values that developed in response to the rank-conscious pomp and hierarchy of the British military,[38] and the open discussion and informal criticism implicit in Special

Forces culture is universally admired. However, military Australians posted to mainstream conventional units prefer formality and more rigid styles of behaviour, and were uncomfortable with an ally whose soldiers could talk and discuss military issues so openly—and even join trade unions.

It has been argued that this perception that the Dutch are tolerant and non-martial is incorrect, and Zaalberg has claimed that 'the cliché of the Dutch as a traditionally peace-loving, non-militaristic and culturally sensitive people' was in fact at odds with actual Dutch military practice in Afghanistan which could be highly kinetic.[39] This reality was also noticed by some Australians. According to Lieutenant Colonel Jason Blain, 'A lot dis the Dutch as soft and weak. I tell you my experience is they focused on getting out there and achieving results. An interesting lot who don't want to be seen so much as professional soldiers.'[40]

The Australian Defence Force's strict no-fraternisation policy restricting sexual contact between fellow soldiers seemed bizarre to Dutch soldiers. Conversely, Australian soldiers presumed high levels of fraternisation took place among the Dutch. But this was just one of many cross-cultural differences. The Dutch had unisex showers, something which for many Australians seemed to confirm all their deepest suspicions of European behaviour, and the image of Dutch males in the gym was problematic. The practice of wearing lycra or spandex tights without the modesty shorts that were mandatory for Australian soldiers was so offensive to Australian soldiers that a Facebook page emerged to conduct discussion of the 'problem.'

Norms of political correctness was another area where cross-cultural challenges emerged. In this sphere Dutch practices seemed to be the opposite of American practices. While Americans were more likely to be highly religious and were overtly so in public displays, the Dutch were overtly secular and as well as a military chaplain they had a non-religious equivalent. The Dutch were quite happy to joke and make reference to sexual issues in a far more open manner than their Australian counterparts. Australians were also genuinely shocked by the Dutch Christmas tradition of Sinterklaas and Zwarte Piet (St Nicholas and Black Peter), during which some Dutch soldiers dressed as Christmas elves in blackface makeup.

Dutch culinary culture also seemed foreign to many Australians. On Wednesdays, the Dutch-run mess hall in Camp Holland served Indonesian-style curry dishes, an element of Dutch cultural traditions based on the Dutch colonial experience in the East Indies,[41] but *Blauwe hap* or *Rijsttafel* never entered Australian military terminology. Another Dutch military tradition was to have a seafood brunch on Sunday mornings, which gave many Australians what may have been their first exposure to Dutch *rollmops* or raw pickled herring fillets rolled into a cylindrical shape around a filling. This was not a culinary trend that was greatly admired by the non-Dutch military personnel at Camp Holland,[42] and there were protests about Dutch catering. The complaints about Dutch food eventually reached the Chief of the Australian Defence Force, Air Chief Marshal Angus Houston, who admitted to a government committee that while the Dutch food was 'generally nutritious,' 'the issue is that it's not Aussie food, it's European food.'[43]

Crisis situations could exacerbate cross-cultural difficulties on both sides. After taking part in a helicopter extraction of two wounded Dutch soldiers from the battlefield, combat medic Terry Ledgard had his life-saving treatment of one Dutch soldier challenged by a Dutch trauma nurse when he accompanied his casualty into the Dutch-run hospital in Tarin Kowt. He described her angry responses to his treatment of the casualty leaving him feeling 'disoriented in a Bermuda Triangle vortex of unfamiliar Dutch culture, hostility and situational pressure.'[44]

Borrowing from Other Languages in Afghanistan

A very small number of Netherlands military terms became part of the Australian military vocabulary, reflecting the broader limitations to cross-cultural understanding. The very practical *NATO 9 liner* was used as it was the standard casualty-report form. Other generic military terms were acquired because of the particular nature of the training task in southern Afghanistan. An example is the term *omelette*, from Operational Mentor and Liaison Team (OMLT), referring to a small group of Australian or other ISAF soldiers used to mentor and train the Afghan National Army soldiers.

Geographically significant Afghan terms such as the *dasht* (desert area) and *quala* (compound) slipped into regular military usage, as did *shura* (the Arabic term for 'meeting,' used in both Iraq and Afghanistan). Another term that made the transition from the Iraq war to Afghanistan was *jundi*, the Arabic term for soldier that in Afghanistan was applied to any male in Afghanistan.[45] Infantryman Kyle Wilson, like many Australian soldiers, used Afghan words in the battlefield and these words find their place in soldiers' memoirs of events leading up to an imminent battle: 'I had a bad feeling he was a bad cunt and we followed him. I yelled out '*Waderaja*' (stop) but he ignored me.'[46] However, Afghan languages rarely permeated Australian military consciousness, and did not become part of standard Australian military slang. Unlike Australian soldiers based in France from 1915 to 1918, most Australians were deployed to Afghanistan for fixed periods of up to eight months rather than several years, and did not spend rest and relaxation time in the company of a supportive local population. During their deployment to Afghanistan, they lived apart from the civilian population in secure military camps and patrol bases when not on patrol, and thus had limited opportunity to interact in everyday manner with the local civilian population. Troops mentoring the Afghan National Army who were posted to remote patrol bases alongside Afghan soldiers had greater contact with soldiers and of necessity learnt more Afghan terms, but this contact became more constrained as 'green on blue' killings (killing of a coalition soldier by a rogue Afghan soldier) increased in the later years of the Australian deployment.

Analysis of the Australian Experience of Communication in Iraq and Afghanistan

American expressions dominated both wars, which is unsurprising given the vast number of deployed US troops, the influence the United States has on global culture, and their superpower status. There are various possible reasons why Dutch military terminology did not become part of the Australian military lexicon. The very fact that the United States were the coalition leaders during the war on terror since 2001 gave the United States primacy, and would have made it difficult to any other linguistic military culture to have displaced that of the United States. A further explanation could be that the linguistic differences between Dutch and English meant that Dutch usage of terms was not readily apparent to many Australians, limiting the likelihood of the adoption of non-English terms. It should also be emphasised that the Dutch are a talented and educated multilingual people, and large numbers of Dutch military personnel spoke English, further limiting the transmission of Dutch military language to the Australian lexicon. English was after all the mission language and a global language—and Australians did not need or bother to learn Dutch, so had fewer reasons to pick up Dutch vocabulary.

Another reason might relate to Australian perceptions of their own status as fighters and of their perceptions of the status of the Dutch as fighters. Australians perhaps liked to see themselves as being closer to the more warlike Americans and far removed from the ostensibly less warlike and consensus-driven casual Dutch, whose much-praised counterinsurgency policy of civil-military cooperation[47] appeared to some Australians to be a soft approach. A series of dismissive Australian comments on the much more significant Netherlands military presence in Uruzgan adds weight to this possible explanation. American perceptions that their NATO allies were not doing enough to support the fighting effort led to the American joke that the acronym ISAF (word on the sleeve of Dutch troops) stood for 'I saw Americans fighting.' It is ironic, in a situation where Australia actually had a disproportionately smaller military involvement in Afghanistan than the United States, that this American joke was adapted by Uruzgan-based Australians into 'I saw Australians fighting.' Mullins recalls the snide explanation that 'Dutch' stood for the phrase 'don't understand the concept here,'[48] and Masters observed that Australian soldiers had another apparent explanation of the international country abbreviation for the Netherlands (NLD), this being that it stood for 'no one likes Dutch.'[49] There have been Australian claims that the Dutch did not provide enough support for Australians.[50] Counter to this and despite Australian presumptions of their own warlike nature, it should be noted that there had also been instances of Dutch claims that Australians refused to support them in battle, because of more restrictive Australian rules of engagement.[51] This issue of who was the most warlike is not the focus of this chapter, but the key point might lie not so much with the reality of Dutch-Australian military cooperation, but in the Australian perceptions of this cooperation.

The perception of Australian military superiority would have also puzzled the Americans when the Dutch left in 2010. Despite having more troops in Uruzgan than other nations, the Australians insisted on being under American command (Combined Team Uruzgan) until 2012, to avoid the political cost of provincial leadership. This chapter does not explore what allies thought of Australians in Iraq and Afghanistan, but a Lowy Institute publication titled 'inconsequential confused and timid' is telling.[52] In his evaluation of alliance relations in the Iraq war Jim Molan noted: 'The British called us "the new French" and the US saw us as just another ally that needed to be carried. The Americans are far more polite than the British.' Such comments bear out the assessment that Australian participation in the wars was small scale and focused on alliance building rather than military victory.

Conclusion

In conclusion, the Australian military experiences in Iraq and Afghanistan are of interest in terms of the study of Australian military culture. Australians faced the challenge of engaging in cross-cultural communication and linguistic exchange with English-speaking and non-English-speaking allies, and significant differences existed in different cases. This chapter has explored the social history of Australian military communication with allies in Afghanistan and Iraq, and shows that the tradition of borrowing language during war continues, but it also suggests that the global power of English, plus the status of the United States as a major ally that Australians interact with on a regular basis, has meant that the United States has been the dominant linguistic source for Australian borrowing of foreign military terminology in the current era. It also demonstrates that despite apparent cultural similarities, cross-cultural differences meant that communication between allies could be problematic. Based on the Canadian experience, Brian Selmeski has pointed out that cross-cultural competence in war needs to go further than better briefings, additional language training, knowledge of the enemy, and knowledge of international relations.[53] Understanding the ways in which ordinary members of the military understand cross-cultural communication with allies will do much to advance understanding and shape future experiences. Past research shows cultural diversity in multinational force operations can be the source of both weakness and strength,[54] and the likelihood of future service in coalition operations makes examination of past practice significant.

Australians in the wars in Iraq and Afghanistan adopted a range of terms from their allies. The adoption of such insider terms occurs for a variety of reasons. It can be based on an admiration of another military culture, or can reflect the impact a dominant military culture has had on a subordinate military culture, with the duration of time cultures have been in contact with each other also being a factor. A further consideration is that soldiers want to adopt what become 'military chic' expressions in order to take on the representation of real soldiers, presenting themselves as experienced and well-travelled warriors. Using terms and language acquired in the war zone denotes experience and can provide the user with insider status, becoming the mark of the veteran.

Australians served in the war on terror after the Australian government's decision to commit to these conflicts as a military-alliance partner in Afghanistan and Iraq. In both wars, Australian commitments were relatively small scale and Australians did not seek an autonomous role but remained engaged as subordinate elements of larger coalition formations. The Australian military had to manage the obvious challenge of linguistic and cross-cultural communication with unfamiliar Afghan and Iraqi allies, but linguistic and cross-cultural communication problems were also significant in relations with ostensibly more familiar coalition allies.

Notes

1. Shane Bryant with Tony Park (2010), *War Dogs: An Australian and His Dog Go to War in Afghanistan* (Sydney: Macmillan), p. 51.
2. I use the term military to refer to troops or soldiers, as in members of the Army, Navy, or Air Force.
3. For a detailed exploration of a range of these terms, see Amanda Laugesen (2005), *Diggerspeak: The Language of Australians at War* (Melbourne: Oxford University Press).
4. Richard Fotheringham (2009), 'Speaking a New World: Language in Early Australian Plays', *Journal of the Australasian Universities Language and Literature Association*, 111, pp. 1–20, here p. 5.
5. Nathan Mullins (2011), *Keep Your Head Down: One Commando's Brutally Honest Account of Fighting in Afghanistan* (Sydney: Allen and Unwin), pp. 80–81.
6. The term MEAO encompassed Australian military activities in both Iraq and Afghanistan, as well as in bases and on ships throughout the Arabian Gulf, but the focus of this chapter is on Iraq and Afghanistan.
7. Hilary Footitt and Michael Kelly (eds) (2012), *Languages and the Military: Alliances, Occupation and Peace Building* (Houndmills: Palgrave Macmillan).
8. Rachel Woodward and K. Neil Jenkings (2012), '"This Place Isn't Worth the Left Boot of One of Our Boys": Geopolitics, Militarism and Memoirs of the Afghanistan War', *Political Geography*, 31:8, pp. 495–508.
9. Synne L. Dyvik (2016), '"Valhalla rising": Gender, Embodiment and Experience in Military Memoirs', *Security Dialogue*, 47:2, pp. 133–150; Lamberta Hendrika Esmeralda Kleinreesink (2017), *On Military Memoirs: A Quantitative Comparison of International Afghanistan War Autobiographies* (Boston, MA: Brill); Julien Pomarède (2018), 'Normalizing Violence through Front-line Stories: The Case of *American Sniper*', *Critical Military Studies*, 4:1, pp. 52–71.
10. While uniformed members of the military dominate this study, defence civilians and former members of the military also form part of this group of Australians attempting to communicate with allies during war.
11. Richard Gehrmann (2017), 'Enemies of the State(s): Cultural Memory, Cinema, and the Iraq War', in Jessica Gildersleeve and Richard Gehrmann (eds), *Memory and the Wars on Terror* (Cham: Palgrave Macmillan), pp. 69–89.

12. Jim Molan (2008), *Running the War in Iraq* (Sydney: HarperCollins), pp. 23–24; 40.
13. James Prascevic (2014), *Returned Soldier: My Battles: Timor, Iraq, Afghanistan, Depression and Post-Traumatic Stress Disorder* (Melbourne: Melbourne Books), p. 92.
14. This is despite specific targeting of this group. See Anthony John (2013), 'From Institution to Occupation: Australian Army Culture in Transition', *Australian Army Journal* 10:3, pp. 187–202, here p. 191.
15. Hugh Smith (1995), 'The Dynamics of Social Change and the Australian Defence Force', *Armed Forces & Society*, 21:4, pp. 531–51, here p. 12.
16. See Issares Surachestpong (2016), 'A Needs Assessment of Intensive Language Teaching at the ADF School of Languages', PhD thesis, Victoria University.
17. Paul de Gelder (2011), *No Time for Fear* (Camberwell: Penguin), p. 93.
18. Ben Gooley, Matt Lines, and Tom Larter (2012), 'OMLT – in contact', in Dave Allen (ed), *War in the Valleys: 7th Battalion Battle Group (MRTF-1), Afghanistan, October 2008 to June 2009* (Wilsonton: Ryter Publishing), p. 36.
19. Molan, *Running the War in Iraq*, p. 310.
20. Paul Field (2017), *Gimme Shelter: Stories of Courage, Endurance and Survival from the Frontline and Back Home* (Richmond: Echo), pp. 6–7.
21. Graeme Dobell (2014), 'The Alliance Echoes and Portents of Australia's Longest War', *Australian Journal of International Affairs*, 68:4, pp. 386–96, here pp. 288–89.
22. Molan, *Running the War in Iraq*, pp. 23–4. See also Gary McKay (1998), *Delta Four: Australian Riflemen in Vietnam* (Sydney: Allen & Unwin), pp. 215–23.
23. Jim Hammett (2008), 'We Were Soldiers Once: The Decline of the Royal Australian Infantry Corps?', *Australian Army Journal*, 5:1, pp. 39–50.
24. On occasions in Iraq, the British actually thought Australians were reluctant to become engaged in combat. John Blaxland (2014), *The Australian Army from Whitlam to Howard* (Melbourne: Cambridge University Press), pp. 241–42, pp. 246–47. For a comparison of the Canadian and Australian deployments, see Kim Nossal (2009), 'Making Sense of Afghanistan: The Domestic Politics of International Stabilization Missions in Australia and Canada', *International Journal*, 64:3, pp. 825–42.

25. Bryant, *War Dogs*, pp. 62–3.
26. Prascevic, *Returned Soldier: My Battles*, p. 83.
27. For examples of this, see Evan Wright (2005), *Generation Kill* (London: Corgi), and Chris Kyle (2012), *American Sniper* (New York: Harper).
28. Tom Gleeson (2008), *Playing Poker with the SAS: A Comedy Tour of Iraq and Afghanistan* (Sydney: University of New South Wales Press).
29. There have been significant changes in the Australian Defence Force since a highly publicised sex scandal in 2011. See Jessica Carniel (2017), 'Death and the Maiden: Memorialisation, Scandal, and the Gendered Mediation of Australian Soldiers', in Jessica Gildersleeve and Richard Gehrmann (eds), *Memory and the Wars on Terror* (Cham: Palgrave Macmillan), pp. 237–62, here pp. 251–55.
30. See, for example, the memoir of Kayla Williams (2005), *Love My Rifle More Than You: Young and Female in the US Army* (London: W. W. Norton & Company).
31. Paul Field (2017), *Gimme Shelter*, p. 228.
32. This was to become the American-led Combined Team Uruzgan following Dutch withdrawal and transfer of command in 2010.
33. Australians had served briefly under Dutch command in Java in 1942. See Andrew Faulkner (2008), *Arthur Blackburn, VC: An Australian Hero, His Men, and Their Two World Wars* (Kent Town: Wakefield Press), pp. 340–47; and Tom Gilling (2018), *The Lost Battalions* (Sydney: Allen and Unwin).
34. Chris Masters (2012), *Uncommon Soldier* (Sydney: Allen & Unwin), p. 119.
35. René Moelker, Joseph Soeters, and Ulrich vom Hagen (2007), 'Sympathy, the Cement of Interoperability: Findings on Ten Years of German-Netherlands Military Cooperation', *Armed Forces and Society* 33:4, pp. 496–517, here p. 513.
36. Jimmy Thompson and Sandy MacGregor (2015), *Tunnel Rats* vs *the Taliban* (Sydney: Allen and Unwin), p. 138.
37. See Dave Allen (ed), *War in the Valleys*, p. 14.
38. James Brown (2013), 'Fifty Shades of Grey: Officer Culture in the Australian Army', *Australian Army Journal*, 10:3, pp. 244–54, here pp. 248–49.
39. Thijs Brocades Zaalberg (2013), 'The Use and Abuse of the "Dutch Approach" to Counter-Insurgency', *Journal of Strategic Studies*, 36:6, pp. 867–97, here p. 891.

40. Chris Masters (2012), *Uncommon Soldier* (Sydney: Allen & Unwin), p. 269. For an understanding of Dutch approaches, see Martijn Kitzen (2012), 'Close Encounters of the Tribal Kind: The Implementation of Co-option as a Tool for De-escalation of Conflict – The Case of the Netherlands in Afghanistan's Uruzgan Province', *Journal of Strategic Studies*, 35:5, pp. 713–34.
41. Matthijs Kuipers (2017), '"Makanlah Nasi! (Eat Rice!)": Colonial Cuisine and Popular Imperialism in The Netherlands During the Twentieth Century', *Global Food History*, 3:1, pp. 4–23.
42. Seth Robson (2010), 'At Tirin Kot, U.S., Dutch and Australians Serve Together, Observe Cultural Quirks', *Stars and Stripes*, August 20 2010, https://www.stripes.com/news/at-tirin-kot-u-s-dutch-and-australians-serve-together-observe-cultural-quirks-1.115410
43. Rob Taylor (2009), 'Australia's Troops Aghast at Dutch Food', Reuters 4 June 2009, https://www.reuters.com/article/us-afghanistan-food/australias-troops-aghast-at-dutch-food-idUSTRE5523ZE20090603
44. Terry Ledgard (2016), *Bad Medicine: A No Holds Barred Account of Life as an Australian SAS Medic During The War in Afghanistan* (Melbourne: Viking Penguin), pp. 122–23.
45. Nathan Mullins (2011), *Keep Your Head Down: One Commando's Brutally Honest Account of Fighting in Afghanistan* (Sydney: Allen and Unwin), p. 81.
46. Field, *Gimme Shelter*, p. 117.
47. Zaalberg, 'The Use and Abuse of the "Dutch Approach" to Counter-Insurgency'.
48. Nathan Mullins (2011), *Keep Your Head Down*, p. 90.
49. Masters, *Uncommon Soldier*, p. 119.
50. Ian McPhedran (2010), 'Dutch Left Australian Soldiers for Dead in Afghanistan', *Perth Now* 22 October 2010. https://www.perthnow.com.au/news/dutch-left-australian-soldiers-for-dead-in-afghanistan-ng-662402792fd7f286c5bd6042990ac985
51. Tom Hyland (2008), 'Diggers "Let down" Dutch Allies in Deadly Battle with Taliban', *The Age*, 20 January 2008, https://www.theage.com.au/world/diggers-let-down-dutch-allies-in-deadly-battle-with-taliban-20080120-ge6mj6.html
52. Jim Molan (2017), 'Australia in Iraq 2002–2010: Inconsequential, Confused and Timid', *The Interpreter*, 10 March 2017, https://www.lowyinstitute.org/the-interpreter/australia-iraq-2002-2010-inconsequential-confused-and-timid

53. Brian Selmeski (2007), *Military Cross-cultural Competence: Core Concepts and Individual Development.* (Centre for Security, Armed Forces & Society, Royal Military College of Canada).
54. Efrat Elron, Boas Shamir, and Ben-Ari (1999), 'Why Don't They Fight Each Other? Cultural Diversity and Operational Unity in Multinational Forces', *Armed Forces & Society*, 26:1, pp. 73–97.

Section III

Strategies of Communication and Language Teaching

The Implications of War for the Teaching of Japanese Language in Australian Universities, 1917–1945

Jennifer Joan Baldwin

The teaching of languages was part of the curricula of Australian universities from their foundation. Australian universities had taken as their models the universities of Cambridge, Oxford, and Trinity College, Dublin, where language teaching was already firmly rooted. Such universities taught the classical languages, modern languages, and some Asian (then known as 'Oriental') languages. Australia, however, only partially followed the pattern of language teaching from these universities. Australian universities began with the classical languages only. These were seen as an essential part of a liberal education for the young men who would become leaders of the colonies in society, business, and government. This was followed by the introduction of two modern languages, French and German, seen as useful and commercially applicable in the period of rapid change leading up to the turn of the twentieth century.

Oriental or Asian languages began in Australia in rather different circumstances. Unlike the scholarly context for the teaching and study of

---

J. J. Baldwin (✉)
University of Melbourne, Parkville, VIC, Australia
e-mail: baldwin.j@unimelb.edu.au

Oriental languages in Britain and Ireland, the first Asian language to be taught, Japanese, was introduced in Australia as a very practical language. It was considered to be the case that Australia needed to have an understanding of the contemporary affairs of Japan, whose expansionist activities in the early twentieth century prompted Australia to consider very carefully its own security.

The University of Sydney introduced Japanese in 1917 in the closing years of the First World War, and the University of Melbourne introduced Japanese in 1919, although it had begun to be taught informally a couple of years before. Japan was an ally of Australia in the war, so teaching continued at the University of Sydney through the war's final years. At both the Universities of Sydney and Melbourne, the Japanese language continued to be taught through the 1920s and 1930s in spite of increasing concern about the possibility of Japanese imperialist expansion in the Pacific region. It could be argued that global concerns about Japanese intentions fed the fortunes of Japanese language teaching up until the Second World War. Studying the language had increasing value, such as enabling access to contemporary commercial and political news from Japanese newspapers.

However, with the entry of Japan into the Second World War in December 1941, the situation changed dramatically, particularly at the University of Melbourne. At Melbourne, drastic staff changes required a succession of new teachers, who were often appointed on an informal basis. At the University of Sydney, academics became involved with the defence forces assisting in the teaching of Japanese.

This chapter charts the beginnings of Japanese tertiary teaching in Australia, the reasons for that beginning, the vastly different backgrounds of the teachers of Japanese at the Universities of Melbourne and Sydney (the major universities in Australia at that time), and the negative effects of the Second World War on that teaching and its teachers. There are four men integral to this narrative, all teachers of Japanese language, two at the University of Sydney and two at the University of Melbourne: at Sydney, James Murdoch, a Scot by birth, and Arthur Sadler, an Englishman, and at Melbourne, Mowsey or Mōshi Inagaki, Japanese by birth, and Rev. Thomas Jollie Smith, a Scot by birth. The story of their teaching spanned both the latter years of the First World War and all the years of the Second World War.

The University of Sydney

Japanese-language teaching began at the University of Sydney in 1917 after discussions in 1916 between the Department of Defence and the Australian High Commissioners in London and Tokyo about suitable candidates for a university-level position.[1] The initiative had come from the Minister for Defence, George Pearce, who was apparently fearful that Japan might at some point in the future make war on Australia.[2] While Australia and Japan were allies during the First World War, the Australian government was nevertheless concerned about Japanese expansion into the Pacific after several earlier conflicts in Asia: the Sino-Japanese War of 1895, the Russo-Japanese War of 1905, the takeover of Korea by Japan in 1905, and subsequent colonisation in 1910. We now turn to taking a closer look at the two key teachers of Japanese at the University of Sydney, James Murdoch and Arthur Sadler.

James Murdoch: The Scot

The need to teach Japanese was at the time said to be motivated by the fact that competence in the Japanese language would facilitate the growing commercial relations between Japan and Australia. But there was clearly more behind this reasoning. An ability to undertake censorship work was also discussed as a necessary requirement for the successful candidate. James Murdoch, who had been living in Japan for some twenty-five years, had married his second wife, a Japanese woman, and taught in Japanese schools and tertiary institutions while writing his Japanese history.[3] He was, at the age of sixty-one, the successful candidate. What was not generally known, according to the historian Ailsa Zainu'ddin,[4] was that the appointment was largely paid for by the Department of Defence.

Australia had only achieved Federation in 1901 and much of its foreign policy was following that of Great Britain. However, Australia was now moving towards its own independent foreign policy relevant to its region. Integrated into this development of an increasingly independent foreign policy was a concern about defence, motivated in part by anxiety over the possibility of increased Asian strength in the region.

From 20 March 1917, Murdoch taught on Mondays and Tuesdays at the University of Sydney, starting with about eighty students.[5] Murdoch was also required to travel down to Royal Military College, Duntroon, near what was to become Canberra, for three days a week. Duntroon had been set up in 1911 to train future officers for the Australian Army. French and German were the languages traditionally taught at the College.[6] Murdoch's first Duntroon class had eight students, apparently chosen for being the most competent in language learning. The intention was to train interpreters for the Australian Army that the Department of Defence could send to Japan.[7] Not only did Murdoch teach Japanese at the University of Sydney and Duntroon but he was also involved in the introduction of Japanese language teaching at Fort Street Boys' High School. It is said that he never lost his Scots accent and his Japanese was underlined by a broad Scots burr!derlined by a broad Scots burr![8]

As the historian Misuzu Chow has noted, Murdoch insisted on having native speakers to assist him and, after a trip back to Japan in late December 1917 that lasted to early January 1918, he brought back two people to assist him in his work.[9] Koide Nanzi was to teach at the University of Sydney and Miyata Mineichi was to teach at Fort Street Boys' High School. The arrangement for secondary-school teaching of Japanese had been approved by Peter Board, the then-Director of Education in New South Wales.[10] In late 1918 Murdoch returned again to Japan, coming back to Australia in March 1919 with his wife. He also brought someone else with him: his brother-in-law Okada Rokuo, who was to take Japanese classes at Duntroon to 'drill the cadets in practical conversation and penmanship.'[11] Murdoch returned each year to Japan, ostensibly to visit Japanese relatives, but also to assess the current state of contemporary Japanese politics and society. In this latter regard, he reported to Edmund Piesse, Director of Australian Military Intelligence, both by letter and in person. Murdoch was careful in sending coded letters from Japan as there was the possibility of the Japanese intercepting his correspondence.

Apart from his teaching, Murdoch also undertook censorship work for the Australian government, translating intercepted Japanese documents. Australia was particularly concerned about the simmering possibilities for Japanese military expansion and possible espionage activities.[12] Many letters between Murdoch and Piesse are held in the archives at the National Library of Australia and attest to Murdoch's role in reporting on Japanese activities. Although Murdoch's contribution went well beyond teaching the Japanese language, the teaching of Japanese at the University of Sydney continued in those last years of the First World War. Murdoch's elevation to the role of Professor of Oriental Studies in 1918 was a joint arrangement between the University and the Department of Defence designed to keep him in Australia as he was so useful in his wider activities.[13] However, James Murdoch died in 1921 at the age of sixty-five.

Arthur Sadler: The Englishman

It was again at the instigation of the Department of Defence that a replacement for Murdoch was sought.[14] The University of Sydney was fortunate to quickly recruit another Japanese lecturer to fill the professorial chair in Oriental Studies, Arthur Sadler, who began at the University in 1922. Sadler, who was born in England, was a scholar of Hebrew and Assyrian, and had been teaching Latin and English in Japan and studying Japanese. He had been married before in England, but in 1916, in Tokyo he married his second wife, an Anglo-Japanese woman. Sadler taught at the University of Sydney until his retirement in 1948 when he returned to England. He wrote copiously on Japanese history, Japanese art, and classical and modern literature, and read widely in Japanese. He was renowned for his translations of Japanese poetry into English. There is little evidence, however, according to Chow, that he was ever involved in advising political leaders on the affairs of Japan as his predecessor Murdoch had been. Sadler was more a man of letters.[15] While Sadler became the constant in the Oriental Studies Department at the University of Sydney, there was a whole succession of other teachers of Japanese over the next twenty years.

Into the 1930s and the War Years

One of the many language teachers of the interwar period was Okada Rokuo, who went from Duntroon to teach at the University of Sydney for the next three years as a lecturer. When his contract expired at the University, he continued to teach at Fort Street and North Sydney High Schools as well as Sydney Church of England Grammar school, eventually leaving to return to Japan in January 1927.[16] At Duntroon, Japanese classes were taken by Jeffrey F. M. Haydon, appointed as Professor of Modern Languages. Another Japanese lecturer, Kitakoji Isamitsu, taught at the University of Sydney from late 1926 to the end of 1928.[17] Japanese teaching at the University of Sydney continued, although by 1928, the teaching at Duntroon had dwindled to merely an annual visit of monitoring, supervision, and examinations.[18]

Duntroon discontinued its Japanese language training in 1937, according to a document Jennifer Brewster found in the Australian archives. It was stated: 'This language is of little general cultural value and being almost a life-time study, the time spent on it at the College is practically wasted unless its study can be continued afterwards at universities, and in Japan and it is not possible to arrange this entirely.'[19] Nevertheless, teaching of Japanese at the University of Sydney continued with Sadler, and there were various native-speaking Japanese lecturers at the University throughout the Second World War.

The situation for Japanese language teaching changed dramatically after the Japanese began the Pacific War in December 1941. Knowledge of the Japanese language was now deemed to be of crucial importance for Australia's national defence and security interests. Duntroon's disenchantment with, and abandonment of, the earlier Japanese teaching arrangement with Sydney University had proven to be premature. Now the involvement of Sydney University academics in Japanese-language training was required once again.

There was an urgent need to recruit and train Japanese linguists, although this took several years to set up. Max Wiadrowski, an Royal Australian Air Force (RAAF) Intelligence officer with Japanese language ability, argued persuasively for a Japanese-language training facility which was established in Sydney in March 1944. Classes were conducted at the University of Sydney under the direction of Professor Sadler,[20] assisted by Joyce Ackroyd[21] and Margaret Lake.[22] This was reinforced with further evening instruction by military linguists as the university instruction alone was considered too academic for practical military application. Students included RAAF, Army, and Navy personnel. An arrangement for the teaching of Japanese between the University of Sydney and the RAAF School of Languages lasted from July 1944 till July 1945.[23]

Although the Second World War had increased the need for Japanese-language study and many of the linguists produced were employed with the Occupation Forces in Japan after the war ended, student numbers at the University of Sydney itself declined and no new students were enrolled after 1950 with the subject consequently discontinued.[24] Japanese was not taught again until 1959.[25] As Brewster put it, Japanese was now on the backburner. Chinese and Russian were seen as more strategic languages than Japanese for Australia's immediate interests because of the new 'cold war' and the Communist revolution in China.[26]

The University of Melbourne

The situation at the University of Melbourne was very different. While there had been moves as early as 1913 to consider introducing a wider range of languages, including Japanese, there was a reluctance to expend the funds which this would have required. Then, with the outbreak of the First World War, the possibility of languages expansion was put aside for the much more urgent considerations of the management of the University as staff and students enlisted to fight. Eventually, however, the University of Melbourne did introduce Japanese-language teaching but not as part of a degree course. In the first instance, this teaching was led by the unlikely collaboration between a Presbyterian minister, Reverend

Thomas Jollie Smith, and a Japanese national and native speaker of Japanese, Mōshi Inagaki.

Rev. Thomas Jollie Smith: Scottish Presbyterian Minister

Thomas Jollie Smith, the son of a Scottish Presbyterian minister, was born in Scotland and came to Australia as a child with his family. He was educated at the University of Melbourne and was a brilliant scholar, achieving honours in language and logic, and subsequently becoming a Presbyterian minister himself. After serving in a parish in South Australia, and spending a year as a lecturer in Hebrew at the University of Melbourne, he was, from 1905 to 1922, minister of the Ewing Memorial Church in East Malvern (Melbourne). According to Uniting Church theologian Ian Breward,[27] Jollie Smith wanted to undertake missionary work among the Japanese in Korea in 1916, and to this end had mastered Japanese on his own. However, his call to this work was stymied by the Japanese Government who at that time ruled Korea through their military forces.[28]

Through his connection with the University of Melbourne, Jollie Smith was part of a group who lobbied the university in 1917 over the need to teach Japanese.[29] In August 1918, the University, through the Faculty of Arts, came up with the idea of instructors, with fee-for-service teaching that would not cost the University anything.[30] Jollie Smith was already teaching Japanese informally at this time.[31] In 1917, Senkichi Mowsey Inagaki (known as Mōshi) began teaching Japanese privately in Melbourne, and in 1919, Jollie Smith and Inagaki officially began teaching at the University of Melbourne, pioneering Japanese studies. This partnership ceased in 1922, when Jollie Smith was appointed to a Chair in Hebrew and Old Testament Studies at the Theological Hall at Ormond College, University of Melbourne. Jollie Smith died in September 1927. From 1922, Mōshi Inagaki was the sole instructor in Japanese for the evening classes that were run. This appointment received the strong support of Edmund Piesse, a former pupil of Inagaki, and, as we saw earlier, Director of Military Intelligence.[32]

Mōshi Inagaki: Japanese National

Mōshi was born in Shizukoa, Japan, in 1880. He came to Australia in approximately 1906, arriving first on Thursday Island. He travelled south and made his home in Melbourne. He enrolled in art classes at the National Gallery of Victoria where he met Rose Allkins; they married in 1907 at the East St Kilda Congregational Church. According to various sources[33] he worked as a waiter, a laundryman, and an artist's model. He also taught Japanese privately.[34] Inagaki was refused naturalisation when he married and was rejected when he tried to enlist in the Australian Imperial Force (AIF) in 1915.[35] His wife always insisted he was tertiary educated in Japan but there is no firm evidence of this. Apart from his teaching at the University, he was also involved in Japanese-language programmes broadcast on Radio 3LO in the 1930s.[36] He also maintained a connection with the National Gallery of Victoria, assisting director Bernard Hall in sorting and cataloguing Japanese artefacts.[37]

Inagaki's teaching of Japanese as the sole instructor at the University of Melbourne continued until 1941. He was also involved in Saturday-morning Japanese teaching at MacRobertson Girls' High School (MacRob) in South Melbourne. From 1936, his daughter, Mura Inagaki, twenty-eight years old at the time, taught Japanese at the Methodist Ladies College.[38] When the news of the Japanese bombing of Pearl Harbour on the morning of 7 December 1941 reached Australia, Inagaki, fifty-one years old at the time, was immediately taken from his home and interned at Tatura in Victoria for the rest of the war. This was the fate of many Japanese living in Australia. Leslie Oates, who had attended those Saturday-morning classes at MacRob from 1939 to 1941 as a teenager, indicated that in late 1941, because of Inagaki's internment, Oates' Intermediate Certificate Japanese examination paper was marked by Rose Inagaki.[39]

Letters archived at the University of Melbourne reveal how Inagaki's wife Rose pleaded with the University for assistance. They were not interested. The Registrar argued that Inagaki was not a regular member of staff and merely an instructor. Even Inagaki's connections with influential men whom he had taught or knew professionally came to nothing. He had taught such men as Edmund Piesse, Peter Russo (later an Australian authority on Japanese affairs), Longfield Lloyd (trade commissioner to Japan), and Alexander Melbourne (who wrote many reports on foreign policy with China and Japan).[40] Sir John Latham, who had endorsed his original appointment, declined to assist. By the time of Inagaki's internment, Piesse was dead, as were Bernard Hall and Thomas Jollie Smith. Peter Russo and Longfield Lloyd were still alive. Former students were not supportive, but rather were critical of Inagaki's teaching at Tribunal hearings into his case.[41] Inagaki was never wholly embraced by the University, and Melbourne University had never given the formal commitment to Japanese-language teaching that the University of Sydney had. So, Inagaki remained in internment, as did many Japanese people in Australia during the war. Sadly, Rose died in 1943, so when Mōshi was released, he agreed to voluntary deportation back to Japan. He departed Australia on 1 January 1947, after spending thirty-five years (more than half his life) in the country. He left with the blessing of his married daughter, Mura, thirty-eight years old at the time.

Japanese-Language Teaching at the University Melbourne After 1941

Once Inagaki was interned, the University of Melbourne was faced with a problem: how to continue Japanese-language instruction for those in the middle of a course. Entries in the University Calendars confirm that Japanese continued to be taught for the next few years, with different teachers working for short periods of time and often recruited in an ad hoc manner. Each of these teachers had been born in Japan and, as it turned out, spent periods of time working in intelligence services or censor work for the Australian government during those latter years of the Second World War. In March 1942, the University Registrar, Mr Foster, contacted George Gregory who worked as an interpreter in the Intelligence Department, Southern Command, at Victoria Barracks in Melbourne. Rather obliquely, Mr Foster indicated that they were seeking an instructor 'in the absence of the university's regular instructor in Japanese.'[42] Mr Gregory's appointment was subsequently endorsed by the

University Council on the recommendation of the Dean of Arts, Max Crawford.

Gregory, who was fluent in Japanese, had arrived in Australia in early 1941. He had been raised and educated in Japan, the son of a Japanese mother and a Scottish father.[43] He also did broadcasts in Japanese for Radio Australia. In June 1942, he wrote to Professor Crawford indicating he needed to give up one of his classes and recommended Charles Souza Bavier as a substitute instructor for the third-year class. Bavier, he said, had been born in Switzerland, educated in Japan, was naturalised as an Australian, and had served with the AIF at Gallipoli in the First World War. After several lecturing commitments in Japan, he had come back to Australia.[44] Gregory indicated that Bavier had been working for the Department of Defence and as a broadcast monitor for the Department of Information.[45] Bavier's background was even more international than Gregory knew. In fact, he had served in the revolutionary forces in China around 1911 and, just before the start of the Second World War, was recruited into the British intelligence service, MI5, as an undercover agent gathering intelligence about Japanese movements in Singapore.[46]

It appears from archived correspondence that the Dean of Arts and the Registrar accepted Gregory's statement of Bavier's qualifications, offering Bavier the position and seeking no other confirmation of the veracity of his qualifications.[47] In the event, Bavier did not teach the third-year class for very long, just one term. On 18 August 1942, Gregory wrote to inform the university that Bavier had to leave Melbourne and go to Brisbane for an indefinite period, and that he, Mr Gregory, also had to resign his classes due to the pressure of his other commitments. As before, Gregory recommended a substitute, Mrs Selwood, the wife of the Presbyterian minister at Cowes, on Phillip Island.[48] Mrs Selwood, who was part-Japanese, had arrived in Melbourne in November 1941 from Yokohama, via Hong Kong. She, with her husband and two daughters, had secretly left on one of the last evacuation ships from Japan. This was the last chance of getting passengers out before the start of the Pacific War. Mrs Selwood, according to the *Horsham Times*, had formerly been a teacher in a Japanese high school.[49]

In early 1942 the language skills of Mrs Selwood were a welcome addition to the Army Japanese Training School being run at the Olderfleet

Building in Melbourne. She became the chief instructor of this School from 1942 to 1945.[50] Mrs Selwood's services were much in demand. Having now lost both Gregory and Bavier as instructors in Japanese, there was an urgent need for the University to replace them. Because her Army work was daytime only, Mrs Selwood gladly took up the position as Japanese instructor at the University starting in September 1942. The University made an attempt to see if Bavier might be returning to Melbourne and could take the third-year class again but as he was so uncertain of his movements due to the Government's need of him, they dropped this idea. So from the beginning of 1943, Mrs Selwood agreed to take all the Japanese instruction. She did this right through until the end of 1945.[51]

The year 1945 was the last year of any of the instructorships, Japanese included. Over the four years from early 1942, the teaching arrangements were very patchy and recruitment procedures very informal, as previously described. The University concluded that these informal, and often temporary, arrangements that had developed over the years were not satisfactory, but rather an embarrassment for the University. As a consequence, all instructors were told their positions would not be renewed for 1946 as all instructorships were to be abolished.[52] Japanese teaching ceased and was not taught again until introduced formally as part of a degree course in 1965.

Conclusion

As we have seen, the advent of Japanese-language teaching at the University of Sydney towards the end of the First World War was prompted by a fear of Japanese military aggression. It was largely taught by Westerners, with native Japanese speakers assisting. Then with the beginning of the Second World War, when Japanese linguists were urgently needed, it became expedient to involve the University of Sydney in the teaching of Japanese to military personnel.

At the University of Melbourne, however, Japanese language teaching was thought to be useful for commercial reasons, but was introduced in the cheapest possible way and not well supported by the University administration. When Japan's entry into the Second World War forced the internment of Inagaki, the sole Japanese teacher, the University enabled Japanese-language teaching to continue but in an ad hoc and piecemeal way. As far as the University was concerned, Inagaki was not their concern. They did not support him at his internment appeal and washed their hands of him.

As has been demonstrated, Japanese-language teaching in Australia was directly affected, first by the fear of war and then by the advent of war, and this prompted the need to develop language teaching at the University of Sydney. However, the government's internment activities in the Second World War impacted negatively on Japanese-language teaching at the University of Melbourne, reflected in the treatment of Inagaki. This, however, was not the end of the narrative about the effects of war and Japanese-language teaching at these two universities.

Once Australia and Japan were no longer at war, for a time Japanese-language teaching in Australian universities ceased. Another but different phase of 'war' and conflict had begun: the cold war with the Soviet Union, the fallout from the Chinese Communist Revolution, and the creation of the newly declared nation of the People's Republic of China. How universities reacted to these issues in their language offerings is another story waiting to be told.

Notes

1. Jennifer Brewster (1996), 'You Can't Have a Failure Rate of 75%: Idealism and Realism in the Teaching of Japanese in Australia 1917–1950', in Helen Marriott and Morris Low (eds), *Language and Cultural Contact with Japan*, (Clayton, Vic.: Monash Asia Institute, Japanese Studies Centre, Monash University), pp. 4–39, here p. 5.
2. D. C. S. Sissons (1987), 'James Murdoch (1856–1921): Historian, Teacher and Much Else Besides', *The Transactions of the Asiatic Society of Japan*, 4th series, vol 2, pp. 1–57, here p. 45.
3. Marjorie Jacobs (1953), 'Oriental Studies in the University of Sydney', *The Australian Quarterly*, 25:2, pp. 82–90, here p. 83; Senate of the University of Sydney (1919), 'Report of the Senate of the University of

Sydney for the year ended 31 December 1918' (from the Calendar of the University of Sydney 1919), p. 648.
4. Ailsa G. Thomson Zainu'ddin (1988), 'The teaching of Japanese at Melbourne University 1919–1941', *History of Education Review*, 17:2, pp. 46–62.
5. Brewster, 'You Can't Have a Failure Rate of 75%', p. 6.
6. Misuzu Hanihara Chow (2003), *The Study of Japan in Australia: A Unique Development over Eighty Years* (Kyoto: International Research Centre of Japanese Studies), p. 20.
7. Sissons, 'James Murdoch (1856–1921)', p. 48; Jacobs, 'Oriental Studies in the University of Sydney', p. 82.
8. Sissons, 'James Murdoch (1856–1921)', pp. 20, 47.
9. Chow, *The Study of Japan in Australia*, p. 19.
10. Brewster, 'You Can't Have a Failure Rate of 75%', p. 8; Harold Wyndham (1979), 'Board, Peter (1858–1945)', in *Australian Dictionary of Biography*, http://adb.anu.edu.au/biography/board-peter-5275, accessed 12 April 2018.
11. Brewster, 'You Can't Have a Failure Rate of 75%', p. 8.
12. Chow, *The Study of Japan in Australia*, p. 26; Neville Meaney (1996), *Fears and Phobias: E.L. Piesse and the Problem of Japan 1909–1939* (Canberra: National Library of Australia), pp. 7, 13.
13. Brewster, 'You Can't Have a Failure Rate of 75%', pp. 6, 7.
14. Chow, *The Study of Japan in Australia*, pp. 34–35.
15. Chow, *The Study of Japan in Australia*, pp. 34–35.
16. Brewster, 'You Can't Have a Failure Rate of 75%', pp. 10–11; Meaney, *Fears and Phobias*, p. 14.
17. Brewster, 'You Can't Have a Failure Rate of 75%', pp. 11, 13.
18. Brewster, 'You Can't Have a Failure Rate of 75%', p. 10.
19. Brewster, 'You Can't Have a Failure Rate of 75%', p. 14.
20. Joyce Ackroyd (1986), 'Japanese Studies: Then and Now', *Japanese Studies*, 6:1, pp. 13–18, here p. 13; Chow, *The Study of Japan in Australia*, p. 43.
21. Joyce Ackroyd, Japanese language academic, University of Sydney 1944–47, later Canberra University College, Australian National University, and the University of Queensland. See Chow, *The Study of Japan in Australia*, p. 43; Brewster, 'You Can't Have a Failure Rate of 75%', p. 30.

22. Jacobs, 'Oriental Studies in the University of Sydney', p. 84; Colin Funch (2003), *Linguists in Uniform* (Clayton, Vic.: Monash University, Japanese Studies Centre), p. 55.
23. Barry Turner (1983), 'Outhouses of Excellence: The Development of the RAAF School of Languages', *Defence Force Journal*, 38, pp. 18–24, here p. 21; Funch, *Linguists in Uniform*, p. 55.
24. Jacobs, 'Oriental Studies in the University of Sydney', p. 86.
25. A.D. Stefanowska (1984), 'In memoriam: A.R. Davis 1924–1983', *Japanese Studies* 4:1, pp. 17–18, here p. 17.
26. Jennifer Brewster (1989), 'You can't have a failure rate of 75%! Administrative and pedagogic concerns of Australia's Wartime Teachers of Japanese', JSAA conference abstract, Japanese Language Teaching in Australia, in *Japanese Studies*, 9:2, pp. 10–35, here p. 13.
27. Ian Breward (1988), 'Smith, Thomas Jollie (1858–1927)', in *Australian Dictionary of Biography*, http://adb.anu.edu.au/biography/smith-thomas-jollie-8486, accessed 13 March 2017.
28. Ian Jenkin (1991), *In Search of His Kingdom, the Ongoing Mission of Ewing Memorial Church East Malvern, a Centenary History*, (East Malvern, Vic.: Ewing Memorial Church), p. 28.
29. Faculty of Arts, University of Melbourne, 'Centenary of Japanese language,' https://arts.unimelb.edu.au/e/centenary-of-japanese-language#history, accessed 13 April 2018.
30. Report to the Council from the Faculty of Arts on the question of Instruction in Japanese, 16 August 1918, UMA, Office of the Registrar 1999.0014, file no. 1918/151.
31. He would have been known in the University as he had lectured in theology at Trinity College and Ormond College and in the Faculty of Arts in logic.
32. Faculty of Arts, University of Melbourne, 'Centenary of Japanese language,' https://arts.unimelb.edu.au/e/centenary-of-japanese-language#history, accessed 13 April 2018.
33. Masayo Hayakawa (1990), 'Moshi Inagaki and Japanese Residents in Australia 1906–1947', unpublished BA (Hons) thesis (University of Melbourne), pp. 49, 50.
34. Ailsa G Thomson Zainu'ddin (1985), 'Is it a Crime to Marry a Foreigner?', In Marilyn Lake and Farley Kelly (eds), *Double Time: Women in Victoria—150 years* (Ringwood, Vic.: Penguin Books), pp. 335–43, here p. 336.

35. Juliet Flesch and Peter McPhee (2003), 'Moshi (Mowsey) Inagaki (1880–1947)', in *150 years: 150 stories* (Melbourne: History Department, University of Melbourne), p. 90.
36. Funch, *Linguists in Uniform*, p. 30.
37. Gwen Rankin (2013), *L. Bernard Hall: The Man the Artworld Forgot* (Sydney: New South Publishing in association with the State Library of Victoria), p. 191.
38. Ailsa G. Thomson Zainu'ddin (1982), *They Dreamt of a School: A Centenary History of Methodist Ladies' College Kew 1882–1982* (Melbourne: Hyland House), p. 229.
39. Leslie Oates, personal communication, 2 July 2012.
40. Richard Selleck (2003), *The Shop, The University of Melbourne, 1850–1939*, (Carlton, Vic.: Melbourne University Press), p. 643.
41. Hayakawa, 'Moshi Inagaki and Japanese Residents in Australia 1906–1947', p. 61.
42. Foster to Gregory, 24 March 1942. University of Melbourne Archives. 1999.0014, 1943/414 (unit 298).
43. Funch, *Linguists in Uniform*, p. 42.
44. Charles Souza Bavier is more likely to have been born in Japan after his father's affair with a European woman. His father abandoned him and left Charles to be brought up by his Japanese mistress, Chika.
45. Gregory to Crawford, 6 June 1942. University of Melbourne Archives. 1999.0014, 1943/414 (unit 298).
46. Jeria Kua (2016), 'Book review', *Pointer, Journal of the Singapore Armed Forces*, 42:3, pp. 70, 71.
47. Crawford to Foster, 17 June 1942, Foster to Bavier 26 June 1942. University of Melbourne Archives. 1999.0014, 1943/414 (unit 298).
48. Gregory to Sussex, 18 August 1942. University of Melbourne Archives. 1999.0014, 1943/414 (unit 298).
49. Our correspondent, 'Evacuees left Japan secretly', *Horsham Times*, 18 November 1941, p. 3.
50. Brewster, 'You Can't Have a Failure Rate of 75%', pp. 26, 27; Turner, 'Outhouses of Excellence', p. 20; Funch, *Linguists in Uniform*, pp. 42, 44.
51. Selwood to the Registrar, 4 January 1943. University of Melbourne Archives. 1999.0014, 1943/414 (unit 298).
52. Registrar to Selwood, 29 November 1945, University of Melbourne Archives. 1999.0014, 1945/442 (unit 350).

Effectiveness of Intensive Courses in Teaching War Zone Languages

Yavar Dehghani

The Australian Defence Force School of Languages (DFSL) is a unique institution that develops and conducts most intensive language training for selected Australian Defence Department personnel in specified Languages Other Than English, in order to enable them to conduct joint, combined and/or interagency operations, and other Defence business in support of the Australian national interest. The DFSL offers courses in various Asian, Pacific, Middle Eastern, and European languages. The languages that are offered are taught in an intensive method ranging from 3 months to 12 months. In all instances, students attend the course five days a week for the duration of the course and each day they study for six periods. They are also required to study at least two hours a night at home.

The literature on teaching intensive courses is not extensive, but most of what has been reported supports the notion that the quality of the teaching and learning experience in an intensive course is comparable to when the same subject matter is taught in a longer format, particularly

Y. Dehghani (✉)
Defence School of Languages, Melbourne, VIC, Australia
e-mail: Yavar.dehghani@defence.gov.au

© The Author(s) 2020
A. Laugesen, R. Gehrmann (eds.), *Communication, Interpreting and Language in Wartime*, Palgrave Studies in Languages at War,
https://doi.org/10.1007/978-3-030-27037-7_5

when the instructional quality is high. In a review of the literature related to the use of intensive courses in higher education, Daniel included a section on teaching practices and concluded that intensive courses stimulated discussion and fostered creative teaching.[1] Specifically, she noted that successful intensive courses are well planned, employ organised and structured activities, utilise a multitude of teaching strategies, and focus on learning outcomes and careful student assessment.

Lee and Mroczka determined from their review of the literature that time per se may be relatively unimportant if instructors deal effectively with the learning environment.[2] In particular, they proposed instructors set clear learning outcomes, recognise individual learning differences, create positive classroom environments, consider using short but frequent assignments, and provide regular feedback and support to students. Building on her earlier research findings and those of others, Scott concluded that intensive courses have benefits, including more focused learning, more collegial classroom relationships, more in-depth discussions, and stronger academic performance when certain instructional and classroom attributes are present.[3]

Types of Courses Offered by the DFSL

There are different types of courses based on the job requirements of the students, including:

- Tactical Interaction course (8–10 weeks)
- Operational Engagement course (35 weeks)
- Strategic Engagement course (46 weeks)
- Basic Language course (12 weeks)
- General Language (GL) course (46 weeks)

The course that will be introduced and discussed in this chapter is the General Language course, which runs for 46 weeks. During this time, the staff train linguists in the target language within a year at an appropriate level so that by the conclusion of their training course, they can communicate with native speakers of that language. The levels that the students should reach at the end of the course are determined by the Australian Defence Language Proficiency Scale (ADLPRS), and these language descriptors are explained below.

Summary of ADLPRS language descriptors (intermediate level):

Speaking	
2	*Partially effective.* Speaker is quite effective when working within most general and familiar/specialist topics, but otherwise quality of communication is inconsistent. Speaker has enough vocabulary to convey meaning on most general functions, and familiar/specialist topics, but is limited outside that range; can differentiate many common shades of meaning. Speaker achieves accuracy in most uncomplicated constructions, but occasional errors of word order may occur, and some English influence is evident in sentence patterns. Pronunciation may show noticeable English influence, but few errors or hesitations occur. Pauses or hesitations do not significantly inhibit interaction, and speaker has some flexibility in linking statements or changing the direction of conversation.
2+	*Generally effective.* Speaker is able to convey meaning on a range of general and specialist topics, although attempts to convey more subtle/conceptual information may be unsuccessful. Speaker has enough vocabulary to speak on general and specialist topics, but not always with high precision or clarity; and successfully differentiates many shades of meaning. Range of grammatical patterns is adequate for most interactions, and speaker routinely achieves accuracy in uncomplicated constructions, although some English influence may be evident. Pronunciation may show some English influence, but errors rarely cause any problems. Pauses or hesitations do not significantly inhibit interaction, and speaker has moderately good flexibility in linking statements or changing the direction of conversation.

Listening	
2	*Straightforward.* Listener displays **accurate, complete, and specific comprehension** of material consisting largely of narration/description of events/processes/things, or straightforward reporting of statements/opinions. Subject-matter is mainly tangible/concrete, although some simple conceptual material may be present. Overall structure of material is clear, but some moderate complexity of reasoning is possible. Vocabulary covers most general functions and familiar/specialist topics; significant elements of a more informal/familiar style may be present. Material may include a significant proportion of more complicated sentence structures, some quite long, but all generally clear. Material is delivered slightly more slowly and clearly than normal, and may be in a slightly non-standard accent.

	Listening
2+	*Mainly uncomplicated and/or tangible.* Listener displays **accurate, complete, and specific comprehension** of material consisting primarily of narration/description, or reporting of others' words, although presentation may be slightly conceptual or analytical. Subject-matter is generally tangible/concrete, but moderately conceptual material may also be present. Overall structure of material is generally clear; reasoning may be moderately complex. Vocabulary covers a range of general and specialist topics; style ranges from formal to informal/familiar. Some of the sentence structures may be quite long or sophisticated. Material is delivered with normal clarity and at a normal pace, and may be in a slightly non-standard accent.
	Reading
1+	*Simple.* Reader displays **accurate, complete, and specific comprehension** of material consisting mainly of simple narration/description of events/processes/things, or simple reporting of statements/opinions, on mainly tangible/concrete subject-matter. Structure of material is simple and easy to follow, and complexity of reasoning is low. Vocabulary is limited to familiar topics/functions and some specialist areas, and meaning is usually readily apparent; elements of a more informal/familiar style may be present. Sentence patterns tend to be mainly simpler types, but all have clear structures. Material normally uses standard printed form of script/characters, but may use clearly presented non-standard or handwritten form.
2	*Straightforward.* Reader displays **accurate, complete, and specific comprehension** of material consisting largely of narration/description of events/processes/things, or straightforward reporting of statements/opinions. Subject-matter is mainly tangible/concrete, although some simple conceptual material may be present. Overall structure of material is clear, but some moderate complexity of reasoning is possible. Vocabulary covers most general functions and familiar/specialist topics; significant elements of a more informal/familiar style may be present. Material may include a significant proportion of more complicated sentence structures, some quite long, but all generally clear. Material normally uses standard printed form of script/characters, but may use clearly presented non-standard or handwritten form.

Writing: Alphabetic (Non-Roman) Scripts	
1+	*Limited.* Some effective communication is usually achieved, but writer displays limited range and accuracy. Vocabulary is limited to familiar topics/functions and some specialist areas, enabling the conveying of general information, but significantly limited outside that range; errors of word choice may be frequent. Writer can accurately produce most simply structured sentences; some errors of word order may occur, and influence of English sentence patterns may be evident even in simpler constructions. Writing may seem awkward and disjointed, with limited flexibility in linking or extending statements. Writer can recall and produce most letters, and achieves moderate speeds in doing so, but with quite a few errors. Writer has only partial ability to transliterate unknown words.
2	*Partially effective.* Writer is quite effective when working within most general and familiar/specialist topics, but otherwise quality of communication is inconsistent. Writer has enough vocabulary to convey meaning on most general functions, and familiar/specialist topics, but is limited outside that range; can differentiate many common shades of meaning. Writer achieves accuracy in most uncomplicated constructions, but occasional errors of word order may occur, and some English influence is evident in sentence patterns. Above paragraph level, writer has only partial flexibility in linking statements or changing the direction of discussion. Writer can recall and produce all letters, with only occasional errors; production is partly automatic, with moderate speeds and few errors. Writer has quite good ability to transliterate unknown words.

Writing: Alphabetic (Roman) Scripts	
2	*Partially effective.* Writer is quite effective when working within most general and familiar/specialist topics, but otherwise quality of communication is inconsistent. Writer has enough vocabulary to convey meaning on most general functions, and familiar/specialist topics, but is limited outside that range; can differentiate many common shades of meaning. Writer achieves accuracy in most uncomplicated constructions, but occasional errors of word order may occur, and some English influence is evident in sentence patterns. Above paragraph level, writer has only partial flexibility in linking statements or changing the direction of discussion. Spelling/punctuation/use of capitals is usually correct; writer can spell out most unknown words.

Writing: Alphabetic (Roman) Scripts	
2+	*Generally effective.* Writer is able to convey meaning on a range of general and specialist topics, although attempts to convey more subtle/conceptual information may be unsuccessful. Writer has enough vocabulary to convey meaning on general and specialist topics, but not always with high precision or clarity; and successfully differentiates many shades of meaning. Range of grammatical patterns is adequate for most interactions, and writer routinely achieves accuracy in uncomplicated constructions, although some English influence may be evident. Writer has moderately good flexibility, at and above paragraph level, in linking statements or changing the direction of discussion. Spelling/punctuation/use of capitals is almost always correct; writer can spell out almost any unknown words.
Writing: Character-Based Scripts	
1+	*Limited.* Some effective communication is usually achieved, but writer displays limited range and accuracy. Vocabulary is limited to familiar topics/functions and some specialist areas, enabling the conveying of general information, but significantly limited outside that range; errors of word choice may be frequent. Writer can accurately produce most simply structured sentences; some errors of word order may occur, and influence of English sentence patterns may be evident even in simpler constructions. Writing may seem awkward and disjointed, with limited flexibility in linking or extending statements. Writer can recall and produce characters for most known vocabulary, and achieves moderate speeds in doing so, but may make quite a few errors.
2	*Partially effective.* Writer is quite effective when working within most general and familiar/specialist topics, but otherwise quality of communication is inconsistent. Writer has enough vocabulary to convey meaning on most general functions, and familiar/specialist topics, but is limited outside that range; can differentiate many common shades of meaning. Writer achieves accuracy in most uncomplicated constructions, but occasional errors of word order may occur, and some English influence is evident in sentence patterns. Above paragraph level, writer has only partial flexibility in linking statements or changing the direction of discussion. Writer can recall and produce characters for most known vocabulary; production is partly automatic, with moderate speeds and few errors. Writer can transliterate a few simple personal/place names for which characters are not already known.

Translating	
1+	*Simple.* Translator is able to **comprehend** and **translate accurately** and with adequate expression, material consisting mainly of simple narration/description of events/processes/things, or simple reporting of statements/opinions, on mainly tangible/concrete subject-matter. Structure of material is simple and easy to follow, and complexity of reasoning is low. Vocabulary is limited to familiar topics/functions and some specialist areas, and meaning is usually readily apparent; elements of a more informal/familiar style may be present. Material consists mainly of shorter sentences with fairly simple and clear structures. Material normally uses standard printed form of script/characters, but may use clearly presented non-standard or hand-written form.
2	*Straightforward.* Translator is able to **comprehend** and **translate accurately** and with adequate expression, material consisting largely of narration/description of events/processes/things, or straightforward reporting of statements/opinions. Subject-matter is mainly tangible/concrete, although some simple conceptual material may be present. Overall structure of material is clear, but some moderate complexity of reasoning is possible. Vocabulary covers most general functions and familiar/specialist topics; significant elements of a more informal/familiar style may be present. Some sentence structures may be longer or more complicated, but all are generally clear. Material normally uses standard printed form of script/characters, but may use clearly presented non-standard or hand-written form.
Interpreting	
1+	*Simple.* Interpreter can **comprehend** and **interpret accurately** and with adequate expression, material consisting mainly of simple narration/description of events/processes/things, or simple reporting of statements/opinions, on mainly tangible/concrete subject-matter. Structure of material is simple and easy to follow, and complexity of reasoning is low. Vocabulary is limited to familiar topics/functions and some specialist areas, and meaning is usually readily apparent; elements of a more informal/familiar style may be present. Material consists mainly of shorter sentences with fairly simple and clear structures. Material is delivered more slowly than normal, and in a standard accent; segments do not exceed 20 words.

96   Y. Dehghani

Interpreting	
2	*Straightforward.* Interpreter can **comprehend** and **interpret accurately** and with adequate expression, material consisting largely of narration/description of events/processes/things, or straightforward reporting of statements/opinions. Subject-matter is mainly tangible/concrete, although some simple conceptual material may be present. Overall structure of material is clear, but some moderate complexity of reasoning is possible. Vocabulary covers most general functions and familiar/specialist topics; significant elements of a more informal/familiar style may be present. Some sentence structures may be longer or more complicated, but all are generally clear. Material is delivered slightly more slowly than normal, and may be in a slightly non-standard accent; segments do not exceed 35 words.

Defence Force School of Languages (DFSL) (2019), 'Australian Defence Language Proficiency Scale (ADLPRS)'

Course Timetable

As previously stated, the classes run for six periods a day for five weeks. A sample weekly timetable is provided below:

Effectiveness of Intensive Courses in Teaching War Zone... 97

Week 3 Timetable

	Period 1 0800–0850	Period 2 0855–0945		Period 3 1005–1055	Period 4 1100–1150		Period 5 1300–1350	Period 6 1355–1445
Mon	Revision	New materials	Morning break	Speaking	Writing	Lunch	Language lab	Interpreting
Tue	Grammar	New materials		Speaking	Reading		Language lab	Translating
Wed	Revision	New materials		Speaking	Writing		Language lab	Interpreting
Thu	Grammar	New materials		Speaking	Reading		Language lab	Translating
Fri	Revision	New materials		Speaking	Writing		Culture	Culture

The Classroom Environment

A system of continual reinforcement underpins training on the General Language course, and the first period of the day is allocated to the revision of the previous lessons, before new lessons are introduced in the second period of each day. The lesson topic varies each day. The same topic is practiced in speaking, writing, listening, and translation and interpreting periods on the same day. On the subsequent day, the vocabulary and grammar of the lesson is revised in the first period. In this manner, the vocabulary, grammar, listening, and conversation about the same topic is practised throughout the day and the students learn it rather than having to practise after hours. However, they need at least 2 hours of extra classwork to absorb the new vocabulary that they learn each day (a minimum of 30 words).

Using Transliterations

Most of the languages taught at the DFSL use non-Roman scripts, including Arabic, Persian, Korean, Chinese, and Japanese. Starting language teaching by introducing the script would however make the students more confused in the early stages of language learning. If such an approach were followed, they would need to concentrate on learning the newly introduced vocabulary, grammar, and culture of the new language, while simultaneously spending much of their time learning the actual characters in the script. To avoid this, we now introduce the language lessons for the first month or two in transliteration, and leave the introduction of the script for later when students have overcome their confusion about how the structure of the language works, and have learnt some introductory vocabulary. This gives them the confidence to progress to learning a more complex and challenging script.

Our experience has shown that this method is more beneficial than the traditional method where the lessons are introduced in their written script from the beginning of their language training. The traditional example of such language teaching is of the Saturday language schools, where community languages are taught to children of migrant parents in the same way they would have learnt their first language. Most of these students lose interest in learning their community language because this unfamiliar script occupies their class time more than speaking, listening, and other more instantly applicable skills.

Benefits of Intensive Courses

The first advantage of intensive learning is the simple issue of chronological frequency—in other words, students learn the language more often. With a short interval between classes, it is much easier to practise each day's lessons, ask questions, and get feedback rather than put it on hold until another week. Exposure is also very high. Students talk to their teachers each day in the target language and they are given a large quantity of new vocabulary and grammar to learn. They learn more material but in small, discrete packages of information. Their vocabulary will be more extensive, and they will have a chance to learn more complex grammatical structures than would otherwise be the case.

Intensive Language Classes are intense! In a language course in a regular tertiary setting, students usually study 50 minutes of class time followed by 23 hours of activities (and sleep) before the next language class. They may spend an hour or more doing homework, listening to tapes, and conducting other revision activities for that one hour of class. But if students experience six hours of class per day, they are going to have to do at least two hours of homework per day, and maybe more. The DFLS students make flashcards and carry them around; they write new vocabulary every day directly on their cards, and test themselves constantly. At the end of the course, the result of such intensive training is that they end up with thousands of flash cards that they have gradually learned.

The Structure of the Course

As previously stated, a General Language course (GL) runs for 46 weeks, 5 days a week from Monday to Friday and with 6 periods of 50 minutes each day. Six 'macro' skills are taught in the course: speaking, listening, reading, writing, translating, and interpreting. Each of these skills are taught for at least one period a day, and the greatest level of emphasis is given to speaking, which runs for two periods each day.

In the speaking period, students are divided into pairs and are required to role play the conversation they have studied in the new lesson. This pair work and role play makes them ready for speaking in the target language.

Interpreting Skill

The students who are deployed to war zones mostly concentrate on developing interpreting skills. Although all macro skills are important in learning language, interpreting is a real on-the-job and practical task that they will be required to undertake. To be able to interpret between two people in two different languages, the interpreter should also have good listening and speaking skills.

Interpreting is a language skill which is not really taught along with the other four macro skills (speaking, listening, reading, and writing) in mainstream second-language courses. This skill, which is used mostly for job-related tasks, needs a relatively high proficiency in the second language, and thus it is usually taught to students in an intermediate or advanced course.

One of the unique second-language environments in Australia where students learn interpreting as a fundamental part of their jobs is the DFSL. Interpreting skills are taught in the intensive language courses along with other macro skills. At the conclusion of their course, language learners are able to perform interpreting tasks effectively, and to deploy their skills in a war zone situation. The National Australian Association for Translators and Interpreters is the only organisation besides DFSL that runs interpreting classes.

Challenges in Interpreting

There are various challenges that students can encounter in interpreting:

- Remembering words and phrases
- Short memory issues

- Self-correction
- Hesitation
- Mixing the direction
- Using English words
- Not being familiar with original word and phrase

In addition, the issue of cultural appropriateness is also one that is important for interpreters, and is especially of concern for service personnel deployed to war zones. While minor cultural inappropriateness would not prevent the conveying of meaning, it could potentially negate or undermine a linguist's effectiveness in certain situations. The cultural appropriateness of the language used is therefore a significant factor to be considered in assessment of interpreting, especially at higher levels. The interpreting sample below is derived from the DFSL's *Pashto Coursebook*,[4] and provides an example of styles of conversation used in such instances.

Interpreting Sample

The dialogue below is a sample of interpreting practice dialogues where one student acts an the Australian person, the other student, as the local person and the third student as the interpreter between them:

1	Australian:	Local, how are you feeling?
2	Interpreter:	حفيظه. څنګه احساس کوې؟
3	Local:	بوازي خوشحال يم چي تا سره يم. دا ډېر ښه احساس دى چي سلامت يم. نيکمرغه يم چي ژوندى يم.
4	Interpreter:	Just happy to be here with you. It feels good to be safe. I am lucky to be alive.
5	Australian:	Yes, I hope you are feeling much better. You certainly look better compared to when you arrived at the base. Please tell me what happened to you.
6	Interpreter:	هو، هيله کوم چي نور ښه به احساس وکړې. يقيناً چي ته د هغه وخت په پرتله ښه ښکارې که چې قشلې ته راورسيدې. لطفاً ما ته روايه چي تا ته څه دريښن شول
7	Local:	زه يو مرستندوى يم. زه د هلمند ولايت په وروکي ساختاني پروژه کي د درې مياشتو لپاره/ څخه کار کوم. ما د مارجي په ولسوالۍ کي د خلکوسره خبرې کولي چې يو سړى ما ته ور کړ چې په موټر کي يې کښينم
8	Interpreter:	I am an aid worker. I have been working in Helmand Province for three months on small construction projects. I was in Marja town talking to the people when someone walked up to me and ordered me into their car.

(continued)

(continued)

9	**Australian:**	Just like that? In front of everyone?
10	**Interpreter:**	په همدا ډول؟ د هريوه(د ټولو) په مخکي؟
11	**Local:**	هو. هريوه. (ټولو) وليدل. هغه راغلو او ټوپک یې ما ته ونیو او ویې ویل، چې د هغه سره ولاړ شم.
12	**Interpreter:**	Yes. Everyone saw. He walked up and pointed a gun at me and told me to go with him.
13	**Australian:**	And then what happened?
14	**Interpreter:**	او بیا څه پیښ شو؟
15	**Local:**	هغه زه خپل موټر کې کښېنیولم او زما سترګې یې وتړلې. وروسته هغه زه یو ځای ته بوتلم او یوې وړې کوټې ته. یې تېله کړم. هغې کړکۍ نه درلودلې. ما فکر کاوه چې هغه با ما ووژني خو یوازې سترګې په لاره او سترګې په لاره وم
16	**Interpreter:**	He took me to his car and blindfolded me. Then he drove me somewhere and pushed me into a small room. It had no windows. I thought he is going to kill me but I ended up just waiting and waiting.
17	**Australian:**	Did he speak to you at all? Was there anyone else there?
18	**Interpreter:**	هغه تا سره په مجموع کې خبري وکړې؟ هلته بل څوک وۀ؟
19	**Local:**	نه، هغه یوازې ما ته ویل چې چپ شه. زه مطمین یم چې هغه یو کس و. هماغسې چې زما سترګې تړلې وې.. ما هیڅ نه لیدل او هیڅ نه اوریدل
20	**Interpreter:**	No, he just kept telling me to shut up. I'm pretty sure it was only one person. As I was wearing a blindfold I could not see a thing and I could not hear anyone else.
21	**Australian:**	Did he take any of your belongings?
22	**Interpreter:**	هغه ستا کوم شی واخیست؟
23	**Local:**	هغه زما بټوه او بوټان واخیستل. اوه، او زما کوته.
24	**Interpreter:**	He took my wallet and my shoes. Oh, and my ring.
25	**Australian:**	And how did you escape?
26	**Interpreter:**	او ته څنګه وتښتېدلې؟
27	**Local:**	څو ساعته وروسته ما د څلکو غږونه واورېدل او په چیغو مې شروع وکړه. تقریباً نیم ساعت وروسته خلک.. راغلل او دروازه یې ماته کړه. او بیا یې دلته راوستلم
28	**Interpreter:**	After a few hours I heard people outside so I started yelling and yelling. After about thirty minutes people came and broke down the door. Then they took me here.
29	**Australian:**	How long would you have been locked up for?
30	**Interpreter:**	د څه مودې لپاره بند وې؟
31	**Local:**	شاید ۳ یا ۴ ساعته.
32	**Interpreter:**	Probably about three or four hours.
33	**Australian:**	So, do you remember where this place is?
34	**Interpreter:**	نو، ستا دا ځای په یاد دی چې چېرته دی؟
35	**Local:**	دا د دې ځای په شمال کې و، شاید تال کلې/ قلي ته نږدې، هغو څلکو چې زه یې وژغورلم، به لارۍ کې د نیم ساعت لپاره پټ کړم، یقیناً نه پوهېږم چې دا ځای چېرته دی؟
36	**Interpreter:**	It was north of here, maybe near Tall Kala. People who rescued me hid me in their truck for about half an hour so I do not exactly know where the place is.

(continued)

(continued)

37	Australian:	You are a very lucky man, Local. Whoever kidnapped you had not planned it very well. He does not sound like Taliban—they usually do not behave like in that way—but who knows? He could have just been a thief who was wondering what to do with you next.
38	Interpreter:	حفيظه، ته یو ډېر نيکمرغه سړی يې! هغه چا چې ته يې اختطاف کړی وې (تنبتولی وې) صحيح پلان يې نه و. جوړ کړی. هغه طالب نه برېښي — هغوی داسې رفتار نه کوي — مګر څوک پوهېږي؟ کېدای شي چې هغه يو غل و او نه پوهېده چې تا سره يا / وروسته څه وکړي
39	Local:	زه ډېر نيکمرغی احساس کوم.
40	Interpreter:	I feel very lucky.
41	Australian:	Well, we will organise for you to be taken back to Kabul. Have you spoken to your family yet?
42	Interpreter:	بنه، موږ به تاسو ته د کابل د بېرته تګ تياری ونيسو. تاسو تر اوسه د خپلې کورنۍ سره خبرې کړې دي؟
43	Local:	هو، منه. ما ن ن سهار خپلې مېرمنې سره خبرې وکړې. هغه ډېره حيرانه وه خو هغه بنه ده.
44	Interpreter:	Yes, thanks. I spoke to my wife this morning. She was very shocked but she is fine.
45	Australian:	That is good. OK I suggest you rest right now and we will let you know when your travel to Kabul is ready.
46	Interpreter:	دا بنه ده. سمه ده، تاسو ته وړانديز کوم، اوس آرام وکړئ او تاسو ته به روايو چې د کابل سفر، کله وخت، تياريږي.
47	Local:	سمه ده.. ستاسو د ټولو مرستو څخه مننه.
48	Interpreter:	OK. Thank you for all your help.

From the Australian Defence Force School of Language (DFSL) (2010) *Pashto Coursebook*.

Culture and Language

As we know, culture and language exist in a close relationship with each other. Cultural sensitivities in one society do not always exist in the other. There are also words and phrases in one language or another which are closely connected with cultural contexts, and we cannot translate them out of the context of their culture.

Language without culture is artificial and in abstraction. The close relation between language and culture has been noticed in the related literature for a long time. It is also noted that language is only understood when it is placed in its cultural setting.[5] There is a connection between language and identity of a social group.[6] Thus, understanding the culture of a language helps the speaker to identify with the language community of that language and makes him an insider to the culture. It is not possible to understand culturally loaded words and phrases without knowing their cultural background. McKay says that to use a language for special purposes, one needs to learn the culture associated with the aspects of the discourse.[7] The students on a course such as the General Language course should not only be able to speak and interpret in the language, but also need to be familiar with the culture, as cultural misunderstanding is as dangerous as communication breakdown in a war zone.

Therefore, one of the main non-language subjects that is taught in these intensive courses is cultural sensitivities. These are as important, and sometimes more important than the language itself, as we know that communication can be significantly hampered without cultural context. Some of these sensitivities that are taught to Afghan language students are discussed below, and their significance is obvious:

- Highly formal language for elderly and women: The language register that is used for addressing women and elderly is highly formal and cannot be mixed with the colloquial language.
- Avoid giving orders to the elderly: As a young person, you are not supposed to order an elderly person to do anything. There is of course an exception to this during military operations and in emergencies.
- Avoid extending legs or lying down in front of older people: It is not polite to extend your legs while sitting, or to lie down, when older people are present.
- Avoid swearing: You should not swear at anyone, even at your colleagues. Swearing is a big insult in this culture and it is used in fighting. Using obscene language such as F-word should be avoided.
- Avoid showing affection with the opposite sex in public: People do not show affection with their partner in public in Afghan culture and it is very insulting to others if you do engage in public displays of affection.
- Avoid eating or drinking in public during Ramadan: During the month of fasting (Ramadan), you should avoid eating and drinking in public.
- Avoid drinking alcohol: You should avoid drinking alcohol in public or while the locals are present.

- Avoid touching female body parts or initiating a handshake: As a male, you should never touch any body part of a female, greet them with a handshake or kiss them while greeting. Avoid deliberately mixing women with men. Avoid leaving a female and a male alone in a room. Always let Australian women face Afghan women or Afghan co-workers face Afghan women. Avoid making a date with an Afghan or making any kind of sexual reference. If you do not know a female's name, call her sister.
- Avoid interfering with prayers and religious ceremonies.
- Do not enter a mosque with shoes on or accompanied by dogs.
- Do not joke about religion or unnecessarily comment about religion.

Other cultural instructions are also provided to students:

- Conversion of dates: The Afghan calendar is different from the Gregorian calendar and it was 1397 in the year 2018. To convert the date, the student needs to add 621 years. The students learn how to convert the dates, as the locals in rural areas may not necessarily know about other calendars and it is important to know the date in local calendar.
- Addressing people: People are addressed by using a title of Mr or Mrs or by their job title, which is followed by the surname, with an example being Mr. Mohammadi, Engineer Ahmadi. In these languages, the title comes either before or after the job. Except in the case of referring to children, close friends, and relatives, addressing people by their first name is considered offensive.

There are also some phrases with different meanings based on different contexts. To use them in the correct way, students need to understand the context well. An example is *befarmäyin,* which literally means 'you may order.'[8] This phrase has many different politeness denotations based on different contexts as follows:

- 'How can I help you?' context: for example, when you enter a shop and say hello and the shopkeeper says *befarmäyin.*
- 'Come in' context: for example, when you knock on the door and the person inside says *befarmäyin.*

- 'Here you are' context: for example, when you are going to pay the money for your purchased items in the shop, you give the money to the shopkeeper and say *befarmäyin*.
- 'Please go on, continue' context: for example, when you are talking and someone interrupts, and then he apologises and tells you *befarmäyin*.
- 'Take a seat' context: for example, when you enter somewhere and the person inside offers you a seat and says *befarmäyin*.
- 'You go first' context: for example, when you are entering somewhere with someone else, you say to him *befarmäyin*.

In addition, there is also a need to understand kinship terms. Many relationship terms are culture-related, that is, they vary according to types of relationships between people in a specific culture, and the rules that apply to those relationships. There are relationship terms in English that do not have an equivalent in some other languages, for example: de facto, partner, gay and lesbian, and bisexual relationship. In Dari, the variety of relationships is limited and it is mostly defined through marriage. However, there are also kinship terms that do not exist in English. Some examples include:

- Uncle: *Ka ka* (paternal)/*mama* (maternal)
- Aunt: *ama* (paternal)/*khala* (maternal)
- Cousin: *pesar ama* (aunt's son, paternal)/*dokhtar mämä* (uncle's daughter, maternal)
- Wife's sister: *khiyäshna*

Another culture-related linguistic component is the use of swear words. Swear words differ from one language to another, as they are often culture-related. For example, these words are very insulting in Afghan culture:

- خر (Donkey)
- سگ (Dog)
- گاو (Cow)

In-Country Training (ICT)

In-Country Training (ICT) is a discrete component of longer language courses, and it runs for two weeks. The students and their instructors travel to the target language country to put their language competence into practice in the native language environment and culture. This training takes place towards the end of the course and is a real-world test to show how much each student has mastered the language and how well they can communicate with the native speakers. There are three main tasks for students to complete during these two weeks: interviewing native speakers on a topic of interest to them in the target language, collecting the results of the interview, and compiling a report in the target language. These tasks are performed every morning and students can meet different people to interview them in various locations, including shops, offices, schools, parks, and so on.

Since this is their first real encounter with the target language and culture, and with native speakers, sometimes this can be overwhelming for the students, and they can panic that they do not know any language. However, towards the end of the ICT period, they begin to get used to the situation they are in, grow in confidence, understand more, and generally start to communicate better.

Conclusion

This case study has provided an overview of the range of DFSL intensive language courses, with a specific emphasis on the year-long General Language course, and has explained the level of language required, the daily syllabus of a sample course, cross-cultural training, and an example of interpreting. The intensive courses enable the DFSL students to learn the target language within a year to a level that allows them to effectively communicate with native speakers when deployed to operations in countries like Afghanistan. Familiarity with the language and culture helps with communication, and prevents misunderstandings and clashes because of communication breakdown. As a result, this can save lives.

Experience has shown that carefully selected students can be taught to a high level of competency in intensive language environments that can allow them to reach functional levels of language ability. Repeated periods of instruction with carefully structured mixtures of language learning and cultural training, combined with daily revision, has led to positive outcomes for students. The real-world experience of operational deployments in war zones has shown the efficacy of these learning methods.

Notes

1. E. L. Daniel (2000), 'A Review of Time-shortened Courses Across Disciplines', *College Student Journal*, 34:2, pp. 298–308.
2. S. L. Lee and M. Mroczka (2002), *Teaching in Intensive Course Formats: Towards Principles of Effective Practice* (Baltimore, Maryland: Paper presented to North American Association of Summer Sessions Annual Conference).
3. P. A. Scott (2003), 'Attributes of High-quality Intensive Courses', *New Directions for Adult and Continuing Education*, 97, pp. 29–38.
4. Defence Force School of Language's *Pashto Coursebook* (2010).
5. J. P. Gee, G. Hull, and C. Lankshear (1996), *The New Work Order: Behind the Language of New Capitalism* (Sydney: Allen & Unwin), pp. 1–23.
6. C. Kramsch (2001), *Language and Culture* (Oxford: Oxford University Press), p. 65.
7. S. McKay (2002), *Teaching English as an International Language* (Oxford: Oxford University Press), p. 85.
8. Y. Dehghani (2009), 'Challenges in Translating Culturally Loaded Words and Phrases' (Canberra: Paper presented to AARE Annual Conference), p. 5.

The Challenge of Strategic Communication in Multinational Military Operations: Approaches by the United States and Germany in the ISAF

Jasmin Gabel

Over the last century, we have seen drastic changes to the way humans conduct war. In recent decades, new forms of technology allow warfare to be conducted safely from behind a computer screen, minimising the necessity to deploy troops on the ground. And while wars are still fought between two nations over territory, the war in which much of the Western world has been embroiled since the beginning of this century is not as easily defined in terms of its ultimate goals. Western nations have poured endless resources into a 'War on Terror' for close to two decades.

The 'War on Terror' has changed our understanding of warfare as well as the strategic approach to war, increasing the number of joint multinational operations and requiring lengthy missions. Multilateral warfare has been growing in importance since the United States, Great Britain, France, and the USSR allied to defeat Nazi Germany. After the Second World War, international organisations such as the North Atlantic

---

J. Gabel (✉)
Independent Scholar, Berlin, Germany

Treaty Organization (NATO) and the United Nations were founded on the principles of lasting peace between their members. But despite this goal, member states have not been inclined to relinquish their military assets; rather, they have employed the strategy of creating a form of codependency, training forces together, and jointly carrying out peacekeeping missions.[1]

The International Security Assistance Force (ISAF) was formed in response to the need for establishing security in post-Taliban Afghanistan after the September 11 attacks and the subsequent defeat of the Taliban in 2001–02. ISAF is to date the biggest joint military undertaking ever. It operated in Afghanistan between 2001 and 2014 and at one time comprised of fifty-one nations. The global community had experienced multinational military cooperation before, with the NATO military commitment to peace in former Yugoslavia being a relevant example. But no previous mission had come close to the ISAF mission in terms of size or cooperational efforts. The extensive and diverse intercultural character of the mission resulted in many different challenges, one of which was the need for the coordination of public communication by its member states.

A variety of communication strategies can potentially be used for multinational military operations such as the ISAF mission. In ISAF, one hub of strategic communication lay with NATO, an entity of which many of the most significant ISAF contributor nations were members. However, as is common in multinational deployments, every nation involved also had its own communications strategy tailored specifically to their own national audience. Such diversity might not have been as significant an issue prior to the existence of social media, the Internet, and globalisation. But in a day and age in which information is easily shared and disseminated globally within minutes, individual narratives, especially when contradicting each other, can quickly lead to public-relations nightmares for all involved.

This chapter explores the question of whether it is possible in such large multinational deployments to create unified messages about the mission, its motivations, and its objectives. To answer this question, the chapter analyses and compares the communicational strategies of the US Department of Defense and the German Bundesministerium der

Verteidigung (BMVg). The United States and Germany were chosen as subjects because both were major contributors to the ISAF mission; additionally both nations are NATO members and Western democracies.

The chapter begins by looking at the concept of political discourse and the relationships between the media, political actors, and the public to identify the legitimising power behind political opinion and how such opinion can be influenced. Next, the base narratives of the United States and Germany are explored. These narratives are distinct from each other: the United States draws on its origin myths of an American civil religion, 'manifest destiny' and American exceptionalism; the German base narrative has its roots in the country's post-Second World War reconstruction period with themes of multilateralism and anti-militarism. The assumption is that these base narratives, which are at the very core of a nation's cultural understanding of itself, serve as essential themes to influence public opinion. Press releases by the German and American defence ministries are then analysed through the method of frame analysis. This method considers whether base narratives can be seen to have influenced each country's communicational themes during the ISAF mission.

Legitimising Political Action

Power is assigned and legitimised through political discourse. This discourse consists of regulated connections and formations of statements.[2] In essence, discourse can be defined as the arena in which reality is constructed and power to determine reality is assigned. Power in this context is what governs and limits discourse. As Susanne Kirchhoff argues, the 'governing process occurs through repressive mechanisms, which allow for a restriction on what can and can't be said within a society.' It can therefore be determined that power and discourse share an interrelation with each other. Following Kirchhoff's argument further, 'executive action has to continuously be communicated for it to even be legitimisable' because the 'exercise of power in a democracy is dependent on the will of the people.'[3] In other words, in a democratic state, those who exercise authority can only do so if they are deemed a legitimate power by the public. If this legitimacy is eroded, so too is their capacity to undertake political action.

The arena of political discourse can be seen as inhabited by three major players: political actors, the media, and the public. But access to and space within this arena are not equally distributed between the three. In our modern societies, the media serves as a kind of referee of public discourse. The media is what Altschull calls an 'agent of power.'[4] Discourse represents the public forum in which legitimacy may be created, questioned, and arranged. Yet access to active participation is often restricted to the elite. It is the media that 'regulates this access to discourse and frames the statements of other actors through their reporting.'[5] Because the media prefer hegemonic positions, this restricted access is often granted to those with authority.

Social media has shaken up and challenged these dynamics. For example, we were all witness to the significant influence citizen-journalists had during the Arab Spring, and social-media 'bots' continue to ignite political feuds.[6] Nevertheless, traditional media, though weakened in the age of social media, has for now been able to hold onto its unique position and legitimacy. It could be argued that this is particularly true in the discourse arena that legitimises militarised political action, as this continues to be a closed sphere, to which only a select few are privy.

Politics and the Media

Political actors recognise the influence the media has on public opinion.[7] Therefore, many try to establish a trade-off of sorts between themselves and the media. In such circumstances, if the media publishes favourable coverage, they are granted more exclusive access. Freedom of the press remains one of the fundamental beliefs in many Western democracies. But journalists depend on getting access to exclusive information (a 'scoop'). This makes them dependent on sources—the higher up the better—that are willing to leak information.[8] The fine line between 'working your sources' and 'selling out' is not always obvious and clear. The difference between free and state-run media may be glaring in some instances, but sometimes the boundaries can be unclear. It is assumed that the public's demand for honest and high-quality reporting maintains the integrity of the media.[9] But the relationship between media and the state, and their interdependence, requires ongoing scrutiny.

In times of war, the media are often more compliant in following the government's narrative. The government also seems to be more inclined to use the media as a tool in coercing the public during periods of armed conflict. Erin Sahlstein Parcell and Lynne M. Webb argue that:

> War, or even the threat of war … tends to reverse the normal role between the press and the state, such that rather than serving as a check on power, the press falls in line and becomes a conduit for official state pronouncements.[10]

This governmental media-management works structurally by offering the press access to the governmental defence apparatus.[11] The doctrine of agenda control theorises that the level of news coverage assigned to a given issue correlates directly with the weight voters will give this issue when evaluating politicians. It is therefore of little wonder that governments vie for the media to pick up their line of argument. Ian Stewart and Susan L. Carruthers argue in their study on war, culture, and the media that:

> Military and political leaders attempt to influence the messages coined by the media, believing that media coverage will determine the depth of national and international support on which they can hope to rely for their objectives.[12]

Civil-Military Relationships

In legitimising militarised political action, the government may be vying for the media to pick up certain narratives to influence public opinion.[13] But to determine which narratives can be fruitful, a civil society's relationship with its military must be understood as well. The civil-military relationship can be defined as the direct and indirect dealings that ordinary people and institutions have with the military, legislative haggling over funding, regulation and use of the military, and complex bargaining between civilian and military elites to define and implement policy.[14]

The level of scepticism or trust between military and civil institutions is often rooted in a state's cultural history regarding these institutions. This historical relationship influences the way journalists feel inclined to investigate and report on military matters. Hence,

> cultural differences also shape the ways that military operations are represented in the U.S. and [Germany] illustrating distinct civil-military constitutions and distinct bodies of politic and therefore quite different wars.[15]

The public, the media, and political institutions (in our case, the military) are in an interdependent relationship in which all try to influence each other, and all are dependent on each other. How a military approaches these relationships and how it frames its actions (such as the use of military force) to influence a likely successful outcome depends on the cultural makeup of the target audience. Even within liberal democracies, cultural differences define the political discourse in which a military has to legitimise its actions and therefore influences how each military force chooses to communicate any given amount of information.[16]

If a government decides to push for the action of war, it needs to enter the realm of political discourse and utilise communication strategies that are rooted in culture and ideology in order to coerce the emotions and opinions of the public. If done successfully, this will lead to majority support of the given political action, thus legitimising the government's going to war. One therefore has to understand the audience's ideologies and base narratives to establish effective communication strategies within this legitimising context. These ideologies and base narratives can vary considerably, even between nations that may seemingly have shared values such as freedom and democracy. Therefore, different communication approaches need to be utilised in order to legitimise the same political action.

Exploring the Base Narrative of the United States

The armed services have for a long time been regarded as the most trusted institution by civilian Americans, continually coming out on top in polls on public opinion towards national institutions.[17] Similarly, soldiers have long been held in higher regard than the average citizen.[18] The origins of this type of present-day American militarism are rooted deeply in the nation's past. When committing the United States to large-scale armed conflict, presidents have time and again demonstrated a strong preference for explaining what is at stake in terms of classic American ideology.[19] At the centre of this ideological language is the concept of American civil religion and the myths of manifest destiny and American exceptionalism.

In the founding of the United States, the deeply Protestant character of the nation provided 'a religious dimension for the whole fabric of American life.'[20] This close association of Protestantism and American identity created a 'seamless web of shared beliefs.'[21] The inherently religious national character influenced the development of American institutions.[22] The term 'American civil religion' was coined by Robert N. Bellah in 1967 and has since been adopted by social scientists in discussing the set of beliefs, symbols, and rituals, many drawn from American history, that are used to express American faith in the political process. The creation of such a public religion serves as the bedrock of the 'sacred legitimation for the American capitalist and democratic system.'[23] For example, the American constitution is often regarded as a sacred document, transcending any particular time and place.

'Manifest destiny' describes the origin myth of the United States, stipulating that the creation of the nation was an act of Providence. God led the people to this land so that they could build a new and exceptional social order, and then 'bring light unto all other nations.'[24] It is the creed of the divinely assigned task to reshape the world in its image and be a 'moral compass to the world.' In modern times, those Americans deployed to all corners of the globe are thought of as providing this moral compass.[25] Whereas manifest destiny focuses on the mission and duty God assigned to the American people as a chosen people, 'American exceptionalism' describes the conviction that the United States and its people are unique and exceptional in character, purpose, values, and history.[26] These central themes are particularly well suited for contexts of conflict because they help to 'articulate the country's status, roles and policies in relation to the world community.'[27] When militarised action is framed in this context it is immediately presented as a 'good deed' that helps to inspire others to become more like the United States.

Even though militarism has seen its ups and downs in the United States and was widely challenged in the 1960s and 1970s during and after the divisive Vietnam War, all was forgotten after the events of 9/11, when the nation seemed to suffer a sort of historical amnesia.[28] 9/11 gave birth to a new American militarism, which, according to Bacevich, 'draws much of its sustaining force from myth.'[29] Politicians discovered that 'a sentimentalized version of the American military experience and an idealized image of the American soldier'[30] sell and translate well into votes.

When the ISAF mission was underway, 'widespread, almost automatic support for th[e] doctrine of American Exceptionalism persist[ed].'[31] It seemed, Bacevich observes, that 'at the crossroads of religion and politics, little of consequence [had] changed.'[32] History has proven that American civil religion, manifest destiny, and American exceptionalism are a perfect breeding ground for patriotism and militarism and thus ultimately a convincing justification for armed conflict. For this reason, the military and defence apparatus has continued to employ such rhetoric in its communication strategy.

Exploring the Base Narrative of Germany

Much European history of the seventeenth to nineteenth century is marked by war. First, the kingdoms and then the nations across Europe were in constant battle either with each other or with their own people. In Germany, the one hundred years prior to the end of the Second World War were marked by revolutions and constant regime changes, the instability of the Weimar Republic, and ultimately the horrors of the Nazi regime. The Nazis of course built the backbone of their agenda on the ideal image of a German or Aryan. But the concept of a single

Germany identity had not existed a hundred years prior. It was during the middle of the nineteenth century, when the concept of nation-states swept across the Western hemisphere, that a unified German identity began to form and the Prussian project to create a unified German nation-state became a significant narrative in German political culture.[33]

Through the Nazi regime's megalomaniacal distortion of the nationalist narrative, the mere concept of nationalism was rendered unusable as a future national narrative. 'The dominant national framing was shattered by the total defeat of Hitler's Reich.'[34] This left Germans insecure about the democratic project and purged of any nationalist base narrative.[35] Not only was there no clear historical or nationalist narrative to draw from but the country was divided into two for decades to come. As a result, the two German nations had to rebuild themselves independently and from the ground up, both physically and mentally.

Out of the trauma and confusion of the Second World War, Germany had the considerable task of rebuilding itself. It should be clarified at this point that I will be referring to the Federal Republic of Germany (FRG) or West Germany when I refer to Germany during the period of 1949–1990. Although both West and East Germany had to rebuild themselves, the decision to focus on the FRG was made because it was this German nation that ultimately dictated the discourse and base narrative of the unified Germany that we have today.

Under occupation, Germans were forced to rid themselves of the ideologies they had been indoctrinated with before 1945. But the immediate post-war society had difficulties consolidating this guilt while simultaneously finding room to cope with their own suffering. It took fifteen years before the collective conscience could even begin turning its focus on the suffering of the Holocaust.[36] Previously, the balance between language and silence had gone so far that it had in some sense become ritualised,[37] so far that this generation has become known as the silent generation.

However, as Jarausch and Geyer observe, 'Effectively, many Germans were undergoing something akin to a conversion, a remaking of a sense of themselves, of body and soul. Germany was becoming a different country.'[38] Central to this conversion was reconciliation with the past, a process that I would argue the country continues to undergo to this day.

This reconciliation effort has at its centre the admission of guilt for the crimes committed under Nazism. This guilt has since become transgenerational and symbolic.[39] West German society managed to embrace a collective guilt and collective moral responsibility for the Jewish genocide and the rise of Hitler and his henchmen. The survivors' striving to forget, rebuild, and regain stability, which is specific to post-war Germany, has come to be summarised by historians under the term *Vergangenheitsbewältigung* (literally, coping with the past). The new German base narrative was thus founded in the experience (and repudiation) of the Nazi regime. Guilt, responsibility, reparations, and atonement are central to it.

The country did go through significant changes in the second half of the twentieth century and after, most notably the unification that came with the end of the cold war. But there are still 'few countries in which pacifist sentiments find a deeper political resonance than in Germany.'[40] The experience of the Third Reich and the Holocaust continues to inform German foreign- and security-policy approaches. And, as Thomas Risse observes in his study on German political culture, the values of multilateralism and peaceful conflict settlement have seen almost no change in recent years.[41] As such, they remain the bedrock of the modern German base narrative and represent the leitmotif for German strategic culture and communication strategy.

Frame Analysis of the Deutsches Bundeministerium der Verteidigung (German Defence Ministry) and the US Department of Defense

In order to understand how these base narratives influence the communication strategies of their nations, I will use a frame analysis to compare all press releases related to the ISAF Mission published by both the Bundeministerium der Verteidigung (BMVg) and the US Department of Defense (DoD) between 2001 and 2014. The methodology is based on the approach taken by Romy Froehlich and Burkhard Rüdiger, whose study focused on political public relations by analysing the framing strategies in press releases of German political parties and ministries.[42]

Frame analysis allows us to recognise the different lenses employed by, for example, communication strategists. Each frame is defined by a clear pattern of statements, keywords, and catchphrases. Isolating these repetitive patterns leads to the identification of specific frames.[43] Frames can be understood as lenses through which we view a given subject. They shape interpretations by classifying, organising, and interpreting a given subject.[44] Frames can be either thematic or positional. Thematic frames look at thematic aspects of an issue and provide an interpretation on how an issue should be seen or discussed in public debate. Position frames provide a specific ideological or political outlook taken on an issue.[45]

As a first step in this study, all press releases by the BMVg and DoD pertaining to the mission of the ISAF and Operation Enduring Freedom in the time frame of 2001–2014 were put into broad topical categories based on general recurring topics presented in the given report.

Fourteen different categories were identified (see Table 1). These categories were: casualty reports, international meetings, reactions to press reports, specific operation details, gear, troop visits, unit rotation/deployment, detainee transfer, medals, progress reports, fiscal reports, official statements by the Secretaries of Defence, surveys, and other.[46]

In the next step, of the fourteen categories, I selected just two categories to continue with a more detailed frame analysis: 'international meetings' and 'official statements by the Secretaries of Defence.' These two categories were chosen for two reasons. First, both categories occurred frequently in both countries, and second, these press releases tended to offer more information than press releases from other categories, and therefore, they were more useful in identifying frames and patterns.

Forty-three press releases from the DoD and twenty-eight press releases from the BMVg were analysed. Overall thirteen frames could be identified. Out of those thirteen frames, seven were identified as thematic frames and six were identified as position frames. The DoD used ten frames: five position and five thematic frames. A total of 112 frame mentions were noted in forty-three press releases. The BMVg used nine frames: four thematic frames and five position frames. It had a total of forty-eight frame mentions in its twenty-eight press releases.

Table 1 Topical categories of press releases

	Casualty reports	Unit deployment/ rotation	Detainee transfer	Medals	Surveys	Official statements by SecDef	International meetings	Reaction to press reports
DoD	1641	44	31	6	–	21	20	6
BMVg	12	6	–	–	2	6	20	5
	Specific operation detail	Gear	Troop visits	Progress report	Fiscal report	Other	Total (without casualty reports)	Total
DoD	10	6	7	5	2	15	176	1817
BMVg	3	10	11	–	–	7	70	82

Froelich and Rüdiger write that 'in order to influence which aspects of an issue are given attention during a political and/or public discussion, political players [must] put the issue into certain thematic frames.'[47] Out of the seven thematic frames that were identified, only two, 'no terrorist safe haven' and 'pride in troops,' overlapped between the DoD and the BMVg (see Table 2). While the US Department of Defense thematically focussed primarily on Afghanistan not becoming a terrorist safe haven again, the Bundesministerium der Verteidigung highlighted the importance of the troops and their value within the greater NATO mission.

Position frames, as opposed to thematic frames, communicate the plans and solutions which political players want to see dominating public discourse.[48] The position frames showed a higher correlation between the two countries than the thematic frames (see Table 3). Both countries used four out of the six identified frames, and both countries used five different position frames in their press releases.

Thus, each made use of one position frame the other did not use. Interestingly, those frames that were only used by one side were strongly emphasised wherever they were used. The German BMVg put by far most of their attention towards the importance of a joint civil-military engagement (64%), a frame not employed by their American partners. The Americans on the other hand put a lot of their focus on emphasising the building of an enduring partnership with the Afghans. While the BMVg did not use this frame, it was the frame that the American side used second-most often (21%), second only to 'Afghan military leadership' (43%).

Table 2 Thematic frames in press releases

Thematic frames	DoD (n = 43)	BMVg (n = 28)
A free Afghanistan	17	–
A stable Afghanistan	–	32
Troop valour	22	–
Democracy for the Afghan people	17	–
Pride in troops	15	5
Troop impact within ISAF	–	38
No terrorist safe haven	30	26
Total	101	101

Table 3 Position frames in press releases

Position frames	DoD (n = 43)	BMVg (n = 28)
Afghan military leadership	43	18
Important partnerships	10	11
Enduring partnership	21	–
Afghanistan mission progress	17	*
Safety of the homeland	9	7
Joint civil-military engagement	–	64
Total	100	101

*Fewer than 5%

When looking jointly at all fourteen frames, the DoD's use of frames seems more balanced than the BMVg's use of frames (Table 4). Their percentage span lies between 5% and 22%, whereas the Germans' frame usage spans from >5% to 38%. The distribution between position frames and thematic frames was fairly balanced on both sides, although both defence departments showed a greater tendency towards position frames.

The Germans (58%) had a slightly greater tendency towards position frames than the Americans (52%). Within the BMVg's frames, one stood out in particular. Table 4 shows that 'joint civil-military engagement' is by far the single most implemented frame, presenting a thirty-eight percentage point usage. With the second-most implemented frame, 'troop impact within ISAF,' the frequency of implementation is already down to 15%. For the DoD, this drop is much smaller. Their most-used frame, 'Afghan military leadership,' showed usage of twenty-two percentage points. It drops down to 14% with their second most used frame, 'no terrorist safe haven.'

The analysis shows that the dominant themes of each defence department align with the countries' base narratives. The US themes predominantly focused on Afghanistan not becoming a terrorist safe haven again by empowering the country's military force: in other words, remaking the country in the image of the United States. This aligns perfectly with the narratives of manifest destiny and American exceptionalism. In comparison, on the German side, one theme stood out above all others. The BMVg particularly highlighted the theme of

Table 4 All frames used in press releases

All frames	DoD (n=43)	BMVg (n=28)
A free Afghanistan	17	–
A stable Afghanistan	–	32
Troop valour	22	–
Democracy for the Afghan people	17	–
Pride in troops	15	5
Troop impact within ISAF	–	38
No terrorist safe haven	30	26
Afghan military leadership	43	18
Important partnerships	10	11
Enduring partnership	21	–
Afghanistan mission progress	17	*
Safety of the homeland	9	7
Joint civil-military engagement	–	64
Thematic frames	48	42
Position frames	52	58
Total	100	100

*Fewer than 5%

joint civil-military relationship, effectively establishing a narrative firmly rooted in multilateralism and anti-militarism.

Conclusion

Overall, this comparison showed that each country's communication strategy aligned with its nation's base narrative and that clear differences in approach and language between the two were observed. The frames implemented by the United States only were 'a free Afghanistan,' 'troop valour,' 'democracy for Afghan people,' and 'enduring partnership.' All of these are reflective of core values of the American civil religion. They effectively utilise the narratives of American exceptionalism and manifest destiny and build moral arguments for intervention based on the missionary character of a United States that has at its core the duty to protect and serve while bringing democracy to the world.

The German press releases, by contrast, showed the use of themes such as 'a stable Afghanistan,' 'troop impact within ISAF,' and 'joint civil-military engagement' that embody the norms that make up German political culture. Such frames relate effectively to the sentiments of multilateralism and anti-militarism. The interconnectivity of Germany and its NATO partners is brought to the forefront, while simultaneously stressing the aid-worker character of the mission rather than the combat aspect. As such, both countries' defence departments strategically employed narratives that aligned with their core values towards militarised political action and in so doing managed to legitimise their country's involvement in the mission until it was completed.

The analysis showed that the communicational strategy of a government's defence apparatus relies on base narratives, values, and myths to effectively legitimise its political action in public discourse. This means we can assume that a multinational mission will always consist of as many domestic narratives as it has members. The legitimising forces within a nation will continue to dictate the communication strategies of defence departments. These dynamics will continue to make it impossible for all these nations to come up with an effective, united communication strategy. Ultimately, the societal and cultural frames which continue to constrain governments, along with social media, may even serve as a significant check on governments by their public. Global citizens will be given the chance to view and question contradicting news and misinformation fed to us by our defence apparatuses and hold representatives accountable.

Notes

1. A term that in itself might very well be a point of contention. Peacekeeping missions were in their inception very much defined by their impartial character and the fact that they were not allowed to employ force. In the twenty-first century, as international actors became more heavily involved in global conflicts, the character of peacekeeping missions morphed into an increasingly active role, more akin to an international police force. Alexandra Novosseloff (2016), 'Emily Paddon Rhoads: "Taking Sides": The Challenges of Impartiality in UN Peace Keeping Operations', *Peace Operations Review* https://peaceoperationsreview.org/

interviews/emily-paddon-rhoads-taking-sides-the-challenges-of-impartiality-in-un-peacekeeping-operations/. Accessed 12 March 2019.
2. Hubert Knoblauch (2000), 'Der Krieg, Der Diskurs Und Die Paranoia Der Macht. Michel Foucaults Verteidigung Der Gesellschaft', *Soziologische Revue* 23:3, pp. 263–68, here p. 266.
3. Susanne Kirchhoff (2010), *Krieg mit Metaphern: Mediendiskurse über 9/11 und den "War on Terror"* (Bielefeld: Transcript-Verl), p. 47.
4. Altschull, cited in Kirchhoff, *Krieg mit Metaphern*, p. 65.
5. Kirchhoff, *Krieg mit Metaphern*, p. 6.
6. Chris Baraniuk (2018), "How Twitter Bots Help Fuel Political Feuds" *scientificamerican.com*. https://www.scientificamerican.com/article/how-twitter-bots-help-fuel-political-feuds/. Accessed 12 March 2019.
7. Shanto Iyengar (2011), *Media Politics: A Citizen's Guide*. 2nd ed. (New York: W. W. Norton & Co), p. 232.
8. Ian Stewart and Susan L. Carruthers (eds) (1996), *War, Culture, and the Media: Representations of the Military in twentieth Century Britain*. (Trowbridge, UK: Flicks Books), p. 2.
9. Kirchhoff, *Krieg mit Metaphern*, p. 15.
10. Erin Sahlstein Parcell and Lynne M. Webb (eds) (2015), *A Communication Perspective on the Military: Interactions, Messages, and Discourses*. (New York: Peter Lang), p. 162.
11. Iyengar, *Media Politics: A Citizen's Guide*, p. 232.
12. Stewart and Carruthers, *War, Culture, and the Media*, p. 2.
13. Kirchhoff, *Krieg mit Metaphern*, p. 50.
14. James Burk (2002), 'Theory of Democratic Civil-Military Relations', *Armed Forces & Society* 29:1, pp. 7–29, here p. 7.
15. Athina Karatzogianni (ed.) (2012), *Violence and War in Culture and the Media: Five Disciplinary Lenses*. (London: Routledge), p. 144.
16. Rashed Uz Zaman (2009), 'Strategic Culture: A "Cultural" Understanding of War', *Comparative Strategy* 28:1, pp. 68–88, here p. 68.
17. Andrew J. Bacevich (2013), *The New American Militarism: How Americans Are Seduced by War*. Updated edition (Oxford: Oxford University Press), p. 23.
18. Service members commonly receive benefits such as priority boarding and reduced prices on different goods, and in public discussion their voice is often elevated to a higher moral ground.
19. Robert L. Ivie (2005), 'Savagery in Democracy's Empire', *Third World Quarterly* 26:1, pp. 55–65.

20. Robert N. Bellah (1988), 'Civil Religion in America', *Daedalus*, pp. 97–118, here p. 99.
21. Cecilia Elizabeth O'Leary (1999), *To Die for: The Paradox of American Patriotism*. (Princeton, NJ: Princeton University Press), p. 15.
22. Raymond F. Bulman (1991), '"Myth of Origin," Civil Religion and Presidential Politics', *Journal of Church and State*, 33:3, pp. 525–39, here p. 535.
23. Bulman, '"Myth of Origin," Civil Religion and Presidential Politics', p. 535.
24. Coles (2002), 'Manifest Destiny Adapted for 1990s' War Discourse', *Sociology of Religion*, 63:4, pp. 403–26, here p. 406.
25. Coles, 'Manifest Destiny Adapted for 1990s' War Discourse', p. 416.
26. Stephen M. Walt (2011), 'The Myth of American Exceptionalism', *Foreign Policy*, 11, https://foreignpolicy.com/2011/10/11/the-myth-of-american-exceptionalism/. Accessed 12 March 2019.
27. Coles, 'Manifest Destiny Adapted for 1990s' War Discourse', p. 403.
28. Ivie, 'Savagery in Democracy's Empire', p. 202.
29. Bacevich, *The New American Militarism*, p. 97.
30. Bacevich, *The New American Militarism*, p. 97.
31. Bacevich, *The New American Militarism*, p. 122.
32. Bacevich, *The New American Militarism*, p. 122.
33. Konrad Hugo Jarausch and Michael Geyer (2003), *Shattered Past: Reconstructing German Histories*. (Princeton, NJ: Princeton University Press), p. 39.
34. Jarausch and Geyer, *Shattered Past: Reconstructing German Histories*, p. 101.
35. Jarausch and Geyer, *Shattered Past: Reconstructing German Histories*, p. 46.
36. Wulf Kansteiner (2006), *In Pursuit of German Memory: History, Television, and Politics after Auschwitz*. 1st ed. (Athens, OH: Ohio University Press).
37. Leslie A. Adelson (2000), 'Touching Tales of Turks, Germans, and Jews: Cultural Alterity, Historical Narrative, and Literary Riddles for the 1990s', *New German Critique*, 80 https://doi.org/10.2307/488635, pp. 93–124.
38. Jarausch and Geyer, *Shattered Past*, p. 9.
39. Wulf Kansteiner, *In Pursuit of German Memory*, pp. 4–5.
40. Thomas U. Berger (1998), *Cultures of Antimilitarism: National Security in Germany and Japan*. (Baltimore, MD: Johns Hopkins University Press), p. 194.

41. Thomas Risse (2004), 'Kontinuität Durch Wandel: Eine "neue" deutsche Außenpolitik', *Aus Politik Und Zeitgeschichte*, 11, pp. 24–31, here p. 28.
42. Romy Froehlich and Burkhard Rüdiger (2006), 'Framing Political Public Relations: Measuring Success of Political Communication Strategies in Germany', *Public Relations Review*, 32:1, pp. 18–25, here p. 20.
43. Froehlich and Rüdiger, 'Framing Political Public Relations', p. 20.
44. Ervin Goffman (1974), *Frame Anlysis: An Essay on the Organization of Experience*. (New York, NY: Harper & Row).
45. Froehlich and Rüdiger, 'Framing Political Public Relations', p. 20.
46. Froehlich and Rüdiger, 'Framing Political Public Relations', p. 20.
47. Froehlich and Rüdiger, 'Framing Political Public Relations', p. 20.
48. Froehlich and Rüdiger, 'Framing Political Public Relations', p. 20.

Section IV

Experiences of Interpreters in Wartime and After

'Rediscovering Homeland': Russian Interpreters in the Wehrmacht, 1941–1943

Oleg Beyda

Every invading army conveys its message first through brutal force, guns, shells, and bullets, and only later occupies itself with explaining to the locals that in fact they come in peace and providing reasons it might be a good thing to be occupied. Communication with the occupied population is always conducted through language specialists who either come from within the army itself and who have cultural knowledge and foreign-language skills, or those who are recruited on the ground. Those who come from the second group usually experience endless problems as they can be seen to be collaborators.[1] Despite the outright genocidal nature of the campaign the Wehrmacht unleashed in the USSR in June 1941, the Germans needed to address the issue of how to talk to people.

Some studies argue the significance of foreign languages at the centre of conflict: 'foreignness' and foreign languages are key to understanding what happens in war.[2] In multi-lingual and multi-national settings, which are inevitable during both occupation and in instances of cooperation

O. Beyda (✉)
University of Melbourne, Melbourne, VIC, Australia
e-mail: oleg.beyda@unimelb.edu.au

with allied countries, the interpreter's role is of vital importance. This is not just true of any given individual engaged in mediating the language, but also of translators as a group.³ Social approaches to the topic of war interpreters have only recently started attracting scholarly attention.⁴ This chapter aims to add to this growing area of study.

Unaccepted Defeat

Those people belonging to a national diaspora can be a source for identifying able language specialists; during the German-Soviet War, White Russian émigrés took on the role of interpreters. In the Russian Civil War, the White Army was defeated and suffered a hasty exodus from Crimea in November 1920.⁵ The Russian fleet, numbering some 150,000 people, civilians and military men alike, including the entire First Army Corps, landed in Turkey.⁶ While the Cossacks went to Lemnos,⁷ the First Army Corps, roughly 26,000 men, went to Gallipoli.⁸ Three years of internment in a makeshift camp followed, beset by enormous hardships. This experience left an indelible mark on these now stateless Russians, an experience that only hardened them in their beliefs that the fight against Bolshevism would be revived sooner or later.⁹

From 1921, the last leaving the camp in May 1923, the members of the White Army began to scatter across Europe and the world. Former soldiers and officers took up low-paying jobs as coal miners, carpenters, bellboys, and taxi drivers. Yet they refused to give up their identity. 'Russia abroad,' the term coined by interwar émigrés to describe their extraterritorial nation, articulated an alternative version of 'Russianness,' different and even hostile to the Soviet one. This 'alternative Russia' produced and maintained its own set of holidays, a rich press and publishing, and charitable, educational, and professional institutions, underpinned by non-Soviet Russian culture and a fervent Orthodox Christianity. Despite being geographically diverse, these exiled Russians created a modern imagined nation.¹⁰

White Russians also created their own defence force. In order to preserve the identity of the White Army, if not the actual entity itself, on

1 September 1924, a unique organisation was formed, known as the Russian All-Military Union (ROVS).[11] Lieutenant General Pyotr Nikolaevich Wrangel, the commander-in-chief of the White forces and an architect of the emigré evacuation, headed this organisation, which he himself had established.[12]

Not only was ROVS intended to maintain the cohesion of the former White Russian movement, it was explicitly intended to mobilise émigrés for a possible war against Soviet Russia. In fact, ROVS was a disguised demobilised army, and its structure and internal cohesion built upon the camaraderie of the Civil War veterans and their conviction that the war was not over yet. Participation in the organisation was on a voluntary basis.[13] Because of their fierce anti-communist convictions as well as their language skills, in 1941 these exiled Russians constituted one of the important pools of recruits for the Wehrmacht.[14]

Language and the Army

As early as 1935, Russians had appeared in the Wehrmacht's system of language training.[15] The army worked with *Reichsfachschaft für das Dolmetscherwesen* (RfD, Imperial Association for Interpreting), a body of language professionals, headed by Otto Monien,[16] that was responsible for most of the language manuals and guides used by the defence force.[17] The RfD worked with career linguists and a number of universities (such as Heidelberg University). This ensured a steady supply of experienced specialists.[18]

Nazi Germany had an administrative system of *Wehrkreis* (military district) that provided an uninterrupted flow of recruits into the army. Each *Wehrkreis* had a *Dolmetscher-Kompanie* (Interpreter Company) attached to it. 'Company' here refers to a bureaucratic formality to identify a body of men: Berlin's 'Company' was 1200 men strong, whereas Dresden had a tenth as many men.[19] When conscripted, a recruit who knew any foreign language to a reasonable level of expertise was sent to the respective district's Company for screening, a process which included oral and written examinations to certify proficiency. Three grades could be awarded: grey card (*Sprachkundiger,* 'language assistant,' or rudimentary knowledge), yellow card (*Übersetzer*, 'translator,' or mediocre level), or red card (*Dolmetscher*, 'interpreter,' or fluent in the language).[20]

Depending on proficiency results, the prospective interpreter was then assigned a *Sonderführer* (Special Leader, hereafter Sdf) rank, was trained in special military terminology, and from there sent to a selected military unit, headquarters, prisoner of war (POW) camp, or propaganda formation.[21] On commencement of the war in August 1939, men with specialised skills, but without the necessary military training, could be promoted to non-commissioned officer (NCO) or officer supervisory positions as Sdf.[22] This rank had been introduced in 1937. While not a regular soldier, an Sdf held a rank equivalent to that of his military counterparts, the so-called *Stellengruppe*.[23] Sdf 'G' (*Gruppenführer*) was Corporal; Sdf 'O' (*Oberfeldwebel*) Company Sergeant Major; Sdf 'Z' (*Zugführer*) platoon leader, same level as Lieutenant; Sdf 'K' (*Kompanieführer*) Company leader, an equivalent to that of Captain; Sdf 'B' (*Bataillonsführer*) Major; and Sdf 'R' (*Regimentsführer*) Colonel, a short-lived, rare rank that was abolished by March 1940.[24]

In Berlin, a special sub-institution existed that was preoccupied with the replenishment of qualified personnel, *Dolmetscher-Lehrabteilung* (Interpreter Department). This was an integral part of the *Oberkommando der Wehrmacht* (Supreme High Command of the Wehrmacht) and an umbrella organisation for all the Companies.[25] Various specialists who had knowledge of Russian culture worked there, including linguists and historians of Russia.[26] The head of the Russian-language section was a famous Slavist, Maximilian Braun, who was born in Saint Petersburg in 1903.[27]

The Germans never trusted Russian nationalists and were afraid of political rivalry, and so repeatedly banned émigré personnel from service in the army.[28] However, there is enough evidence to show that at the unit level, these bans were in fact ignored, since the German army, driven by military necessity, was in need of people that were familiar with the Russian language.[29] In the occupied territories, Germans transmitted their orders almost completely through interpreters.[30]

For the role of interpreter in the occupied territories, the Wehrmacht preferred to use Germans, but Russian émigrés became the 'general exception' to the rule because of their fluency in the language.[31]

Recruitment of Russians was thus carried out in a semi-unofficial fashion. For example, shortly before the invasion of the USSR, on 13 June 1941 at a special meeting in Danzig, 'representatives of the German Army appealed to the Russians with an offer to voluntarily join the army as interpreters, mentioning that in such a post, Russian officers were especially desirable.' Colonel of the Life-Guard Finlandskii Regiment, Dmitrii Khodnev, was the first to answer the German call.[32] Khodnev was subsequently attached to the supply department of the 36th Motorised Division, where he served for a few months in 1941, before being demobilised.

Some of the exiles from the Russian Empire were from the Baltic and had German ethnic backgrounds that made them highly desirable for interpreter positions.[33] Exactly how many bilingual Baltic Germans took part in the German-Soviet War remains unknown, as do their exact functions.[34] Under the racial laws of the time, Baltic Germans were not considered to be 'Russians'; therefore, they were not treated as a group of 'useful aliens' that otherwise would have produced a steady documentary trail. Ethnic Russian émigrés, many of them not even having citizenship of the respective country they resided in, were a different story and are somewhat easier to identify in the documentary record. While it is difficult to estimate absolute numbers of *Russian* émigrés who were sent to the USSR as interpreters, we can estimate some figures. By May 1943, 1200 interpreters had been sent from Berlin to the Wehrmacht through the Administration of Russian émigré affairs.[35] In addition, 1500 émigrés joined the Wehrmacht from France.[36]

In a Plethora of Roles

Russian exiles who supported the efforts of the Wehrmacht and provided their skills for the German cause constituted a significant group, a few thousand members strong. They are thus one of the most controversial, involved, and compelling cases to analyse.[37] An interpreter, especially one from among the White émigré group, was never merely a machine for transmitting speech. In essence, his role should be considered to be one of mediator. As a cultural mediator, he was not without a certain autonomy, but his influence depended on the circumstances. Because of their nationalistic worldview, most émigrés identified with Russian peasants which aided in building rapport. A peasant was believed to be naturally more inclined to reach out to an émigré interpreter, seen as 'one of ours,' compared to a German officer with no Russian-language skills.[38]

The position of interpreter opened up opportunities that did not exist in other areas of service. Combined with a vague rank that allowed a degree of 'personal freedom,' it could lead to unusual results. Let us consider an example. Viktor Andreev was an emigré who served in the 6th Infantry Division as an interpreter with the rank of officer. He was appointed as inspector of schools in the Smolensk region that was occupied by the division. He thus had the opportunity to influence children's education, and he drew up a plan of instruction for the seven-class school in Sychevka. Russian literature was to be studied by the students, and in singing lessons, teachers were to 'cultivate a knowledge of old Russian national folk songs.'[39] German language and history were also to be studied.

Thus, interpreters had an opportunity to help people, if only on the limited scale of a single village. In this instance, an interpreter personally tried to shape the situation that he found himself in, using his circumstances to work in favour of his goals. Circumstances might, however, dictate that an interpreter could only exercise a purely formal role, and in that case, the possible range of decisions and actions was much diminished. If, for example, an order came for residents to be evicted from their homes, the role of interpreter was reduced to that of an intermediary in bringing suffering to innocent people.[40] He was transformed into being a transmitter of information and a conduit for the malign will of the occupiers, one of whom he in fact was, by virtue of his role and uniform.

The Russian origins of interpreters were a factor in permitting additional access to the population, access employed to the detriment of the occupied population's interests. Peasants might be reluctant to surrender food produce to the occupiers, for example, but would invariably hand it over to one of 'their own' Russians. Thus, interpreters helped the Germans in their (frequently violent) search for scarce food resources.[41] In the 6th Infantry Division, there was a thorough grasp of the distinct advantages to be gained by émigré interpreters. Orders therefore stipulated that the interpreters were to be the first to advance into villages the Germans needed to occupy. The émigrés had the task of explaining to the population that it was 'necessary' for them to evacuate their homes in order to free them up for occupation by German units.[42]

Knowledge of the language was a double-edged sword. The interpreter, as both an émigré and a local collaborator, could, if he wished, exploit this knowledge for his enrichment, since the population depended on his linguistic skills. In her diary, Lidiia Osipova described vividly how Soviet citizens who spoke German exploited this situation in the environs of Leningrad:

> Interpreters represent a force and a major one. Most of them are appalling scum, people who care only for themselves and who try to screw out of the population everything that's possible, and often, even things that are impossible. Meanwhile, the population is completely in their hands.[43]

Sometimes, however, there were disadvantages to not having enough knowledge. Although they were native speakers of Russian, not all the émigrés were particularly fluent in German, and such shortcomings could limit the scope of their activity or change their roles.[44] On 17 June 1941, Andrei Volkov was sent to the 8th Panzer Division. Because of his poor knowledge of German, he was directed to the front line as a *Lautsprecher-Propagandist*, shouting into a megaphone and calling on the enemy to surrender. Volkov made up for his lack of education with his fanaticism. With his fervent belief in German war aims, he won the confidence of the Germans, but this did not lead to his being assigned any particular or better role.[45] To have good command of both languages meant more work for most. In addition, another problem arose: some of the emigrés spoke an old-fashioned Russian, and this could be a significant limitation in their work (although this depended on the assignment of the candidate).[46]

Russian-language skills were particularly important during the initial contact between a Soviet prisoner of war and an émigré interpreter. Many officers of the Sdf rank who knew Russian well were assigned for interrogation or were assigned to look into the issue of defection and propaganda.⁴⁷ It may be supposed that a scared and disoriented Soviet prisoner finding himself in captivity was more inclined to turn for help to a native speaker—that is, a compatriot, rather than a German. However, some émigrés in these situations used their special position to sow death rather than understanding. An anonymous colonel of the Red Army who was captured at the end of summer 1941 described his experiences after the war. As a prisoner in full uniform, he was taken to the German divisional staff headquarters, where an old émigré, in the rank of Sdf, told a German soldier: 'This is a Bolshevik Colonel and we must shoot him.' A German General saved his life, no thanks to the emigré.⁴⁸

A constant background to the activity of the émigré interpreter was the ill-defined and ambiguous nature of his position, since he could be assigned to various roles. Dmitrii Karov (Kandaurov) served initially both as adjutant to a commander and as an interpreter in Army Group North; later, he served as an intelligence officer on the staff of the Eighteenth Army, and in the spring of 1943, he was employed as a propagandist at the front.⁴⁹ The interpreter for *Bau-Bataillon 214*, Mikhail Gubanov, managed the procuring of firewood and saw to the peeling of potatoes.⁵⁰ At the same time, however, the émigrés recognised their special standing as the 'connecting link' between the occupier and occupied.⁵¹

Another facet of the role played by the emigré interpreter consisted of softening the occupation's immediate effects or presenting it in a different light. As we have seen, the interpreter was often trying to convince Russian peasants to comply and collaborate (e.g. in the struggle against Soviet partisans).⁵² In his conversations with the locals, the interpreter usually offered an explanation of German misdoings, occasionally blending it with a promise of future change. Even German crimes were casually explained.⁵³ Typically, locals either believed the interpreter's reassurances, or became too scared of German wrath to disagree. Either way, the outcome of the translator's verbal interference could be positive for the German 'new order.' The émigré Anton Iaremchuk II, who served with the Eighth Italian Army, recalled how in the village of Eraklievo in the winter of 1943 he was talking with peasants in the street. A crowd gathered around him, complaining that the Germans were taking away young people to Germany for forced labour:

> I calmed them down, telling them that sooner or later the Germans would be forced to treat the Russian people well and to restore private property, that Russia throughout its thousand-year history had experienced Tatar, Polish and Swedish invasions and had overcome them all, that it would be the same with the Germans—that they wouldn't rule forever the Russian land they had seized. The young people listened to me attentively—an Italian, who spoke Russian so well … They thanked me for my kind words.[54]

On the grassroots level, the interpreter was an important if largely invisible institution. The role of the interpreter was thus one of the most diverse imaginable. Such a person was the face of the new authorities and a law-giver, while at the same time also a man of the people. Speaking two languages, he was both a Russian and a German. He was someone 'from there,' from distant Europe, who was invested with power and who might somehow help the peasants in the chaos of war or instead might bring more chaos. For the peasants, he was a person with whose aid the most pressing problems might be solved through intercession with the Germans. The interpreter could thus be asked to give advice, to set injustices right, to baptise children, to organise the local government or police, to help cure sickness, or to decide questions of property. Even more importantly, perhaps, he also facilitated German crimes and cruelties. Ultimately, the interpreter served *German* ends first and foremost: he normalised occupation and made Nazi goals more achievable.

Uneasy Conscience

Émigré sources on the topic of relations between the Germans and the civilian population are more notable for accounts of abuses and excesses than for evidence of warm relations. After crossing the Russian border on 7 July 1941, soldiers of the 36th Motorised Division began robbing the peasants of the Pskov region, considering that since everything belonged to the collective farms, private property and individual rights did not exist. The émigré Dmitrii Khodnev tried to intervene, pleading with the German soldiers and seeking to persuade them not to antagonise the local population, but in vain, since the Germans were not prepared to listen, certain as they were of their rapid victory and racial superiority. Khodnev's joy at returning home was clouded by these thefts, and his happiness gave way to disillusionment with the German 'liberation' of Russia.[55]

The émigrés were also witnesses to verbal aggression against Russians. The German soldiers who had gone to Pskov with the interpreter Aleksei Dumbadze frequently cursed Russia to the ends of the earth, a country they believed to be 'difficult, incomprehensible and harsh.'[56] Dmitrii Karov in the autumn of 1942 was outraged at the Russophobic utterances of one of the German officers.[57] A Soviet interpreter working for the Blue Division later claimed that a few émigrés, 'affected by the Germans' hostility,' returned to Spain, rather than continuing to serve.[58]

With the onset of the cold weather late in 1941, German soldiers began stealing from the population not only food supplies but also warm garments. This also did not escape the émigrés' attention.[59] Although an émigré who served near Staraya Russa in January 1942 wrote that the local commandant's office had paid for requisitioned items and issued four kilos of flour per civilian each month, such cases were exceptional rather than general practice.[60]

Ivan Steblin-Kamenskii was horrified by the theft that occurred, although initially he asserted a strange 'justification' for it:

> Along with cordiality one also encounters cruelty—they take the last cow, the last potato or even things like sheepskin coats and felt boots. As for how the population are going to live, they're indifferent—they have the same attitude to them as toward flies, they'll die, and that's how it should be. To a degree this is not only understandable, but also just; after all, the Bolsheviks treated the population much worse. War is a terrible thing, with all its consequences and with the destruction it brings.[61]

Over time, the number of thefts and cases in which Wehrmacht soldiers showed a disregard for human life increased his unfavourable view of the Germans:

I endure everything with feelings of great sadness. I cannot defend the population. I see them deprived of their last possessions, and I cannot put a stop to the wilfulness of the soldiers. In general, it is very painful to me to see this new, unfamiliar side of the German soldier, without any human feelings, who despite having more than enough to sustain himself takes the last essentials from women and children. It sets me in turmoil, enrages, insults me, and I can do nothing, and have to serve alongside them … I am staggered by the ignorance and lack of education of our Germans. It seems as if they have never heard anything either about Russia or about Bolshevism. They ask: who was Pushkin, a Communist?[62]

Others witnessed much worse. At the end of November 1941, while staying in Novomoskovsk with the Walloon Legion, Rostislav Zavadskii wrote in his diary about the shootings of civilians suspected of being partisans. *Feldgendarmerie* units did this killing, while one Walloon legionary also took part. Belgian officers and soldiers stood by to watch, with some taking photographs. The mother of a young eighteen-year-old boy dug up his body with her bare hands; she left three flowers on him. Witnessing such incidents caused Zavadskii obvious pain and he wrote 'God, save Russia!'[63] There were even interpreters who participated in murder themselves.[64] General Gotthard Heinrici, commander of XXXXIII Army Corps, had a personal interpreter, Lieutenant Hans Beutelspacher, a Russian German who had lost several members of his family to Soviet repression. Heinrici was surprised at the willingness of someone who had been an intelligent university assistant in civilian life to participate in 'combing operations' that invariably ended in the public hangings of dozens of civilians, partisans, and Soviet prisoners of war.

Often, the émigrés would pass these negative incidents through a sort of filter locking their experiences into a kind of 'tunnel vision.' They were trying to compensate for what they beheld with their own eyes by convincing themselves that the situation was not as bad everywhere. Russian émigrés were inclined to deny the scale of the crimes as the norm for German occupation policy, ascribing it instead to 'local excesses.' Even in the spring of 1942 some émigrés serving in the east refused to be fully convinced of the short-sightedness and improvidence of the Germans, who in fact aspired to ultimately enslave the Slavic population of the USSR. For émigrés to fully acknowledge the mistaken nature of German policy was difficult, as this would lead them to suspect that they themselves had backed the wrong cause from the beginning.

By the spring of 1942 it was impossible to deny the mass of negative information on the monstrous way the civilian population and prisoners of war were being treated. A decisive consideration, however, was still the fact that no other force was fighting against the Bolsheviks. In these circumstances, émigrés were still more inclined to regard themselves as mediators between the Germans and the Russian population; that is, if the policy of the Germans consisted of cruelty and pillage, that meant it could be and needed to be changed at the local level with the help of the interpreters and other 'agents of the emigration.'[65]

Since the émigrés were on occupied territory, they sometimes made attempts to appeal to the conscience of the local commanders and asked for policy changes to defend the population. For the most part, these attempts proved futile. The émigrés thus gradually came to realise that they were hostage to the choices they had made. Ideologically, the goals of many émigrés even after the German defeat at Stalingrad in 1943 remained rigidly and unvaryingly anti-Bolshevik, though a note of depression sometimes made its appearance. Sergei Koch, who served in the Ninth Army, recalled:

> This future became especially uncertain and obscure in February (1943), when news was received of the taking of Stalingrad and of a three-hundred-thousand-strong German army perishing amid the ruins. After this all hopes faded of the fall of Bolshevism and the rebirth of Russia. My mood was very sombre, and involuntarily I remembered the years of the Civil War, when my hopes were also replaced by despair. At that time, however, the fight against the perfidious enemy was only beginning, we were young, and still hoped for a continuation of the struggle, for some kind of help from our allies, for the Russian people to come to its senses and overthrow the hated regime. And now? I understood that with the defeat of the Germans the Bolshevik regime would only grow stronger.[66]

In émigré sources, Italian occupiers are recorded as generally having been more humane compared to the Germans. For example, in a village near Kharkov, some children were accidentally blown up by a grenade that had been forgotten by soldiers. In response the Italian interpreter took the mother a box of food; a year earlier the unfortunate woman had lost her husband, whom the Germans had shot.[67] The Germans suppressed private initiative and robbed the population; the Italians did this to a lesser extent, or at least not in such grotesque forms.[68] The émigré interpreters who talked with the senior Italian officers noted these officers' unfavourable attitudes towards inhumane German policies, suggesting to them that the Italians, on the whole, related better to the Russians.[69] Reinforcing the impression of humaneness for the émigrés was the propaganda oriented towards Christianity in Italian leaflets.[70] However, this image was also a simplification. The Italians were generally obediently following German orders, rounding up civilians, taking hostages, and killing peasants while burning their villages.[71]

For the emigré interpreters, it was very important to believe that the Germans took a positive attitude to the local population; this strengthened their confidence that they had chosen the correct path.[72] Adverse cases forced the émigrés to concentrate still more strongly on their role as 'helpers of the population,' while positive examples of German behaviour were seized on. The émigrés were anxious to believe that their ideas about life and the war could find an embodiment in reality. Symbols, events, and examples from their lives were interpreted uniformly from this point of view, and largely through the prism of the Russia of the past and of illusions absorbed during the years of exile.

Conclusion

On 27 June 1942, according to the 'unambiguous order of the *Führer*,' 'the use of Russian emigrants in the Wehrmacht for the struggle in the East' was prohibited and emigrant officers were not to be sent to the front anymore.[73] On 18 August 1942 directive No. 46 was published, which once again prohibited the use of 'emigrants and former leaders of intelligentsia.' After the issuing of the directive, which was signed by Hitler, the demobilisation of emigrant personnel began.[74] While they tried to send the majority home, the Germans were not able to demobilise all émigrés, since they were dispersed over an enormous front and because some commanders turned a blind eye to such instructions.

After the war, most of the émigrés who served under the Germans did not consider their choice to have been in any way mistaken. They continued living in the realm of their own ideas and of the ideology that confirmed them; as it had been in 1920, so it was in 1941, and so it remained after 1945. Their illusions were corrected only with regard to the so-called 'liberating' goal of the Nazis. In the émigré press after the war, the Germans were criticised for their policy of enslavement, which was also determined to be the main cause of their defeat. Some former émigré collaborators went even further, rebranding themselves as 'democratic' and rewriting the history of their roles in the Second World War.[75]

After the war, the White Guards distinguished their own motivation as a group distinct from that of the Germans. The reasons the émigrés had participated in the war were argued to be quite separate. The direct support they had given the Wehrmacht was a 'Russian affair,' even though the émigrés had served in the army and had been German, not Russian, military servicemen. In the eyes of the military emigration, their outburst of patriotic passion remained unsullied. ROVS continued living in its own delusion.

In this fanciful world of the military emigration, it was as though all events were measured by the 'yardstick' of the Russian Civil War. The Second World War as the centre of events was thus displaced. For the émigrés, the centre was not to be found in the conflict between two gigantic powers. The centre and essence of events was the Russian emigration itself, as if the emigration were the key, and the war the lock that the key needed to 'open.' This would in turn bring victory. Also stemming from this view was the conviction of the émigrés that the Germans would not have been able to get by without them, and so were bound to turn to them for help. The émigrés considered that in supporting the Germans in 1941, they were supporting the 'Russian cause.' In the words of Aleksei Polianskii,

> Could I have imagined, in St Petersburg during the war with Germany, and receiving a production order from the pages of His Majesty's Page

Corps on behalf of officers of the Russian Imperial Army, that twenty-six years later I would receive a production order for officers of the German Wehrmacht? And that in donning the uniform of a German officer, I would not feel myself a traitor to my Motherland, but to the contrary, its defender and a fighter for the liberation of Russia from Red usurpers, after being driven to this resort solely for tactical reasons?[76]

A great many émigré interpreters who had seen the German-Soviet front could have signed their names beneath these words. According to the White Guard patriotism of illusions, they were not aiding the enslavement of the Russian people by the Germans because, under the conditions of Soviet rule, they had already lost their freedom. Proceeding on the basis of principles familiar to them, the émigrés wanted to believe, and did believe, that the struggle against Bolshevism would continue, and this faith kept them going for an astonishing amount of time. Yet what the exiles had failed to acknowledge was that as interpreters, however sincere in their anti-Bolshevik patriotism and desire to help unchain their Sovietised kin, they were not only transmitting the orders of a murderous regime, but on a small-scale level, their efforts were in fact abetting a regime whose goals were profoundly murderous and anti-Russian.

Notes

1. See the figure of Izzy the interpreter, an Iraqi working with the Americans, in: D. Finkel (2009), *The Good Soldiers* (New York: Farrar, Straus and Giroux), pp. 154–57.
2. H. Footitt, M. Kelly (2012), 'Introduction', in H. Footitt and M. Kelly (eds), *Languages at War: Policies and Practices of Language Contacts in Conflict*, (Basingstoke: Palgrave Macmillan), pp. 1–15, here pp. 1, 10.
3. P. Kujamäki (2012), 'Mediating for the Third Reich: On Military Translation Cultures in World War II in Northern Finland', in H. Footitt and M. Kelly (eds), *Languages and the Military: Alliances, Occupation and Peace Building* (Basingstoke: Palgrave Macmillan), pp. 86–99, here p. 86.
4. M. Inghilleri and S.-A. Harding (eds) (2010), *Translation and Violent Conflict*. Special Issue of *The Translator: Studies in Intercultural*

Communication, 16:2 (Routledge: London); A. Fernández-Ocampo and M. Wolf (eds) (2014), *Framing the Interpreter: Towards a Visual Perspective* (Routledge: New York); T. Guo (2016), *Surviving in Violent Conflicts: Chinese Interpreters in the Second Sino-Japanese War 1931–1945* (Basingstoke: Palgrave Macmillan); M. Wolf (ed) (2016), *Interpreting in Nazi Concentration Camps* (Bloomsbury: New York); H. Effinghausen (2017), *Zwischen Neutralität und Propaganda—Spanisch-Dolmetscher im Nationalsozialismus* (Berlin: Frank & Timme); P. Kujamäki (2017), 'Finnish Women, German Pigs and a Translator: Translation Consolidating the Performance of "Brotherhood-In-Arms" (1941–44)', *Translation Studies*, 10.3, pp. 312–28, here p. 313.
5. J. D. Smele (2017), *The 'Russian' Civil Wars, 1916–1926: Ten Years That Shook the World* (New York: Oxford University Press).
6. N. A. Kuznetsov (2009), *Russkii flot na chuzhbine* (Moscow: Veche), p. 104.
7. B. Bruno (2009), 'Lemnos, l'île axus Cosaques', *Cahiers du Monde Russe*, 1, pp. 187–230; K. M. Ostapenko, V. (2015), 'Lemnosskii dnevnik', in V. E. Koisin and A. A. Konovalov (eds), *Lemnosskii dnevnik ofitsera Terskogo kazach'ego voiska 1920–1921 gg.* (Moscow: Sodruzhestvo 'Posev').
8. G. F. Voloshin et al. (eds.) (1923), *Russkie v Gallipoli. Sbornik statei, posviashchennyi prebyvaniiu 1-go Armeiskogo korpusa Russkoi armii v Gallipoli* (Berlin: EAG/Druck); K. Acar (2016), 'Rusça kaynaklarda Gelibolu ve Beyaz Ruslar', *Çanakkale Araştırmaları Türk Yıllığı*, 14:20, pp. 1–33.
9. A. Shmelev (2008), 'Gallipoli to Golgotha: Remembering the Internment of the Russian White Army at Gallipoli, 1920–3', in J. Macleod (ed), *Defeat and Memory: Cultural Histories of Military Defeat in the Modern Era*, (Basingstoke: Palgrave Macmillan), pp. 195–213.
10. L. Manchester (2016), 'How Statelessness Can Force Refugees to Redefine Their Ethnicity: What Can Be Learned from Russian Émigrés Dispersed to Six Continents in the Inter-war Period?', *Immigrants & Minorities*, 34:1, pp. 70–91, here p. 72.
11. P. Robinson (2002), *The White Russian Army in Exile, 1920–1941* (Oxford: Clarendon Press).
12. A. Kröner (2010), *The White Knight of the Black Sea: The Life of General Peter Wrangel* (The Hague: Luxemburg Publishing).

13. M. I. Boiarintsev, 'Epokha 1937–1965 gg.', pp. 33–34. Box 1, Mitrofan Ivanovich Boiarintsev Papers (hereafter BAR Ms. Coll/Boiarintsev). Bakhmeteff Archive, Rare Book and Manuscript Library, Columbia University.
14. O. Beyda (2016), 'A Different Russian Perspective or "Their Long Defeat": White Émigrés and the Second World War', in T. Moss and T. Richardson (eds), *New Directions in War and History* (Sydney: Big Sky Publishing), pp. 72–87.
15. A. Reziapkin (2008), 'Voennye razgovorniki. Otkrytiia, kotorye potriasli mir', in G. Pernavskii (ed), *Nepravda Viktora Suvorova* (Moscow: Iauza), p. 418.
16. C. Sinner and K. Wieland (2013), 'Eine translationswissenschaftliche Sicht auf Sprachmittlung im Fremdsprachenunterricht', in D. Reimann and A. Rössler (eds), *Sprachmittlung im Fremdsprachenunterricht* (Tübingen: Narr Verlag), p. 94; C. P. Kieslich (2017), '"Volksgemeinschaft" und "Richtiges Dolmetschen"', in M. Behr and S. Seubert (eds), *Education Is a Whole-Person Process: Von ganzheitlicher Lehre, Dolmetschforschung und anderen Dingen* (Berlin: Frank & Timme), p. 389.
17. The RfD was also responsible for certifying the translation of the proofs of ancestry, an important aspect of every foreigner's legal situation, including Russians. E. Ehrenreich (2007), *The Nazi Ancestral Proof: Genealogy, Racial Science, and the Final Solution* (Bloomington: Indiana University Press), p. 98.
18. Head of the university's Russian section was an émigré, Nikolai von Bubnov (Bubnoff). K. Schultes (2006), 'Die Staats- und Wirtschaftswissenschaftliche Fakultät', in W. U. Eckart, V. Sellin, and E. Wolgast (eds), *Die Universität Heidelberg im Nationalsozialismus* (Heidelberg: Springer Medizin Verlag), pp. 579ff.
19. Interrogation report, interpreter Josef Russ, 33rd Waffen-Grenadier Division der SS 'Charlemagne', 17 April 1945. F. 972, op. 1, d. 299, l. 98. Central Archive of the Ministry of Defence (hereafter TsAMO RF).
20. H. Salevsky (2012), 'Training Translators and Interpreters in Germany: Past and Present', in N. Reingold (ed), *Istoriia perevoda: mezhkul'turnye podkhody k izucheniiu. Materialy mezhdunarodnogo simpoziuma v ramkakh proekta 'Natsional'no-istoricheskie traditsii v perevodovedenii'. Moskva, 15–17 sentiabria 2011 g.*, (Moscow: RSUH), pp. 165–91.

21. Interrogation report, interpreter Josef Russ, 33rd Waffen-Grenadier Division der SS 'Charlemagne', 17 April 1945. F. 972, op. 1, d. 299, l. 98. TsAMO RF.
22. N. Thomas (2002), *The German Army in World War II* (Oxford: Osprey Publishing), pp. 122, 148.
23. A. Schlicht and J. R. Angolia (1996), *Die Deutsche Wehrmacht. Uniformierung und Ausrüstung 1933–1945. Band 1: Das Heer* (Stuttgart: Motorbuch Verlag), p. 305.
24. N. Thomas (1999), *The German Army 1939–45 (3): Eastern Front 1941– 43. Men-at-Arms #326* (Oxford: Osprey Publishing), p. 10.
25. C. Trollmann (2016), *Nationalsozialismus auf Japanisch? Deutschjapanische Beziehungen 1933–1945 aus translationssoziologischer Sicht* (Berlin: Frank & Timme), p. 101.
26. W. Krauss (2004), *Ein Romanist im Widerstand: Briefe an die Familie und andere Dokumente* edited by P. Jehle and P.-V. Springborn (Berlin: Weidler), p. 175; W. Krauss (1997), *Spanische, italienische und französische Literatur im Zeitalter des Absolutismus* edited by P. Jehle and H. F. Müller (Berlin: Walter de Gruyter), p. 576; K. Sydow (2008), 'Die Akzessionsjournale der Preußischen Staatsbibliothek im Hinblick auf NS-Raubgut und die Reichstauschstelle', in H. E. Bödeker and G.-J. Bötte (eds), *NS-Raubgut, Reichstauschstelle und Preußische Staatsbibliothek*, (Munich: K. G. Saur), p. 79.
27. R. Lauer (1985), 'Maximilian Braun zum Gedächtnis', *Die Welt der Slaven*, 30, pp. 203–13, here p. 204; H. W. Schaller (2010), *Die 'Reichsuniversität Posen' 1941–1945: Vorgeschichte, nationalsozialistische Gründung, Widerstand und polnischer Neubeginn* (Frankfurt am Main: Peter Lang), p. 189; J. Dinkel (2009), *Maximilian Braun als Südslavist. Eine akademische Biographie (1926–1961)*, (Munich: Verlag Otto Sagner), pp. 77–80.
28. I. Petrov and O. Beyda (2017), 'The Soviet Union', in D. Stahel (ed), *Joining Hitler's Crusade: European Nations and the Invasion of the Soviet Union, 1941* (Cambridge: Cambridge University Press), p. 373.
29. On military necessity in the Wehrmacht: J. Rutherford (2014), *Combat and Genocide on the Eastern Front. The German Infantry's War, 1941– 1944* (Cambridge: Cambridge University Press). On interpreting in the Red Army: A. Hill (2017), *The Red Army and the Second World War* (Cambridge: Cambridge University Press), p. 27; A. Statiev (2018), *At War's Summit: The Red Army and the Struggle for the Caucasus Mountains in World War II*, (Cambridge: Cambridge University Press), p. 80.

30. S. Lehnstaedt (2012), 'The Minsk Experience: German Occupiers and Everyday Life in the Capital of Belarus', in A. J. Kay, J. Rutherford, and D. Stahel (eds), *Nazi Policy on the Eastern Front, 1941: Total War, Genocide, and Radicalization* (New York: University of Rochester Press), p. 249.
31. Interrogation report, interpreter Josef Russ, 33rd Waffen-Grenadier Division der SS 'Charlemagne', 17 April 1945. F. 823, op. 1, d. 71, l. 197. TsAMO RF.
32. 'Prikaz po ORVS no. 41', 16 June 1941. F. R-5845, op. 1, d. 4, l. 37. State Archive of Russian Federation (hereafter GARF).
33. For example, Baron Achim von Kutzchenbach: T. Diedrich (2008), *Paulus: Das Trauma von Stalingrad. Eine Biographie* (Paderborn: Ferdinand Schöningh), pp. 147, 213, 251, 336.
34. K. Kangeris (1994), 'Kollaboration vor der Kollaboration? Die baltischen Emigranten und ihre "Befreiungskomitees" in Deutschland 1940/41', in W. Röhr (ed), *Okkupation und Kollaboration (1938–1945): Beiträge zu Konzepten und Praxis der Kollaboration in der deutschen Okkupationspolitik* (Berlin: Hühtig Verlagsgemeinschaft), p. 181.
35. B. Dodenhoeft (1995), 'Vasilij von Biskupskij—Eine Emigrantenkarriere in Deutschland', in K. Schlögel (ed), *Russische Emigration in Deutschland 1918 bis 1941: Leben im europäischen Bürgerkrieg* (Berlin: Akademie Verlag), p. 227.
36. K. Schlögel (2006), 'Berlin: "Stepmother" Among Russian Cities', in K. Schlögel (ed), *Russian-German Special Relations in the Twentieth Century: A Closed Chapter?* (Oxford: Berg), p. 62.
37. For the experience of Soviet interpreters: V. Zhdanova (2009), *'Nashim oruzhiem bylo slovo…': perevodchiki na voine/'Unsere Waffe war das Wort…': Translation in Kriegszeiten* (Frankfurt am Main: Peter Lang); B. D. Suris (2010), *Frontovoi dnevnik: dnevnik, rasskazy*, edited by T. B. Trubetskaia and I. I. Galeev (Moscow: ZAO Izdatel'stvo Tsentrpoligraf).
38. Serving with the 52nd 'Torino' Italian Infantry Division, Lieutenant Iurii Sokolov also quickly became an object of interest to the peasants. Suffering from looting by the Italians, the Russian population complained only to Sokolov, calling on him to defend them. I. Sokolov, 'S ital'ianskoi armiei na Ukraine'. *Novyi zhurnal*, No. 142, March 1981, pp. 115–117, 122. In France, some raped women turned to the help of the interpreters since they were often the only ones who, due to their language skills, were able to maintain contact with the local population. B. Beck (2004),

Wehrmacht und sexuelle Gewalt: Sexualverbrechen vor deutschen Militärgerichten 1939–1945, (Paderborn: Ferdinand Schöningh), p. 171.
39. Anlagen zum Tabeguch 6. I.D. 1.4 – 31.12.1942, Anl. 24, 29 June 1942. RH 26-6/66. Bundersarchiv – Militärarchiv Freiburg (hereafter BArch Freiburg).
40. 'Iz sochineniia uchenika 5 klassa srednei shkoly No. 5 Gennadiia Levana', in *Voina glazami detei. Sbornik dokumentov*, Gosudarstvennyi arkhiv Kaluzhskoi oblasti, Kaluga, 1993, p. 45.
41. D. Stahel (2015), *The Battle for Moscow* (Cambridge: Cambridge University Press), pp. 208–09.
42. Besondere Anordnungen, Anlage zum Sonderbefehl des Rgt. vom 21.12.1941. F. 500, op. 12480, d. 59, l. 132. TsAMO RF.
43. O. V. Budnitskii and G. S. Zelenina (eds) (2012), *'Svershilos'. Prishli nemtsy!' Ideynyi kollaboratsionizm v SSSR v period Velikoi Otechestvennoi voiny* (Moscow: Rossiiskaia politicheskaia entsiklopediia (ROSSPEN)), p. 92.
44. D. A. Zhukov and I. I. Kovtun (2012), *RNNA. Vrag v sovetskoi forme* (Moscow: Veche), p. 58.
45. 'Beurteilung des Dolmetschers Andrej Wolkow', 9 March 1943. T-315, R. 498. Washington, DC, National Archives and Records Administration (hereafter NARA).
46. At the beginning of the war, Section Ic of the Eighteenth Army under Major Allmann received a group of émigré recruits that were supposed to be gathering intelligence. Yet their spoken Russian was so different (probably too eloquent, with a touch of outdated terms) from the simplistic Russian the peasants were speaking that it immediately drew unneeded attention to them. D. Karow, 'Entstehung der ersten sowjetischen Einheiten aus Einwohnern der U.d.S.S.R.'. ZS/A–10/3. Archiv des Instituts für Zeitgeschichte (hereafter IfZ-Archiv).
47. M. Edele (2017), *Stalin's Defectors: How Red Army Soldiers Became Hitler's Collaborators, 1941–1945* (Oxford: Oxford University Press), pp. 30–31, 48; O. Buchbender (1978), *Das tönende Erz. Deutsche Propaganda gegen die Rote Armee im Zweiten Weltkrieg* (Stuttgart: Seewald Verlag), pp. 175, 177; K. Zellis (2011), 'Nacionālsociālistiskās Vācijas okupācijas režīma propaganda Latvijā (1941–1945)', PhD Thesis, University of Latvia, p. 57.
48. Probably, this was Georgii Antonov, who collaborated with the Germans from 1942 onwards. Male, 52, Great Russian, Regular Army. Schedule A, Vol. 18, Case 341 (interviewer M.L., type A4), p. 16. Harvard Project on the Soviet Social System. Harvard University, Widener Library.

49. D. Karov, 'Russkie na sluzhbe v nemetskoi razvedke i kontrrazvedke', pp. 22, 137. Box 280, Folder 4. Boris I. Nicolaevsky Collection (hereafter HIA/Nicolaevsky), Hoover Institution Archives, Stanford University.
50. Postcard from Gubanov, 9 December 1941. F. R-5759, op. 1, d. 64, l. 461. GARF. Full biographical reconstruction: O. Beyda (2018), '"Re-Fighting the Civil War": Second Lieutenant Mikhail Aleksandrovich Gubanov', *Jahrbücher für Geschichte Osteuropas*, 66:2, pp. 245–73.
51. 'Voennyi perevodchik'. *Novoe slovo*, No. 77, 26 September 1943, p. 6. Staatsbibliothek zu Berlin, Preußischer Kulturbesitz (hereafter SzB).
52. D. Zhukov and I. Kovtun (2016), *Politsai: istoriia, sud'by, prestupleniia. Izd. 3-e, ispr. i dop.* (Moscow: Izdatel'stvo 'Piatyi Rim' (OOO 'Bestseller')), p. 261.
53. J. D. Enstad (2018), *Soviet Russians under Nazi Occupation: Fragile Loyalties in World War II* (Cambridge: Cambridge University Press), p. 73.
54. A. Gabrieli [A. Iaremchuk II], 'S ital'ianskoi armiei v Rossii. Moia posledniaia (chetvertaia) voina', p. 98. Box 1. Globus Publishers Records (hereafter HIA/Globus), Hoover Institution Archives, Stanford University.
55. D. Khodnev, 'Mesiats v germanskoi armii', pp. 24–25, 31, 34. Box 10, Folder 'Minor Manuscripts'. Finliandskii Leib Gvardii Polk Records (hereafter BAR Ms. Coll/Finliandskii Polk). Bakhmeteff Archive, Rare Book and Manuscript Library, Columbia University.
56. A. Dumbadze, 'Iz zapisok perevodchika'. *Vozrozhdenie*, No. 206, February 1969, p. 42.
57. D. Karov, 'Russkie na sluzhbe v nemetskoi razvedke i kontrrazvedke', p. 166.
58. V. Rudinskii, 'S Ispantsami na Leningradskom Fronte'. *Pod Belym Krestom*, No. 3, 1952, p. 13.
59. 'Tak bylo'. *Suvorovets*, No. 40 (55), 21 October 1949, p. 2. Russian State Library (hereafter RGB).
60. Information Summary of the Administration of I Department of ROVS, 1 March 1942, p. 3.
61. Entry from 21 December 1941. Ivan Steblin-Kamenskii's diary. Archive of Steblin-Kamenskii family (hereafter ASKF).
62. Entry from 30 March 1942. Ibid.
63. R. V. Zavadskii (2014), *Svoia chuzhaia voina. Dnevnik russkogo ofitsera vermakhta, 1941–1942 gg.*, edited by O. I. Beyda (Moscow: Sodruzhestvo 'Posev'), p. 126.

64. J. Hürter (ed) (2016), *Notizen aus dem Vernichtungskrieg. Die Ostfront 1941/42 in den Aufzeichnungen des Generals Heinrici* (Darmstadt: Wissenschaftliche Buchgesellschaft), pp. 64–65, 85–87.
65. N. Sakhnovskii, *Sobytiia 1940–1945 godov i moe uchastie v nikh*, p. 16. Author's private archive.
66. S. Kokh, 'Nizhnee Karlovo (iz vospominanii perevodchika)'. *Chasovoi*, No. 530, August 1970, p. 19. André Savine Collection (hereafter UNC-CH/Savine), Rare Book Collection, Louis Round Wilson Library, University of North Carolina at Chapel Hill.
67. A. Morelli [V. Levashov], 'Na Rodine'. *Chasovoi*, No. 308, May 1951, p. 25. UNC-CH/Savine.
68. A. Morelli [V. Levashov], 'Na Rodine'. *Chasovoi*, No. 309, June 1951, p. 15. UNC-CH/Savine.
69. Ibid., p. 16.
70. A. Morelli [V. Levashov], 'Na Rodine'. *Chasovoi*, No. 311, September 1951, p. 23. UNC-CH/Savine.
71. T. Schlemmer (2005), *Die Italiener an der Ostfront 1942/43. Dokumente zu Mussolinis Krieg gegen die Sowjetunion* (Munich: R. Oldenbourg), pp. 33–38; X. M. Núñez Seixas (2018), 'Unable to Hate? Some Comparative Remarks on the War Experiences of Spaniards and Italians on the Eastern Front, 1941–1944', *Journal of Modern European History*, 16:2, 269–89, here p. 277.
72. Some ROVS wartime reports with such sentiments are available at: K. M. Aleksandrov (2005), *Russkie soldaty Vermakhta. Geroi ili predateli. Sbornik statei i materialov* (Moscow: Iauza, Eksmo), pp. 512–29.
73. J. Hoffmann (1974), *Deutsche und Kalmyken: 1942 bis 1945* (Freiburg: Rombach), p. 98.
74. W. Hubatsch (ed) (1983), *Hitlers Weisungen für die Kriegführung 1939–1945. Dokumente des Oberkommandos der Wehrmacht* (Koblenz: Bernard & Graefe), pp. 201–05.
75. B. Tromly (2016), 'The Making of a Myth: The National Labor Alliance, Russian Émigrés, and Cold War Intelligence Activities', *Journal of Cold War Studies*, 18:1, pp. 80–111, here pp. 83–84.
76. A. Polianskii, 'Russkii Korpus v Serbii, 1941–1945 g.g.', part IV, pp. 29–30. Arranged P(2) PL-POLIA. General Manuscripts Collection. BAR.

Interpreters at Australia's War-Crimes Trials, 1945–1951: From 'Ready-Mades' to 'Happenchancers'

Georgina Fitzpatrick

[I]n Japanese you have got to be very careful in asking questions because there is a big trap if it is a negative question—the Japanese would answer the opposite to us. For example, 'You didn't go, did you?' We'd say, 'No I didn't go.' The Japanese would say, 'Yes you're right. I didn't go.' So they would say yes. You had to be very careful. His answer, 'Yes, he did it.' I had to think. Had I asked the question correctly? I had to really search my ability and … make certain I had got it right because I was conscious of the fact that his life would have been at risk if I had got it wrong. (John Hook in conversation with the author, 11 March 2010)

In the aftermath of the Second World War, 300 trials were held in Australian military courts in eight locations around the Asia-Pacific region, taking place between 1945 and 1951.[1] The accused were suspected of committing war crimes. The majority consisted of Japanese of all ranks and some civilians, but Korean and Taiwanese colonial conscripts also

G. Fitzpatrick (✉)
School of Historical and Philosophical Studies, University of Melbourne, Melbourne, VIC, Australia
e-mail: georgina.fitzpatrick@unimelb.edu.au

© The Author(s) 2020
A. Laugesen, R. Gehrmann (eds.), *Communication, Interpreting and Language in Wartime*, Palgrave Studies in Languages at War,
https://doi.org/10.1007/978-3-030-27037-7_8

faced prosecution. The military lawyers for the prosecution and initially for the defence were Australians operating in English.[2] So too were the President and the Members of the Court who sat in judgement. However, witnesses at the trials, apart from those speaking Japanese as a first or a second language, included people from remote parts of Papua New Guinea and other islands, liberated Indian or Chinese prisoners of war, Chinese civilians from Rabaul, and the occasional German missionary. Not surprisingly, this Babel Tower of languages was an enormous challenge to those running the Australian war-crimes trials. The possibilities of misunderstanding were limitless.

Although there has been a detailed study by Kayoko Takeda of interpreting at the International Military Tribunal of the Far East (IMTFE),[3] little has been published concerning interpreting at the trials of the so-called 'minor' war criminals in the Asia-Pacific region.[4] This chapter explores the efforts made to offer some level of interpretation at the Australian-run trials and will also recount the stop-gap measures put in place to cope with this challenge. Using my interviews with some of the Australian Army interpreters as well as trial transcripts and their associated files,[5] I will outline the situation that was faced, mainly in relation to the Japanese language, and offer some observations on the process.

When the Pacific War began in December 1941, the Australian military authorities scrambled to meet not only the military threat but also to provide skilled linguists. Few Australians had Japanese language skills.[6] Once the Japanese advance in New Guinea was stemmed, both captured Japanese personnel and documents fell into Allied hands. The need for linguists as interrogators and translators became even more desperate. Colin Funch has charted the history of the wartime language schools in meeting this challenge, but it is his account of the formation of the Allied Translator and Interpreter Section (ATIS) in September 1942 that is most pertinent to the trials. An Allied unit based in Brisbane, with growing numbers of US military personnel as well as Australian, ATIS had five main sections: the Translation Section, the Examination Section (responsible for the interrogation of captured Japanese personnel and the preparation of interrogation reports), the Information Section (which collected, collated, and disseminated information), the Production Section (printing and duplicating), and, finally, the Training Section. The last tested and classified all ATIS linguists.[7]

At war's end, provision of sufficient linguists skilled in Japanese became even more difficult. All around the Pacific, thousands of Japanese surrendered in dozens of places, very often to Australian troops accompanied by an interpreter.[8] The situation was overwhelming and the tasks complex. The scale of atrocities committed by Japanese forces, not only against prisoners of war but also against civilian residents in the occupied territories, was well known. With the Allied commitment to prosecute such crimes, more linguists were needed.[9] At each local surrender, they sifted through seized documents and thousands of surrendered enemy personnel to find those suspected of committing war crimes. They interpreted at interrogations and translated statements and captured documents. All the interpreters I spoke to in 2009 and 2010[10] had carried out all or some of these roles before working at Australia's war-crimes trials.

The role of linguists during the war-crimes investigation phase needs further research, but in this chapter I will concentrate on the next phase in the process: the interpreting at the actual trials of war-crimes suspects. Who was available to interpret at the eight locations scattered across the Asia-Pacific—Wewak, Morotai, Labuan, Darwin, Rabaul, Singapore, Hong Kong, and Manus Island—at a time when demobilisation was underway?

Categories of Linguists

Although some of the linguists had been recruited early in the war and may have been eligible for demobilisation, many stayed on to interpret at the trials. They fall into five categories. First, there were what Funch called 'the ready-made' Japanese linguists, consisting mainly of expatriates with pre-war years of residency in Japan under their belt. Second, there were enlisted men (and some women[11]) trained at the various language schools through the war who were prepared to defer demobilisation. And third, there were some self-taught linguists.[12] At the trials, I found two further categories: people on loan from the better-resourced Americans and British and even from the enemy, and a grab-bag of individuals who happened to be on the spot and played a part, from clarifying particular words or phrases to full-scale interpreting. I dub these the 'happenchancers.'

The 'Ready-Made' Linguists

Space prevents me from going into much detail about this group of ready-made linguists, of which there were fifty-one, according to Funch.[13] Many from this group delayed demobilisation to serve at the war-crimes trials, either in the court or behind the scenes.[14] Some of these linguists had been recruited directly from evacuation ships as the following story of a ready-made linguist attests.

By 1941, an initial request from Eastern Command to the Department of Interior for the names and addresses of any evacuees from 'the orient' who were competent in the languages of the area from which they had come 'especially in relation to knowledge of the Japanese language, both written and spoken'[15] had transmuted into a policy where Intelligence Officers attended the docks looking for likely candidates. Among several recruited from passengers evacuated from Yokohama on the last ship to Australia before hostilities commenced—the *An Hui* in late 1941—was Joseph da Costa and also his sister, Maria.[16] Their father had been a businessman in Japan in the pre-war years. His children had received their schooling in Japan and were fluent.

Maria stayed in the Censorship School in Melbourne,[17] training others and translating while Joseph, after his military training, went into the field.[18] At first interpreting when captured Japanese were questioned, he then became an interrogator himself. His Japanese was reputed to be so good that if you put him behind a screen, a suspect would not realise that he was a foreigner. However, he told me that his vocabulary had to be extended to cover legal, military, and medical terms which came up in the trials.[19] He interpreted at eight of the trials at Labuan.[20]

Joseph da Costa, whose interpreting work at the trials comprised an exhausting thirty days, was very conscientious in his approach to his duties. For example, when I asked him about social life in the officers' mess in the evenings, described in jolly detail by one of the prosecuting officers, Captain Athol Moffitt, in his unpublished diary,[21] da Costa told me he didn't attend. Instead, he went to the prisoners' compound to go over what had happened that day in the trial with the accused. He was concerned that those on trial didn't really understand the import of the questioning and the significance of their answers.[22]

Wartime Language Students

The second category of armed-services linguists were those trained at the Censorship School and/or the Royal Australian Air Force (RAAF) Language School.[23] Some years ago, I interviewed or corresponded with five of these: John Hook, John Ferris, the late Gordon Maitland, the late Les Oates, and the late John Wright. And in a sense, I talked to a sixth, the late David Sissons, interpreter at some of the 1946 Morotai trials, whose extensive papers underpinned my chapters in the book *Australia's War Crimes Trials*.[24] I will focus on John Hook's experience to outline some of the problems facing the interpreters when they sat in the courtroom.

During 1946, at trials in various locations, the deficiencies of Australian-born and -educated interpreters became apparent under the pressure of instantaneous interpreting day after day. In Rabaul, where 188 trials were conducted, the practice developed of using bilingual Japanese people, either military or civilian, as the main interpreters, with Australian linguists acting as monitors of the translations. John Hook recalled going into huddles with other monitors and the Japanese nationals to discuss the correct word or phrase to use, while the Court waited for their decision.[25] Hook had studied two units of Japanese at the University of Melbourne before he attended the Censorship School with the purpose of translating documents.[26] He explained:

> We did do conversation with Mrs Selwood. But the crux of the thing really was … we were basically trained in reading and writing. However, when I was sent out into the field with Peter Barbour, we were sent as interpreters so we were thrown into the deep end, after being trained as translators.[27]

Monitoring was adopted because, according to John Ferris, the Japanese interpreters

> spoke excellent English and it soon became clear that their competence in English exceeded our competence in Japanese. So we adopted the practice of using one of them as the principal interpreter, and one of us was always there to help explain any points of difficulty that arose or to interrupt the proceedings if we felt that the Court may have misunderstood an interpretation.[28]

Self-Taught Linguists

Initially, I assumed that no people of Funch's third category were employed at the Australian-run trials as official interpreters. However, after Hook, Ferris, and Barbour were demobilised, two self-taught linguists can be identified as interpreters at Rabaul in 1947: Gus Doddridge and Peter Dimopoulos. Doddridge was used at six late trials.[29] Australian-born, he had taught himself Japanese after the end of the war. According to John Hook,

> He was somebody who came to Rabaul—was involved with interpreting with fairly limited knowledge. But he had been with water transport in Borneo and had quite a bit to do with Japanese seamen. He had picked up some language and I think he was on the outskirts of the trials.[30]

Peter Dimopoulos, born in Greece but resident in Australia from the age of eleven, had learnt his Japanese while a prisoner of war for four years in Singapore and Thailand, and had acted as camp interpreter. The monitoring role of Dimopoulos and Doddridge at the 'Command Responsibility' trial of Major General Hirota Akira was the subject matter of a newspaper report, but neither was officially sworn in as interpreter for that trial.[31]

Borrowed Linguists

The fourth major category consists of linguists borrowed from Australia's Allies and also from the enemy forces. At the end of the war, there were still many American troops stationed in northern Australia. Australian interrogations of captured Japanese personnel were able to benefit from the presence of *nisei* interpreters within the American elements of ATIS.[32] One such was Sergeant R. Y. Miyao, who translated for Captain Douglas Bruce when Bruce interrogated Lieutenant Tazaki Takehiko, self-accused of cannibalism.[33] However, Miyao did not interpret at the subsequent trial of Tazaki at Wewak. Another *nisei* interpreter from the US Army was used. Unfortunately, the list of sworn personnel is incomplete,[34] but a photograph from the trial captures the interpreter seated beside one of the witnesses.[35]

In Hong Kong in 1948, as in Singapore in 1946, the Australian authorities relied upon their British hosts to supply their needs, not always to the satisfaction of the Australian legal officers.[36] Judge Advocate Colonel Brock singled out the quality of the interpreters supplied to the Australian court as 'the most serious deficiency' in the running of the trials. He reported after the first trial that the Court had to go over the written translation and try to put it into 'understandable English,' editing and re-editing. 'Consequently the record of proceedings as it now appears does not give any idea of the work actually involved.' He thus begged for a competent interpreter to be appointed.[37]

In the short term, the British lent Seki Toshio to the Australians for some weeks of the complex Hainan Island trial. Seki had been born in Shanghai, educated in an English school at primary level and then at an American high school. Seki monitored the interpreting in both directions. During the Japanese-to-English interpretation, according to Brock, Seki had to take over 'practically every time.' He also corrected the English-to-Japanese interpretation 'about every third sentence.'[38] When Seki left, Brock calculated that he had saved £300–£350 in lost time.[39]

For the Rabaul trials, captured Japanese personnel often appeared as the main interpreters. Captain Suzuki Heihachirō, born in America but captured at Rabaul among the surrendered Japanese military, interpreted for at least twenty-five trials as the main interpreter, including the trial of General Hirota.[40] He was one of several *nisei* interpreters (second-generation Japanese-Americans) recruited from the Japanese forces.[41]

'Happenchance' Interpreters

The final category of interpreters used at the Australian-run trials were those providing translation as a stop-gap measure. One example occurred when an official observer of the three Darwin trials, Major J. M. L. Hosselet, used one of his many languages to help the Court out in the second trial concerning crimes committed on Timor. On the eighth day of the trial, several days after the questioning of three villagers from

Koepang, the relevant Australian interpreter, Sergeant William Cornish, had probably believed his duties as Indonesian/Malay interpreter were over, and so was not in Court. However, the Prosecuting Officer unexpectedly re-called one of the witnesses for the purposes of rebutting statements made by one of the defendants.[42] As Judge Advocate for the Dutch Forces in Australia, Hosselet was present in the Court. In Java before the war, he had been President of the Court of Justice for Natives, then Public Prosecutor in Surabaya.[43] With Sergeant Cornish absent, Hosselet was sworn in as a substitute interpreter.[44]

Further examples of 'happenchance' interpreting will emerge in the remainder of this chapter. I now turn to an exploration of some instances of interpreting in specific trials.

Interpreting in Practice

Interpreters employed in the Court not only had to contend with specialist military and medical terms[45] but also the rhetorical flourishes of some prosecutors. In his closing address at the second trial, Captain William Cole, Defending Officer at Darwin, criticised the Prosecuting Officer, Major Gerald Ruse. Ruse, Cole suggested, had made a 'fine play on words' during his cross-examination of the Japanese defendant. This approach was condemned in a list compiled for the IMTFE at Tokyo. Prosecutors there were advised against long questions, questions that were complicated, conditional, sarcastic, or negative, and questions hanging on the interpretation of one word.[46] No such advice is recorded as being given at the Australian trials. Cole concluded that Ruse had adopted 'a method good in the Supreme Court of a State, but not in a trial of this nature where the Prosecutor has a statutory duty only and where interpreters have to be employed.'[47]

Cole was mistaken about the employment of interpreters. There was no specific requirement set out in either the Australian *War Crimes Act 1945* (Cth) or the accompanying *Regulations* to provide interpreters.[48] However, in the accompanying forms, there seems to have been an expectation that some level of interpreting would be provided.[49] Every President of the Court had to complete a Certificate of Proceedings, which included 'The Interpreter' as among the personnel and witnesses to be sworn in.[50] This suggests a recognition that the absence of interpretation might impact upon justice.

Evidence in the Australian-run trials was often produced in the form of statements taken from Japanese accused or from witnesses when the alleged crime was being investigated. These statements were read back to the accused by an interpreter for corroboration. But this approach could lead to an injustice, as Captain Cole pointed out in another Darwin trial. Defending Japanese suspected of torturing several Australians captured behind the lines in Timor, Cole criticised the prosecution for relying upon written statements by the accused that included 'remarks which they have not themselves made, but which were made by Australians whose statements were then read to the Japanese.' He gave the example of one of the accused, Sergeant Kitano Tamotsu, being read the statement of one of the victims, Captain Cashman, and confirming it 'as a true record of the events.' Cole pointed out that this method was flawed because the statement which had been translated and read to Kitano was 'lengthy.' He continued:

> There has been great difficulty in getting the interpreters to clearly impart the English meaning to Japanese in evidence in this Court, and it has been necessary to correct minor items. I am quite satisfied that these imperfections of language have caused many of these difficulties and I do suggest that my friend [the prosecutor, Captain Pitcher] did wrong in putting into the mouths of the accused every word.[51]

Two of the interpreters in this trial fell into the second category noted by Funch—those trained at one of the RAAF Language courses.[52]

Even where a trial had the unusual advantage of several bilingual participants, translations of evidence could be disputed. At his trial, Sergeant Sugino Tsuruo objected to the wording of a statement taken from him by an interrogator at Miri in October 1945.[53] When asked why he had not objected when the disputed statement was read to him in Japanese by Captain Davern Wright in November, months before the trial began,[54] he explained that not only had he found the original interrogator 'not very good at the language' but he 'did not get the full gist of the statement' when it was read out to him. He added that he blamed 'the manner in which the statement was read.'[55] Sugino was fortunate that this issue was addressed. He had two 'ready-made' linguists interpreting at his trial—da Costa and Sergeant Donald Mann[56]—and, as his Japanese Defending Officer, Colonel Yamada Setsuo from the Headquarters of the 37th Japanese Army, who spoke English well enough to dispense with translations of evidence from Australians.[57] Yamada was able to convey what Sugino had really meant in the disputed sentence even if it did not save Sugino from a guilty verdict and death by firing squad.

Yamada, who was Defending Officer in seven of the Labuan trials, was an economist educated at the Universities of Tokyo and Oxford.[58] A reporter for the *Argus*, observing the trial, commented that Yamada's English, 'while exotic and laboured, is sufficient to enable him to make himself clear to the Court and he often assists interpreters by explaining some fine shade of meaning of a Japanese phrase.'[59]

In other words, he was yet another example of a 'happenchance' interpreter. Yamada claimed in his closing address to the Court that his English was 'extremely limited' along with his knowledge of jurisprudence in general and Australian law in particular, but he then delivered a wonderfully telling image about his irritation at 'not being able to express my mind fully, like to scratch an itchy spot from outside shoes.'[60] He was sympathetic to the interpreting difficulties, conceding:

> I can well imagine the trouble and difficulty of interpreters to which they have to confront when assisting the interrogation of your officers concerned. However the delicate expression by Japanese who has no English knowledge is very difficult after all, to be conveyed by the interpreters.

He warned of the 'danger' of 'many misinterpretations and misunderstandings ... due to the differences of language spoken.'[61]

Sometimes an accused would intervene in English during his trial. Captain Hoshijima Susumu,[62] for example, who had criticised the translations of his pre-trial interrogation, also found fault with the trial interpreter when he was tried at Labuan. According to prosecutor Athol Moffitt, '[Hoshijima's] great ability with Japanese-English translations was demonstrated ... by his willingness to object and his constant arguments on translations with the interpreter during my cross-examinations.'[63] The interpreter was Joseph da Costa who remembered the exchanges.[64]

Conclusion

Linguists in many guises—as interrogators, translators, witnesses, perpetrators, and, finally, as interpreters at the actual trials—have flitted through this chapter and I have mainly discussed the English-Japanese encounter. There has only been space to skim across the solutions adopted by the Australian military authorities when tasked with providing sufficiently trained interpreters and translators for the vast war-crimes trials process. Further research on the work of specific interpreters and on the provision made for the other languages required at the trials awaits publication.[65]

The piecemeal stop-gap measures adopted at the Australian-run trials between 1945 and 1951 would never pass muster in modern war-crimes prosecutions, such as those at the International Criminal Tribunal for the former Yugoslavia (ICTY).[66] However, the foundations of interpreting in courtrooms, particularly war-crimes courtrooms, were being laid in those post-war years. My exploration of the trial transcripts and accompanying investigation and correspondence files related to Australia's 300 war-crimes trials suggests they offer a fruitful new source for delineating these foundations.

Several principles were established in the Australian trials. First, that suspects and witnesses needed interpreters for the sake of justice, even if that was not a statutory provision in the Australian *War Crimes Act 1945* (Cth) nor the accompanying *Regulations*. Second, there was the recognition that where an Australian linguist was not as advanced as a bilingual Japanese captured soldier, the enemy status of the interpreter would be overlooked and that Japanese captive given the leading interpreting role in the courtroom. Practical, on-the-spot solutions were adopted to fill any perceived inadequacies. From this distance, it is hard to know if all witnesses and all suspects really knew what was going on all the time but, within the constraints of the period, an effort was made to ensure a measure of mutual comprehension.

Notes

1. For an account of the trials in each location, see the author's eight chapters in (2016), Georgina Fitzpatrick, Tim McCormack, and Narrelle Morris (eds), *Australia's War Crimes Trials 1945–51* (Leiden: Brill Nijhoff) PART II: Trial Locations, pp. 373–686. For a full list of the trials with the corresponding National Archives series and control symbols, see Appendix IV, pp. 826–30.
2. Japanese lawyers began to appear for the Defence first at the Labuan trials (from December 3, 1945), then at the Rabaul trials (from December 11, 1945). No Japanese lawyers appeared at Wewak or Darwin nor were they used at the Morotai trials until late January 1946.
3. Kayoko Takeda (2010), *Interpreting the Tokyo War Crimes Tribunal: A Socio-Political Analysis* (Ottawa: University of Ottawa Press).
4. However, there are some studies of interpreting at British-run trials in Europe. See Simona Tobia (2010), 'Crime and Judgement: Interpreters/Translators in British War Crimes Trials, 1945–49', *The Translator*, 16:2, pp. 275–93; Hilary Footitt and M. Kelly (eds) (2012), *Languages at War: Policies and Practices of Language Contacts in Conflict* (Basingstoke: Palgrave Macmillan), especially Chapters 9 and 11. The shortages of linguists and the ad hoc remedies revealed by Tobia and Footitt in relation to the European conflict can be applied to the Pacific War. The big difference, however, is that the explicit class basis of recruitment evident in Britain is not apparent in Australia's ATIS.
5. The trial transcripts are digitised and available through the National Archives of Australia (NAA) website. Associated correspondence and investigative files generated by the Department of the Army which ran the trials may be found in the Melbourne branch of the NAA. Other relevant files are held in Canberra at the Australian War Memorial (AWM). A few files held in the Canberra branch of the NAA have been digitised.
6. This scarcity was recognised as early as 1938 but the outbreak of the European War in 1939 overran any preparations. See the digitised file, 'Study of Japanese Language in the Services', NAA, A816, 44/301/9.
7. Colin Funch (2003), *Linguists in Uniform: The Japanese Experience* (Clayton, Vic.: Japanese Studies Centre) pp. 106–09. Funch provides statistics showing the impressive scale of the work of each section of ATIS.

8. For the statistics on Japanese troops surrendering to Australian forces, see Gavin Long (1963), *The Final Campaigns* (Canberra: Australian War Memorial), p. 555. Funch, *Linguists in Uniform*, pp. 208–11 gives several examples of Censorship School and RAAF Course One recruits thrown into the deep end to interpret at local surrenders.
9. On 26 July 1945, Article 10 of the Potsdam Proclamation issued by Truman, Churchill, and Chang Kai-Shek (and later subscribed to by Stalin) included the following statement of intention concerning the Japanese and war crimes: 'We do not intend that the Japanese shall be enslaved as a race or destroyed as a nation, but stern justice shall be meted out to all war criminals, including those who have visited cruelties on our prisoners,' Neil Boister and Robert Cryer (eds) (2008), *Documents on the Tokyo International Military Tribunal* (Oxford: Oxford University Press), pp. 1–2.
10. John Wright (August 3, 2009), John Hook (March 11, 2010), Joseph da Costa (March 12, 2010), and Gordon Maitland (February 17, 2010). I also had detailed correspondence with John Ferris in 2010.
11. Among the nine women identified by Funch in his list of those trained at the Military Intelligence/Censorship School was Doris Heath (Funch, *Linguists in Uniform*, pp. 283–84). After the war and a period in Tokyo with 2nd Australian War Crimes Section (AWCS), she was sworn in as an interpreter for three of the 'Command Responsibility' trials in 1947 (R172, R173, and R174), the only time a woman was used as an interpreter at the trials.
12. Funch, *Linguists in Uniform*. See his lists of people in Appendix 2, pp. 282–91.
13. Funch, *Linguists in Uniform*, pp. 282–83. They include Harold Williams, an expatriate and former business man in Kobe, whose papers are in the National Library (NLA, MS 6681) and Albert Klestadt, an anti-Nazi German, who used his sailing skills to island hop and sail to Australia just ahead of the Japanese: Albert Klestadt (1959), *The Sea Was Kind* (London: Constable). Williams was his Next of Kin on his enlistment form, NAA, B833, VX128203.
14. For example, George Charlesworth, Henry Hong Choy, and Murray Tindale. Hong Choy was Australian born to a Chinese father (see his service file, NAA, B883, QX27088). Charlesworth, born in Yokohama to a Japanese mother and English father, had worked in Japan before the war. Tindale, the son of missionaries, was educated in Japan.

15. Major A. E. Mander, Intelligence, Eastern Command, to the Dept of Interior, December 1940, NAA, A433, 1942/2/2951, transcribed in Papers of D. C. S. Sissons, NLA, MS 3092, Box 39. This file charts the developing policy.
16. Da Costa was listed as a student aged 19. Others on this ship who were recruited included Arthur Page (formerly Pappadopoulos), born in Yokohama, and Donald Mann, born in Kobe. Page worked as a combat linguist, but Mann interpreted at eleven of Australia's trials at Labuan. They all knew each other in Japan. See Arthur Page (2008), *Between Victor and Vanquished: An Australian Interrogator in the War Against Japan* (Loftus, SA: Australian Military History Publications).
17. For an account of the Censorship School, see Funch, *Linguists in Uniform*, pp. 37–44.
18. For his service file, see NAA, B2458, 3172200. He remained in the Army after the war, retiring in 1972 with the rank of Lieutenant Colonel.
19. Interview with da Costa.
20. They were ML2, ML3, ML4, ML11, ML16, ML17, ML18, and ML28. Apart from ML11, a trial concerning conditions at the Kuching prisoner-of-war camp, these trials concerned crimes committed during the death marches across the island of Borneo from the Sandakan prisoner-of-war camp in mid-1945. Only six men survived. See Georgina Fitzpatrick (2016), 'The Trials on Labuan', in Fitzpatrick, McCormack, and Morris (eds), *Australia's War Crimes Trials 1945–51* (Leiden: Brill Nijhoff), pp. 457–62.
21. Papers of Athol Moffitt, AWM, PRO1378, Box 1, Series 1, item 1: Diary.
22. Interview with da Costa.
23. For an account of the so-called RAAF school which continued until August 1948, see Funch, *Linguists in Uniform*, pp. 57–75. It had intakes of students from the Army as well as the air force. See lists of personnel trained in the various courses in Funch, *Linguists in Uniform*, pp. 283–90.
24. National Library of Australia (NLA) MS 3092. See also Fitzpatrick (forthcoming), 'David Sissons and the History of Australia's War Crimes Trials: A Spectral Interaction in the Archives', in Keiko Tamura and Arthur Stockton (eds), *Bridging Australia and Japan Volume 2: The Writings of David Sissons, Historian and Political Scientist* (Canberra: ANU Press).

25. Interview with John Hook.
26. Funch, *Linguists in Uniform*, p. 284.
27. Interview with John Hook. Mrs. Selwood was one of those recruited from the *An Hui* in late 1941. As a Eurasian, she was given a special entry permit to enter Australia, NAA, A436, 1950/5/921, photocopy in Papers of D. C. S. Sissons NLA, MS 3092, Box 39.
28. Letter to author from John Ferris, January 26, 2010.
29. R177, R179, R185, R186, R187, and R188.
30. Interview with John Hook.
31. 'SA Sergeant Has Last Say in Rabaul Trial', *Advertiser* (SA), 27 March 1947, p. 4. The official interpreter was Captain Suzuki Heihachirō of the Imperial Japanese Army; see transcript of the Hirota trial (R172), NAA, A471, 81653, PART A, p. 23. Dimopoulos and Doddridge could be classified as 'happenchance' interpreters at this trial (see below). Unlike Doddridge, Dimopoulos was never used as an official interpreter.
32. *Nisei* refers to second-generation Japanese-Americans found in both the US and the Imperial Japanese forces.
33. Miyao appears in several photographs taken at the time of the interrogation and held in the collection of the Australian War Memorial. See, for example, 098104.
34. For the named court personnel, see the trial transcript for MW1 (see NAA, A471, 80713, pp. 6–7).
35. The witness, Corporal Yamamoto Hachirō, is turned towards the unnamed interpreter in AWM 099192. From the photographic evidence, that interpreter is not Miyao.
36. The British seemed to have recruited the interpreters from Japan along with the defence lawyers. They retained the best for their own series of trials in Hong Kong. For the arrangements between the British and Australians, see Fitzpatrick (2016), 'The Trials in Hong Kong', in Fitzpatrick, McCormack, and Morris (eds), *Australia's War Crimes Trials 1945–51* (Leiden: Brill Nijhoff), pp. 606–45, here pp. 625–30.
37. Brock to 'Jack' [Flannagan], December 10, 1947, NAA, B4175, 26. This letter went into some detail about how the interpreters missed distinctions between certain words and the time it took to pin down which meaning was intended.
38. Brock to Flannagan, January 20, 1948; Guinn and Brock to OC, 1AWCS, February 26, 1948, NAA, B4175, 26.

39. Seki returned to work at the later trials in November and December 1948. See his testimony about the translation of submitted evidence at the last trial (Hong Kong HK13), NAA, A471, 81654, p. 17.
40. See note 31. Hirota's trial was conducted over several days: March 19–21, 24–29, and 31, and April 3, 1947.
41. Another example is Civilian Interpreter Hattori who interpreted for General Imamura at the surrender on *HMS Glory*. He is present in several photos in the collection of the AWM including 095802. He interpreted at twenty of the Rabaul trials.
42. Isak Annin was recalled on March 28, 1946 to rebut some of Lieutenant Colonel Yutani's statements in the second Darwin trial. His questioning by the Prosecutor, then the Defending Officer, and then the Court may be found in the trial transcript, NAA, A471, 81630, pp. 132–37.
43. Hosselet had been a prisoner of war in Java and spoke Japanese, Malay, Dutch, English, French, and German. 'Darwin War Trials. Defence Testimony', *West Australian*, 25 March 1946, p. 9.
44. He was sworn in on March 28, 1946, NAA, A471, 81630, p. 132.
45. See da Costa's comment at note 19 above.
46. Yuma Totani (2015), *Justice in Asia and the Pacific Region, 1945–1952: Allied War Crimes Prosecutions* (New York: Cambridge University Press), p. 17.
47. Trial transcript for D2, NAA, A471, 81630, p. 146.
48. For the full text of these instruments, see Appendices I and II in Fitzpatrick, McCormack, and Morris (eds) (2016), *Australia's War Crimes Trials 1945–51* (Leiden: Brill Nijhoff), pp. 810–23.
49. Some trials do not name the interpreters. The full slate of languages required for those defendants whose first language was not Japanese was not necessarily catered for.
50. For the wording of the certificate, see Fitzpatrick, McCormack, and Morris (eds) (2016), *Australia's War Crimes Trials 1945–51* (Leiden: Brill Nijhoff), p. 822.
51. Closing Address by the Defending Officer, Captain Cole, Trial transcript for D1, NAA. A471, 80708, p. 139.
52. The Court interpreter was Sergeant Gordon Maitland (whom I interviewed in 2010). At nineteen, the 'youngest interpreter in ATIS' ('Darwin War Crimes Trials Begin Today,' *Argus*, 1 March 1946, p. 24), he had also been sent to Timor to round up Japanese suspected of crimes. The interpreter for the Defence was Sergeant Tom Ridgeway, who had

trained in the second RAAF Language course with Maitland from November 1944 to September 1945: Funch, *Linguists in Uniform*, p. 286.
53. Sugino was tried at Labuan accused of killing prisoners of war during one of the infamous death marches across Borneo in 1945. For his objection see the trial transcript for ML2, NAA, A471, 80716, p. 32. There were two statements presented at the trial (Exhibit A). The first, taken on October 11 through interpreter Corporal P. A. Penklis (pp. 52–53), contained the sentence to which Sugino objected and wanted corrected by the second statement (taken on October 25 through interpreter Matthew Liaw Kon Fatt).
54. Called as a witness, Captain Wright described the circumstances of reading to Sugino the two earlier statements on 26 and 27 November 1945, NAA, A471, 80716, pp. 30–31. Wright was in Borneo with ATIS and 9th Division AIF, May 4, 1945 to January 24, 1946 (see his service file, NAA, B883, VX108129). A barrister and later a Judge of the County Court of Victoria, he had studied some Japanese from a Teach Yourself book before the war and was trained further at the Censorship School (Funch, *Linguists in Uniform*, p. 284) and information from my interview with his brother John Wright.
55. It was read out before an assembled group of twenty-eight Japanese prisoners. And perhaps Wright's accent was difficult to understand.
56. These were among those recruited as linguists when the *An Hui* docked in Australia. See note 16.
57. See the handwritten annotation after Wright gave his evidence that the Defending Officer was 'not requiring a translation.' NAA, A471, 80716, p. 31.
58. Papers of D. C. S. Sissons, NLA, MS 3092, Box 23; Eric Thornton (1945), 'Jap Lawyer Invites Prosecutor to Be His Guest in Japan', *Argus*, 7 December 1945, p. 20. Sissons contradicts almost every assertion made about Yamada by Athol Moffitt in his (1989), *Project Kingfisher* (North Ryde, NSW: Angus & Robertson); a book that so disgusted him with its inaccuracies, he refused to go ahead with a review of it when it came out!
59. Eric Thornton (1945), 'Jap Lawyer Invites Prosecutor to Be His Guest in Japan', *Argus*, 7 December 1945, p. 20.
60. Trial transcript for ML2, NAA, A471, 80716, p. 44.
61. Trial transcript for ML2, NAA, A471, 80716, p. 46.

62. Several photographs and a portrait of Captain Hoshijima Susumu are held in the collection of the Australian War Memorial. See, for example, 133913 and ART22988 respectively. For the trial transcript of ML28, see NAA A471, 80777 PARTS 1–2.
63. Moffitt, *Project Kingfisher*, p. 33. In his unpublished diary, Moffitt referred to the interpreter (whom he did not identify) as *nisei*. Da Costa, with a Spanish mother and part-Portuguese father, had Mediterranean looks. Moffitt wrote that he 'was accepted as the best interpreter here.' Diary entry for January 14, 1946, Papers of Athol Moffitt, AWM, PRO1378, Box 1, Series 1, item 1.
64. Interview with da Costa.
65. An article on the recruitment and employment of Eric Shimada and a chapter on Pacific Islander witnesses and interpretation are in preparation by this author.
66. Nevertheless, even there, similar problems occurred. For an account of the translating and interpreting difficulties of the ICTY, see Ellen Elias-Bursac (2015), *Translating Evidence and Interpreting Testimony at a War Crimes Tribunal: Working in a Tug-of-War* (New York: Palgrave Macmillan).

Interpreting the 'Language of War' in War-Crimes Trials

Ludmila Stern

From the time when the International Military Tribunal (IMT) conducted the 1945–46 Nuremberg trials up until today's trials of the alleged perpetrators in recent military conflicts, interpreting has been key to communication in courts that have involved mutilingual participants. Its impact on evidence, proceedings, and even judgements has been recognised in more recent post-Second World War trials (such as the 1961 Eichmann trial, the 1989 Demjanjuk trial,[1] and the 1986–93 Australian War Crimes Prosecutions[2]) and contemporary trials by international courts and tribunals (ICts): the International Criminal Tribunals for the Former Yugoslavia (ICTY) and Rwanda (ICTR), and the permanent International Criminal Court (ICC).[3] During these trials, distant worlds come together: the western style, often English- and French-speaking, courts, where trials are conducted by counsel and judges, and the world of the accused, victims, and witnesses, who are often brought in from the country of the conflict. These transient participants, on whose evidence

---

L. Stern (✉)
University of New South Wales, Sydney, NSW, Australia
e-mail: l.stern@unsw.edu.au

the trials depend, usually speak the languages or dialects of countries such as Ukraine, the former Yugoslavia, and African countries, and do not speak the language of the court. In these complex multilingual and multicultural environments, where participants come from radically different cultural, linguistic, and legal backgrounds, how do courts ensure that interpreted evidence is presented accurately, and the proceedings are not compromised? What challenges do interpreters experience when interpreting 'language of war,' and how do they overcome them?

Over the years, no matter how different the cases and the courts, war-crimes trials have revealed similar types of interpreting challenges, often of a lexical and semantic nature. Some of these challenges have been triggered by the specialised courtroom discourse of judges and lawyers, others by the evidence of witnesses who speak their vernacular languages, often with regional variations and dialects.[4] In all these trials, a range of challenges occurred in the presentation of eyewitness evidence, including capturing the *realia* denoting the types of localities and dwellings, clothing, seasons and times of the day, and festivals and religious customs. In addition, descriptions of a conflict's setting, military violence, and atrocities against the civilian population were often expressed in a vernacular full of colloquial expressions, idioms, and sayings.[5] Interpreters experienced comprehension difficulties when the meaning of the eyewitness's evidence was unclear. Other difficulties arose when interpreters had to accurately render ideological, political, military, and legal concepts and terms that lack equivalence in the target language (TL).[6] Challenges above the 'word and collocation' level resulted from courtroom-interviewing techniques unfamiliar to witnesses, including the lack of pragmatic clarity of strategic questions.[7]

The success or inadequacy of interpreted communication, miscommunication, and communication breakdown has been associated with interpreters' competence. However, primary participants—counsel and judges—have also been shown to play a key role in effective communication, for example, through understanding witnesses' cultural background and their ability to modify their own strategies in communicating through interpreters. Complexities of interpreted communication in war-crimes trials have been such that they have raised concerns in some legal research[8] about the possibility of effective and accurate interpreted interactions in war-crimes trials.

Approaches to Interpreting in International and Domestic War-Crimes Trials from the Second World War to Today

The Nuremberg trials (1945–46), conducted by the IMT to prosecute major Nazi war criminals, were the first international interpreted trials.[9] At almost the same time, another IMT, this one for the Far East (IMTFE), conducted the so-called Tokyo Trials (1946–48), prosecuting Japanese military personnel accused of war crimes.[10] Criminals from the Second World War were also prosecuted in domestic courts and, until recently, by countries including Germany, the former USSR, the US, the UK, Australia, New Zealand, and Israel. Some of these domestic trials, for example, the 1961 Eichmann and 1989 Demjanjuk trials in Israel, gained much international attention, while the 1986–93 Australian War Crimes Prosecutions attracted less.[11] It took almost 50 years from the end of the war for the United Nations (UN) to create International Criminal Tribunals to investigate and prosecute late twentieth-century war crimes, such as those of the Rwanda genocide (ICTR) and those that took place in the former Yugoslavia (ICTY). With the Rome Statute coming into effect in 2002, a permanent International Criminal Court (ICC 2003) was created to investigate charges of war crimes and crimes against humanity (including genocide and mass murder) and to prosecute the alleged perpetrators in cases that could not be conducted in the country of conflict.

Both domestic and international war-crimes trials have conducted proceedings through interpreters and translators. The Nuremberg trial was the first instance where the then-experimental simultaneous interpreting (SI) in booths was used—an innovative, time-saving interpreting mode that turned out to be so successful that it was adopted by the newly created United Nations and later replaced the consecutive interpretation traditionally used in international organisations.[12] This otherwise successful mode required a high cognitive load with instant decision-making. Where the Nuremberg-based IMT employed interpreters in the four languages of the victorious allies and defeated Germany—English, German, French, and Russian—the Tokyo Tribunal used English and Japanese,[13] and used a combination of consecutive and simultaneous modes. In addition to the official languages of the court, English and French, contemporary tribunals have used the languages of the countries of the conflict for witness testimony and to communicate with the accused and the victims: Kinyarwanda in ICTR and the languages of the former Yugoslavia (Croatian, Serbian, and Bosnian that became known as BCS, and in later trials Macedonian and (Kosovar) Albanian) at the ICTY.

Prior to the Nuremberg Trials, SI had never been used in court, and none of the languages used at the ICTY and ICTR had been used in international settings, with the exception of international negotiations and high-level official visits. Furthermore, as the ICC began to investigate major war crimes committed in African countries, the languages of the victims, witnesses, and accused required the use of vernacular African languages such as Lingala, Acholi, Sango, and Zagawa. These languages had never been used in international interpreting settings before, and some of them have an emerging literacy and virtually no reference materials. It was apparent that in order to work competently in the highly regimented environment of international courts, expecting interpretation of great accuracy in the fast-paced SI mode, interpreters had to be professionally skilled. The ICTs have addressed this problem in many cases by conducting thorough recruitment, testing, and selection of prospective interpreters, followed by induction, mentoring, preparatory practice, and, in more recent cases, extended training in SI.[14] Quality assurance and monitoring have been ongoing throughout the trials. By contrast, in domestic courts, with the exception of the Eichmann trial, mostly untrained, freelance, community interpreters have been employed, requiring the use of the consecutive mode to interpret witness evidence for the court and the whispered simultaneous mode (known as *chuchotage*) of the proceedings for the defendants.

How Court Interpreting Shapes Proceedings and Interpreters' Responses

In the words of Elias-Bursać, 'Translation and interpreting do more than just facilitate the proceedings. They shape them.'[15] Most studies on court interpreting in war-crimes trials include a section or chapter on the way interpreting has impacted the evidence.[16] They point to challenges associated with cross-linguistic transfer of individual terms and concepts, and larger units at the discourse level, that are material to the case or affect the proceedings in more general terms. When interpreting for the witnesses and accused *from the language of the court*, interpreters encounter conceptual and lexical gaps embedded in the courtroom language; these include legal terms and formulaic courtroom routines.[17] At the discourse level, counsel's strategic questions in the adversarial system are not always conveyed accurately and therefore the pragmatic intent of these questions can be misunderstood by witnesses.[18] When interpreting *from the languages of the witnesses* for the court, interpreters report lexical gaps of military or political terms, as well as the vernacular languages and dialects that contain *realia*—untranslatable culture-bound features—along with colloquial expressions, proverbs, metaphors, and other figures of speech. The interpretation of these requires a linguistic shift. It is not surprising that with such challenges, a lawyer may believe that 'the act of interpretation invariably alters the meaning of a speaker's utterances.'[19]

The nature of these challenges in war-crimes trials is not dissimilar to other criminal trials held in domestic courts. Interpreting of inadequate and inconsistent quality impacts the evidence and influences the case outcomes and access to justice.[20] In her study of courtroom discourse in domestic courts, Hale found that interpreters in domestic courts attributed 25% of their difficulties to the interpretation of witnesses' colloquial language, another 25% to legal terms, and 44% to witnesses' incoherent language.[21] To overcome these problem triggers, interpreters in Hale's study showed a tendency to clarify, disambiguate, and polish witnesses' answers.[22] A question arises how interpreters in war-crimes trials address such problems and whether they use similar strategies and solutions.

Studies of interpreting in war-crimes trials show that interpreting challenges are often dealt with on a case-by-case basis. During the Polyukhovich case (1990–92 trial), heard in the Supreme Court of South Australia, some challenges arose from the dialectal use of language and code-switching between Russian and Ukrainian by Ukrainian rural witnesses. Lexical gaps led to inconsistent ways of translating the same language-bound word, for example, the interpretation of *khutor* ranged from 'village' to 'farm' to 'hamlet.' With regard to the interpretation of English legal terms and expressions into BCS, ICTY interpreters also used different interpreting techniques to translate the same legal terms and expressions, ranging from literal, word-for-word translation, to a paraphrase and explanation.[23] Such different solutions point not only to the inconsistent approach by different interpreters in the early days of the ICTY, making the decision a matter of personal choice, but also to interpreters' tendency to align interpretation with the listeners' comprehension, leaning towards explicitation through paraphrase and explanation. Similarly, in the Tokyo trials, originally examined in the Japanese-language MA thesis by Watanabe,[24] Takeda explains that 'interpreter latitude' was exercised 'to facilitate intercultural communication.' That this approach prevailed when interpreting for the defendant[25] leads to question about interpreters' adherence to the ethical tenet of impartiality.

The Role of the Courts and Interpretation Users in Ensuring Interpreted Communication Accuracy

While recognising the role of interpretation users—investigators, lawyers, and judicial officers—in interpreted communication, few studies have focused on the way users have responded to interpreting challenges. Practical responses to unsatisfactory interpreting have included replacing individual interpreters (e.g. the Polyukhovich case[26]) or improving interpreters' working conditions in trials of international resonance (e.g. Martin and Ortega on the Madrid train bombing trial[27]). While in some criminal cases in domestic courts, the judges' efforts to facilitate interpreted communication led to unnecessary interruptions of proceedings[28] and other judges refrained from taking responsibility and facilitating communication, studies of ICTs[29] identify constructive steps by interpretation users, for example, judges recognising and resolving a miscommunication problem or adapting their own communication strategies to assist interpretation and comprehension. A significant theme arising from these studies is the evolution of strategies by international and domestic courts aiming to deal with these interpreting challenges. While domestic courts have attempted to improve interpreters' professional conditions for high-profile war-crimes and terrorism cases through ad hoc measures,[30] ICTs have the advantages of a sound existing infrastructure to ensure interpreting quality and are well positioned to modify interviewing tactics and users' courtroom behaviour.[31]

This chapter is not only about the nature of lexical 'problem triggers' that arise during the presentation of interpreted evidence in court in war-crimes trials and the strategies interpreters have used over 50 years to achieve lexical equivalence. The implications of these decisions for the proceedings, and the way courts and interpretation users have dealt with the problems of interpreting accuracy through the negotiation of meaning, will also be addressed. (The scope of this chapter does not allow us to address other aspects of court interpreting, such as interpreting modes, translation of documents, etc.) In the following section, I identify specific types of lexical challenges pertaining to the 'language of war' during the trials of Second World War criminals in domestic and international courts, and the ways these challenges were addressed at different times. I will focus primarily on the Nuremberg trials and briefly touch upon the Eichmann and Demjanjuk trials and the Tokyo Trials. In this section I will use the existing historical literature.[32] For the discussion of the Australian War Crimes Prosecutions (Polyukhovich and Wagner cases), I will include my insider observations as an interpreter, translator, and researcher for the Australian war-crimes unit, including two 1992 reports commissioned by the Director of Public Prosecutions (DPP) of South Australia and an article.[33]

I then turn to look at the challenges that arose during contemporary trials by ICTs, beginning with the ICTY. I will point to the similarities and differences of interpreting challenges compared to the Second World

War-related trials. I will also discuss the steps undertaken by the ICTY interpreters and court administration to address those challenges, highlighting the evolution in the ICTs' professionalism in resolving interpreting conflicts and the role of the interpretation user. Finally, I will discuss the ICC approaches, showing the legacy of the earlier ICTs. Aside from the literature already cited, I will also use data from unpublished primary sources that I collected during several of my 2001–16 field work sessions at these ICTs, including court observations, post-observation interviews with ICTY and ICC interpreters and other court participants, and some court transcripts.

Interpreting the 'Language of War' in Second World War-Related Trials

Literature on the 1945–46 Nuremberg trials largely focuses on the way language services were organised and operated in proceedings that had to be interpreted simultaneously into four official languages.[34] It discusses issues such as the technical implementation of SI equipment, the recruitment and training of interpreters, their working conditions, quality assurance by the court, and the role of interpretation users.[35] Above all, Gaiba notes universal amazement at the success of this innovative court-interpreting system, but also notes criticism of the interpreting and interpreters with regard to accuracy. Interpreters did receive much praise for dealing with the 'limitless scope of the issues involving technicalities of politics, military terms or the empty phrases of Nazi jargon.'[36] The positive interactions of interpreters with defendants during the trials was also noted,[37] with some defendants even attempting to develop a speaking protocol to assist interpretation. However, there was also criticism from the defence when the interpretation had the potential of impacting evidence. Defence sometimes challenged the translation and interpretation equivalents, for example, running an argument that interpreters allegedly instilled excessive interpretation of their own into meanings or that a mistranslated document led to the sentencing of one of the defendants.[38] Bowen and Bowen have examined not only the arguments surrounding the translation of some terms but also the way in which the court went about resolving them.[39]

During his cross-examination, Hermann Göring, who understood English, contested some of the so-called translation mistakes of Nazi jargon. Göring challenged the English translations by court translators and interpreters, claiming that *Freimachung* [clearance of the Rhine] should be translated as 'clearance' and not 'liberation,' and *niedergeschlagen* as '[legally] beating down [a court case]' rather than '[unlawfully] suppressing.' Göring challenged the use of the term 'final solution' that he himself had used when ordering Heydrich to prepare the extermination of the Jews, claiming that the English translation should rather be 'complete solution.'[40] Bowen and Bowen consider that the arguments about these 'translation mistakes' were in fact not about equivalence problems but were instead used as a conscious delaying strategy by Göring, who knew the full impact of these terms.[41] In order to resolve the matter, the IMT bench accepted the accused's explanation of the meaning of these ideologically charged terms and accepted them as authoritative. Bowen and Bowen conclude therefore that in this very first trial where SI was used, interpreters were not yet accepted as professionals and language experts, not even by the IMT bench. Despite their high level of education and general praise of their skills, because many of them were not professionally trained as interpreters and their use of language was criticised, it gave Göring the prerogative to claim language ownership. Gaiba concurs that the court should have referred to its own language staff rather than allowing Göring to take advantage of the linguistic weakness of the tribunal.[42]

Nevertheless, language staff also had input. The Chief Interpreter and interpreting monitors identified instances of misinterpretation and brought these up with the interpreters. One such instance was that interpreting too literally led to the misinterpretation of some witnesses' intention. Due to an insufficient lag between the speaker and the interpretation, when the German-language 'Ja' was the first word in several witnesses' and defendants' replies and was interpreted as the acquiescing 'yes,' it amounted to the defendants' admission of guilt; instead the discourse marker 'well …' should have been used.[43] Interpreters were instructed by the Chief Interpreter to increase the interpretation lag until the overall meaning of a statement—and the filler—became clear. The monitor also became involved when some interpreters were unable to render accurately the vulgar language of some of the defendants and preserve their register. In one instance, an interpreter was unable to use the word 'brothel,' which was picked up and interpreted by the monitor. In another instance, an interpreter sanitised the phrase *auf die Juden pissen* 'piss on the Jews' as 'ignore the Jews.' In recognition that such euphemisation was 'compromising the impact of testimony on the trial,' the bench removed both interpreters.[44] While the IMT clearly lacked experience in addressing interpretation challenges, these instances also show that it was committed to resolving the potentially damaging impact of interpretation on the presentation of evidence and the proceedings as a whole.

A brief analysis of interpreting in subsequent war-crimes trials conducted in domestic courts shows how interpretation challenges have been addressed, although there is little discussion of specific lexical, semantic, and pragmatic challenges that threatened to interfere with courtroom interactions. Morris refers to the 1961 Eichmann trial held in Israel as being marked by the horrific nature of evidence and Eichmann's excessively long sentences.[45] Without discussing specific aspects of linguistic/interpreting challenges, Morris describes the unprecedented approach by the Israeli German-speaking judges and prosecution—former German refugees from Nazi Germany—who spoke German to communicate with the accused as they acknowledged the linguistic challenges and unavoidable mistakes in interpreting into Hebrew. This unprecedented step of treating the original German words as authoritative was never to be repeated. Further domestic prosecutions of Second World War Nazi collaborators—local police and *gendarmerie*—that took place in the mid-to-late 1980s to the early 1990s, were conducted in a different environment of domestic courts which did not enjoy the IMT infrastructure and the users' awareness; also, they mostly employed community interpreters with no training. During the 1989 trial of the former concentration camp guard Ivan Demjanjuk,[46] for example, the linguistic environment in Israel was far more Hebrew-speaking than it had been during the 1961 Eichmann trial. In her article *Justice in Jerusalem*, Morris raises the question of the substandard quality of the official court-appointed Ukrainian interpreter, whose inaccuracies were picked up by a monitor and became a matter of complaint for the accused and his defence.[47]

The late 1980s–early 1990s prosecutions of former policemen Ivan Polyukhovich and Mikolay Berezovsky and the *gendarmerie* officer Heinrich Wagner, all three of whom had collaborated with the Nazi occupying forces in Ukraine, were carried out in the Supreme Court of South Australia. These prosecutions provide further examples of war-crimes cases that were conducted in a domestic court many years after the event. These cases were treated as murder cases, and not as war crimes.[48] Multiple problems arose during the interlingual communication with witnesses, not all of them relating to interpreting, but many highlighted by interpretation.[49] The domestic court and the interpretation users showed themselves unprepared to adequately handle witnesses from another country and culture, or to manage communication challenges that included interpreting and cross-cultural matters. The fact that the prosecutions dealt with 45-year-old crimes and rural Ukrainian witnesses who were testifying about wartime events created an enormous cross-cultural gap that was magnified in interpretation. Further, different legal cultures of Ukrainian witnesses and the Australian court created a series of misunderstandings during examination and cross-examination. Finally, the fact that the hearings took place in a domestic court in South Australia possibly contributed to an environment that was unconducive to interpreted communication.

Many lexical challenges that arose during the giving of evidence echoed those encountered in the Nuremberg Trials: for example, military terminology relating to the Nazi occupation of Ukraine and the exact denominations of weapons. It wasn't always clear what the generic term *gun* meant, and whether the equally generic *vehicle* meant a car, a van, or a cart. Court interpreters' poor working conditions, such as the lack of case-related background information or the opportunity to prepare, left interpreters unable (and sometimes unaware of the need) to interpret these terms with great precision to determine whether *gun* referred to a handgun, a rifle, or another type of firearm; whether the reference to Jewish residents of the village 'being taken' to the place of execution meant their being taken in a truck, a van, or a cart, or marched on foot. A precise description of uniforms was required during witness testimonies in order to identify whether the accused was a member of the ethnic police (*politsai*), a higher-ranking German *gendarme*, a member of the Wehrmacht, or a volunteer assisting the German police. However, the interpretation of these witness testimonies revealed that the rural Ukrainian witnesses, recollecting events that had taken place almost 50 years previously, were frequently unable to provide a nuanced description of colours. Thus, any dark colour—blue, brown, or dark green—was described as black, and any light colour as white (including blonde hair colour), thus impeding the identification of the accused's affiliation. Another example was the description of a residential location: *khutor* was variously translated as farmstead, farm, hamlet, or even small village. *Dvor* in the context of the trial referred not to 'courtyard' but to 'household'—something that untrained community interpreters may not have been aware of, opting for a literal translation rather than a meaning-based one that would enable the estimation of the size of the village population. As a result, interpreters used different versions at different times, which led to the inconsistent use of terminology in the evidence. At the same time, the prosecution did not follow up these inconsistencies in the testimonies of their witnesses to provide an explanation to the court.

Cultural differences and the risks of literal translation also appeared in references to times and locations. The questions of the Australian counsel included precise identification of months, dates, and times of the day. However, the villagers used rural references based on seasonal and diurnal changes—seasons were described by references to weather ('mud on the roads' for autumn), religious festivals ('after Easter'), and/or the state of the crops ('apples ripe,' 'buckwheat high'), and the time of day was described by position of the sun in the sky (high, low) or religious services (before vespers, at matins).[50] Australian interpreters, unlike interpreters in the Nuremberg trials, did not explicate the original, staying on the side of literal translation. Neither did the prosecution follow this up with the court to explain the meaning of the references. However, some examples of literal translation show the lack of analysis of the overall discourse, as was the case of the literal translation of 'Ja' in the testimony of the Nazi-accused during the Nuremberg Trials. Australian interpreters interpreted the discourse marker *nu?* ('Were you there?'—*Nu?*) literally as 'so?' instead of a more appropriate expression of confirmation that the witness was following the line of questioning ('Yes, I follow you' or even 'Okay'). As consecutive interpreting was used, it was not the interpreter's inability to wait until the end of the question but rather the lack of understanding of the pragmatic meaning of the original discourse marker and that of its accurate cross-linguistic transfer. As a result, witnesses appeared impatient, if not uncooperative, rather than guarded. Another example of a translation that replicated the sound of the original but not the meaning was the translation of *von* [*coll.* 'over there'] with the similar sounding but incorrect *yon*.

It is difficult to ascertain whether witnesses were at times unable to understand the semantic and pragmatic meaning of the questions by the counsel because of the interpretation or the nature of the question. Questions were often excessively long and grammatically complex, containing several embedded clauses and questions within questions. This made it difficult to interpret such questions.[51] Witnesses voicing their inability to understand the question or expressing frustration at the repetitious nature of the question—for example, during cross-examination—brings up another problem of cross-cultural communication not encountered during the Nuremberg Trials and unrelated to interpreting problems: the witnesses could not be easily 'slotted' into the Anglo-Australian courtroom proceedings, they were unable to understand the intention of courtroom questioning strategies, and they failed to understand that certain questions required them to confirm or refute their own earlier statements during the investigation. Witnesses' unfamiliarity with a broader courtroom procedure of cross-examination led them to retract their earlier statements or acquiesce as a show of gratuitous concurrence. While these instances were only in part related to interpretation quality and accuracy, making the description of the crime scenes and the identification of perpetrator unconvincing, they also made the witnesses appear inarticulate, inconsistent, and therefore unreliable, something which was amplified by the interpretation. Importantly, these examples had not caused any misunderstanding during the preliminary investigations and did not transpire in the statements that the same witnesses had given to the Australian investigators. When the witnesses were interviewed at the investigation stage, they were found persuasive, genuine, and consistent. Communication with them did not signal any future challenges. One can surmise that when the same evidence presented during the committal hearings led to misunderstandings, the court did not adequately deal with them,[52] leading to a negative impact on the prosecution cases. While the bench did little to address these misunderstandings, the Director of Public Prosecutions of South Australia considered that the Ukrainian witnesses were disadvantaged.[53] It commissioned two expert reports[54] that outlined communication-problem triggers and identified the ongoing communication difficulties arising from linguistic and cultural differences. Some responsibility for inadequate communication was attributed to the court participants' lack of awareness of the witnesses' cultural differences and their inability to communicate adequately with their own witnesses.[55] Although the court did not allow for the report to be tendered, the bench acted on its recommendations informally and brought in a monitor, another Ukrainian interpreter, to observe the interpreted proceedings and raise any problematic issues.

Discussing the inaction of the bench in assuming responsibility for effective interpreted communication, Morris contrasts the lack of quality assurance in the 1989 Demjanjuk trial to that of Eichmann, 25 years earlier:

> In contrast to the situation at the 1961 Eichmann proceedings, monitoring of the interpretation at the Demjanjuk trial was neither consistently performed nor an objective linguistic matter, despite the fact that all of the Demjanjuk proceedings were broadcast live on both radio and television. The reasons probably lie in the linguistic skills of the two panels of judges, as well as in differences in their attitudes towards and acceptance of responsibility for interpreting quality.[56]

Morris makes an important point about the increased proportion of native Hebrew-speaking population in Israel at the time of Demjanjuk's trial and the effect this had on the attitude towards speakers of other languages. It highlights the attitude of monolingual domestic courts being essentially poorly suited to conduct multilingual proceedings of international resonance. This contrasts with the ICTs such as the Nuremberg IMT, where all the participants, including the judges, communicated through interpreters. The features for which the counsel and judges in domestic courts should take responsibility include a better understanding of witnesses' cultural background (including different legal systems, different expectations, lack of adjustment of interviewing tactics to elderly rural witnesses), leading to their being able to adequately explain witness evidence to the court, such as unpacking references to the local *realia* in clear terms. They could better communicate through interpreters by avoiding lengthy utterances with embedded clauses and phrasing questions clearly. Finally, they should be able to adequately handle situations where witnesses from another legal culture are unable to respond adequately, resulting in refusal to cooperate, retracting earlier statement under cross-examination, and inability to understand the questions.[57]

In contrast, other historical examples, such as the 1949 Tokyo Trials by the IMTFE, show that with the support of the bench, despite the interpreters' lack of qualifications and their imperfect professional skills, interpreting quality can be monitored and miscommunication and errors picked up at an early stage. Citing the Japanese-language study by Watanabe,[58] Takeda describes *kainyu* (intervention) as actions by the monitors and the interpreters to ensure interpreting quality by interrupting proceedings and including:

> All types of behavior of the linguists, including the monitors' interjections and direct interactions with court participants, and the interpreters' 'self-corrections' and direct interactions with court participants.[59]

Divided into three categories, *kainyu* include 'error corrections; changes to an "easier-to-understand" version or additions of explanation; and clarifications, procedural explanations and instructions.'[60] When exercised by the interpreter, however, the two last categories (namely procedural explanations, editing (simplifying) the original, and providing an explanation rather than paraphrasing) raise concerns regarding the interpreter overstepping his or her professional role and potentially violating a code of ethics (e.g. the ICTY Code of Ethics).

Interpreting in War-Crimes Trials in Contemporary ICTs

As in post-Second World War trials, interpreters in contemporary ICTs face challenges of a lexical and cultural nature resulting from differences between Western-style international courts and victims and witnesses whose languages and cultures, including legal, are mostly distant from those of the court. Thus, at the ICTY,

> Like in a national criminal courtroom ... interpreters are confronted with a wide-ranging gamut of witnesses, from factual to expert witnesses ... In the war crimes context expert testimonies can encompass a wide-ranging scope of knowledge and include exceedingly specialized fields of historical, ballistic, medical, psychiatric, political or linguistic analysis.[61]

As in earlier trials, problem triggers arise when interpreters try to convey lexical equivalence with partial or no equivalence in the target language for: military terms and the terminology of military administration; legal concepts and terms, including strategic questions; and the language of witnesses and defendants, from *realia* to expressive colloquial language, essential to describe the conflict and atrocities against civilians. In the ICTs, the success of interpreted communication has been shown to be due to the combination of factors including interpreters with high-quality professional skills, court infrastructure that ensures interpreting quality, and counsel and judges who are aware of the speaker's cultural background and adapt interviewing tactics to a multilingual court to adequately resolve miscommunication.

The examination of the ICTY and ICC recruitment procedure and ongoing quality assurance strategies shows a much greater preparedness in contemporary ICTs for running interpreted trials, in particular by developing a suitable infrastructure through a top-down approach, with language-services units created at the early stages of the courts' existence, a conscious legacy of the Nuremberg IMT.[62] Strategies include rigorous interpreter recruitment and screening, in-house induction and training at the ICC, professional working conditions including preparation and accessibility of case-related materials, and SI teamwork in booths.[63] In contrast to domestic courts, in international courts, interpreter visibility and voice in the proceedings are enshrined in codes, such as the *Code of Ethics* (ICTY)[64] and *Staff Regulations* (ICC). Observations and studies confirm that interpreters 'have a voice in the proceedings' whereby, whether at the request of the bench or unsolicited, interpreters can 'point out errors, advise on language matter, and arbitrate language disputes.'[65] An important development in the infrastructure is the creation of terminology units and interpretation-user awareness raising, including close attention by the court (including the defence) given to the negotiation of meaning of contentious terms and expressions. During these negotiations of meaning, the role of the Conference and Language Services Section (CLSS) and the court's recognition of the interpreters' ultimate expertise has been a significant shift since the earlier war-crimes cases.[66] The greatest challenge, however, has been to raise users' awareness of the interpreting process and 'defend the interpreters' legitimate choice of words and expressions.'[67] However, there is no doubt that interpreting the 'language of war,' in particular in evidence relating to violence against civilians and sexual violence, presents significant challenges to interpreters and, as a result, pushes the boundaries of their agency and the latitude of professional ethics.

Since its establishment in 1993, the ICTY has developed strategies and protocols regarding the negotiation of meaning. Nevertheless, continuous challenges result from working with a number of languages and dialects. In the early days of the Tribunal, interpreters only described differences between Bosnian, Croatian, and Serbian as dialectal and minor, and requiring the interpreters' attention.[68] These included a different denomination of the months in Serbian and Croatian, and of army ranks in different, newly formed armies.[69] One could argue that some types of 'problem triggers' arising from the lack of equivalence of the legal terms and partial equivalence (e.g. English *murder* and French *meurtre*, and *appeal* and *appel*) do not have a material impact on the proceedings, and the somewhat-inconsistent interpreting strategies used by interpreters to interpret legal language had no significant consequence on the cases.[70] However, at least one of the accused challenged the way in which interpreters added 'Your Honour' to his way of addressing the bench politely in his own language.[71]

Interpretation decisions pertaining to 'material' evidence have been prominent, especially as different aspects of meaning have been challenged and negotiated by adversary parties, whether prosecution or defence. The defence that was tasked with monitoring interpreting quality raised challenges at many (especially later) stages of the trials and consistently challenged interpretation, and some debates about the meaning of terms plagued the Tribunal from one case to another.[72] The debate about the meaning of the term *asanacija* [military clean-up operation] and the way of translating it into English[73] arose in at least three cases, and revolved around the prosecution talking about massacres, while the accused denied them. This debate recalls the euphemisms of Nazi language in the Nuremberg Trials. The difference in the terms *komandir* and *komandant* [commander] was discussed by interpreters with regard to the significance of these positions in the early trials,[74] and the negotiation of these terms was brought up by the defence in the later years. This had an impact on the evidence and the degree of involvement of the accused whereby the defence tried to minimise the leadership role of a *komandir*.[75] Apart from these instances, which impacted on the outcomes of the trials and the appeals, the discussion was not limited to the accused's or the witnesses' ownership of the language, but extended even to the involvement of CLLS as the expert unit, including the translation unit, with reference materials and extensive team discussions.

One example of misinterpretation of dialectal differences requiring meaning negotiation was that of *verdhë* as yellow/green/blue colours in the Gheg and Tosk dialects of Albanian. During the investigation, witnesses were shown a colour chart,[76] but during the trials the chart was not used. Tirana-based court interpreters were unaware of the dialectal meaning of *verdhë* as green, and insisted on interpreting it as *yellow* ('the uniforms were yellow') rather than 'blue' or 'green' as in some regions of Kosovo. The prosecution became aware of these problems, eventually resolving them. However, the impact on proceedings was that the defence challenged some witness evidence and the court decision regarding some of the charges.[77] The example of challenges arising from the regional use of colours echoes a similar problem with the Australian War Crimes Prosecutions but shows a significantly more complex approach to resolving these issues. Both cases, however, also point to the disconnect between the flexible way in which investigators gathered their information to build a case, insufficient communication on cultural matters between investigation and prosecution, and the challenges that arise in court where interpreted evidence is open to scrutiny.

The lack of exact equivalents sometimes resulted in interpreters, and eventually speakers, using the BCS loan word when speaking English or interpreting into English, for example, the polysemantic *kum* or the various words for brother-in-law (*šurjak, zet, badžo*).[78] When conveying ethnic slurs, interpreters and translators struggled with the decision as to how to convey them in the English/French interpretation, at times also using a loan word (e.g. *balija*, a derogatory word for 'Muslim' used by Serbian and Croatian soldiers), but not in all instances.[79] Not only did decisions depend on whether the choice of the equivalent would impact the evidence, but also on who was the speaker and whether the word was used with a derogatory intention. These and other examples clearly mark an evolution from the earlier, individual decision-making to a consistent, informed approach where the interpreting unit followed a method that could be defended in court.

Despite in-depth research and discussions to negotiate meaning, unexpected challenges arose during eyewitness examination and the particularly rapid cross-examination, where interpreters in SI respond automatically to challenges:

> In the courtroom the interpreter must make sure to strike an optimum balance when trying to satisfy several equally important interests: the witness's message has to be faithfully rendered, the other participants in the process have to be able to understand the message and gain an insight into the way the message was formulated (the style of the speaker), and the rhythm of the questioning—primarily dictated by the questioning party—should not be disturbed.[80]

This comment is a reminder that despite a thorough discussion of appropriate equivalents, interpreters retain their agency in choosing the equivalents. This is amply illustrated by the challenges at the International Criminal Court (ICC).

The International Criminal Court has benefited most from the experience of its predecessors and the legacy of the Nuremberg IMT and the ICTY. Like these Tribunals, the ICC prepared in advance by creating a sound interpreting infrastructure: it created the Language Services Section (LSS), conducted a 2004 Foundation Round Table, and learnt from the past lessons reinforced by the collaboration between ICTY and ICC.[81] In the case of interpreters in languages of the countries of conflict such as the Democratic Republic of Congo, Central African Republic, or Uganda, rigorous interpreter recruitment is followed by an extended period of training to prepare them for court interpreting in SI in booths in teams. As in the other ICTs, interpreters' professional working conditions include preparation and briefing, and ongoing access to case documents before and during trials. Raising interpretation users' awareness about cultural differences and how to work with interpreters is an ongoing process. Unlike at the ICTY, there is no language-specific cumulative learning effect at ICC because most cases refer to a different country and languages. However, previous experience of the type of lexical challenges anticipated during the interpretation assisted in some of the steps.

As during the Australian War Crimes Prosecutions, the mix of cognate languages and dialects where meanings are commonly misunderstood by interpreters[82] also arises at the ICC. Although to date most of the accused at the ICC come from African countries where French or English are the colonial languages used in administration and education, European interpreters in these languages were at times perplexed by the unexpected meaning of familiar words in the regional variations of English or French. For example, in the description of footwear during his evidence, a Lingala-speaking witness used the French word *bottines* for *military boots*. When the witness was asked, 'What did the non-military civilian army people wear?' the answer was *des pantoufles*, interpreted as *comme des baskets* [like sneakers].[83] French interpreters reported several such regional variations.

Such erroneous comprehension of the African varieties of colonial languages (English and French), leading to a possible misinterpretation using deceptive cognates, can damage the evidence:

And a witness said, 'Vous savez, moi, je suis un chef. Et en tant que chef, quand je me promène, si je vois un attroupement quelque part, je m'arrête pour voir de quoi il s'agit.' And the translator rendered it as 'You know, I'm a chief. And as a chief, if I see a little crowd of people tripping around somewhere I stop to see what's happening.' Which is okay. But in those parts, that is, of Africa, 'Chef' does not exactly mean 'Chief.' 'Chef' is a uniformed officer ... So what he is saying is 'I'm a uniformed officer and if I see a crowd, I have to stop to check because I'm an officer of law and order.'[84]

However, the most common challenge is the lack of lexical equivalents of legal and other official language in the local vernacular languages. In anticipation of linguistic challenges, the ICC created a terminology unit. Whereas at ICTY, a terminology unit was created later than ideal,[85] and its task was to create a database based on the different ways interpreters and translators have been interpreting terms and expressions, at the ICC its task was to coin the lacking courtroom and other terms and expressions. Coining neologisms, using loan words from the colonial languages, paraphrasing—these are strategies to compensate for the lacking equivalents of the commonly used legal terms, such as 'prosecutor,' 'court officer,' 'registry,' and so on. As illustrated by the then-terminologist in an interview, some neologisms are derivations of the existing lexis:

> *Reparation* is a generic term which has, actually, three sub-terms. It can be *restitution, indemnisation, remplacement* [French]. 'Tengeneza' [word pronounced *ten-ge-ne-sah*] which is actually the verb you use when you speak of repairing your bike or repairing your car.[86]

Other terms have been created using the morphological rules of the languages, for example, the neologism *watumba* (prosecutor) was created based on the verb *tumba* (to accuse) and the suffix *wa* indicating the agent.

> We begin by analysing the word *huis clos* (closed session). *Huis clos* means to close a door ... How do we say it in Sango? What do we call a door? ... Before the arrival of the white colonisers our ancestors had this way of closing the entry to their homes; they used to put a kind of a mat made of bark that we call 'pumbo,' they put it in front of the house to prevent the goats

and the sheep to get inside the house and destroy it. So we kept the word 'pumbo' … and we used *durupumbo* to say 'huis clos.' The court officer is a bit like the guard of the door.[87]

Participating in vocabulary development within the terminology unit was part of the trainee-interpreter training as they worked together with the terminologist and linguists, aiming to coin neologisms that would convey legal terms and standard courtroom phraseology following the spirit of their target language.[88] As a result, glossaries of legal terminology and stock courtroom phrases were developed, with translation into Arabic, English, French, Lingala, Sango, Swahili (Congo), and Swahili (Standard).[89]

However, interviews with interpreters and trainers show that opinions on the use of the neologisms have been split, and in the absence of common standards of the vernacular African languages, opinions by external linguistic experts were not necessarily automatically accepted by court interpreters. Some interpreters of African languages expressed concern that the new terms do not align with common usage, and that target listeners will not understand them, opting for loanwords in the colonial language, such as the French *procureur* (prosecutor) instead of *watumba*. Other interpreters argued in favour of the new terms saying that once the neologism is explained when it is introduced the first time, witnesses quickly adjust to it. Another argument in favour of neologisms was that they were introduced into African languages through news updates about the trials by the ICC Outreach Unit broadcast on the local public radio in a village square, thus enriching the languages with new concepts and terms.[90] Observations have also shown that interpreters' agency and desire to convey the message accurately to the listeners leads in fact to ethical dilemmas.[91]

Observations in domestic courts have shown that interpreters are concerned about being clearly understood. Possibly identifying with a 'mother-tongue speaker' leads interpreters towards 'accommodation' of the target listeners.[92] Interpreters' strong sense of alignment with target interpretation recipients, as well as a commitment to maintaining lawyer/witness communication, makes them gravitate towards cultural brokerage,[93] a tendency to overstep interpreters' 'conduit' role and bridge the cultural gap in order to reduce a possible conflict, a feature usually observed in domestic courts. However, this behaviour resonates with that of ICTs' interpreters, for example, at the ICTY:

> ICTY interpreters have to deal with different competing 'loyalties': to the witness, the institution (which includes all the parties in the proceedings), the norm of the highest possible accuracy and neutrality which characterizes a legal environment, and the norm of establishing communication, as an underlying norm of all translatorial activities. In performing their task, ICTY interpreters frequently have to make decisions with ethical implications.[94]

One can argue that, when faced with dilemmas that are not easily resolved, despite training and terminological development, ICC court interpreters make subjective and somewhat intuitive choices to accommodate witnesses' cultural and linguistic expectations. One such form of accommodation in domestic courts is interpreters' language mirroring the language patterns of courtroom professionals.[95] Observations and follow-up interviews with ICC interpreters show that some interpreters also modify their target language pattern in response to witnesses' language varieties.[96] Thus, interpreters use a 'standard' variety of Sango spoken in the Central African Republic with a witness from the rural areas, but they code-switch between the vernacular Sango and the colonial French when interpreting for urban witnesses and former army personnel, who code-switch between the two languages. When interpreting into Sango for a witness, the interpreters' intra-sentential switching includes the French interrogatives *Est-ce que* ...? followed by Sango. 'Establishing communication' at all cost seems to push the ICC interpreter(s) beyond the responsibilities they can possibly achieve within their role, for example, by expanding a paraphrase into a paragraph-long explanation as, for example, with the term 'huis clos' (closed session):

> It's our role to communicate with the witness. It's our role to make him understand what 'closed session' is. We say, 'Mr Witness, now the mics, the cameras, everything is switched off. You can speak without fear. Only those who are in the courtroom can hear you or listen to you.' That's all, that's

our role. All the Presiding judge or the defence counsel say is, 'We are moving into a closed session.' But it's up to us to explain to a witness what happens behind the scenes.[97]

ICC interpreters' alignment with the language of the target recipient and their accommodation is also manifested through euphemisation, with cultural framing becoming paramount for interpreters. An example from another international tribunal, the ICTR, explains euphemisation as being culturally motivated by witnesses (shame, modesty, pain of recollection) and partly by lexical gaps.[98] Thus, in the absence of the word 'rape' in Kinyarwanda, victims used either synonyms that diminished the violence of the act or the French loan *viol*.[99] Similarly, ICC interpreters explain that when interpreting eyewitness evidence of sexual violence, they replace taboo terms denoting genitals with euphemisms (*mon corps d'homme/de femme*). They explain this euphemisation by saying that vernacular African languages lack equivalents of French anatomical terms used by the counsel, and the existing synonyms are vulgar and offensive.[100] Interpreters fear that unless their interpretation is culturally appropriate to the witness, it may lead to the counsel's loss of face, and negatively impact the progress of the examination of witnesses. The above examples show that the interpreter can exercise their decision making, and interpreting that involves decisions regarding the interpretation of sexual taboos involves a significant degree of freedom based on the understanding of cultural appropriateness.

Conclusion

Over a period of more than 50 years, lexical challenges in interpreting the 'language of war' generally occupy similar domains in both domestic and international courts: military language, legal language, and vernacular language. Interpreting challenges have included correct comprehension of the original as well as the search for the exact equivalent in the target language. Linguistic challenges, including the uncertainty about meaning due to dialectal differences, lexical gaps, and the lack of standardised language norms, have been compounded by the impact of the interpretation/translation decision on the evidence and even on the trial outcome. When the negotiation of meaning becomes a matter of material importance to the outcome of the trial, proceedings have been delayed because of the time required to resolve a linguistic problem.

At the outset of court interpreting in war-crimes trials, the Nuremberg IMT may not have had the necessary expertise to resolve interpreting and language-related challenges. However, the Languages unit ensured the quality and accuracy through the training and preparation of interpreters, and interpreter monitoring throughout the trials. The interpretation users tried to offset the lack of simultaneous court-interpreting experience by controlling the speed of speakers' delivery. High interpreter visibility in both the Nuremberg and the Tokyo trials allowed interruptions of the proceedings in order to correct errors and resolve misunderstanding. Despite this, when interpreting accuracy was challenged by the accused or defence, interpreters were sometimes blamed for allegedly inserting their own understanding of certain terms into their interpretation, and the court deferred to the accused, and not the language unit or the interpreters, as language experts. Fierce challenges by the defence highlighted the parties' attribution of the impact of interpretation on the evidence and the outcome of the case.

Subsequent interpreting-accuracy problems found an unprecedented resolution when the German-speaking Israeli judges in the 1961 Eichmann trial spoke German to the accused; they were partly motivated by the court's lack of confidence in the interpreters. However, further war-crimes trials in domestic courts[101] showed that domestic courts were not adequately equipped to deal with interpreted evidence. The lack of competent court interpreting was exacerbated by a significant cross-cultural gap—both geo-political and temporal. The impact of dialectal and other regional language differences as well as the lack of interpretation users' expertise in working with interpreters in the Australian cases are likely to have impacted on the quality of interpreted communication. In those cases, we know of no interruptions of proceedings to clarify miscommunication and address the reasons behind communication breakdown with the witnesses.[102] The expert reports aiming to elucidate communication challenges were not accepted by the court and were considered as giving the Ukrainian witnesses an unfair privilege.[103] In these proceedings, interpretation users did not show adequate skill in communicating through interpreters or elucidating for the court the meaning behind the witnesses' answers that did not appear to be clear.

Despite the nature of contemporary military conflicts in geographic regions that span from the former Yugoslavia to African countries, the interpretation challenges encountered in court are unsurprisingly similar: legal and military concepts and terms, and *realia* and idiomatic vernacular language, including dialectal differences. As during the Australian war-crimes prosecutions, at the ICTY failure to convey the correct meaning, an unwitting error, or even a colour nuance can threaten the identification of the accused or result in eyewitness testimony's being rejected by the court. At the ICTY, challenges to interpreters' accuracy became routine, and many requests for meaning negotiation were requested by the prosecution and defence alike. Despite the challenges of the defence and interpreter scapegoating, the ICTY experience has also demonstrated the central role of Language services as an expert authority on meaning, giving the interpreting profession the status it deserves as language experts.

While the ICC continued the legacy of its predecessors, it has gone one step further: it has demonstrated that interpreter training, anticipation of challenges, and pre-emptive actions prepare interpreters and users for these challenges. Despite this, the unanticipated interpreting challenges that arise during fast-paced legal exchanges continue to pose difficulties for interpreters. The multi-lingual courts' 'powerful actors'—counsel and judges—need to have a high level of intercultural awareness; at the same time the courts' language services have to consistently provide them with guidance on how to work with interpreters. Only cooperative actions that help monitor and navigate interpreted communication in court will facilitate an early resolution of misunderstandings and prevent miscommunication. Even though the languages of each ICC case are different, the overall infrastructure, the interactions between participants, and the mapping of procedures make it possible for the court to prepare for future trials in an informed way, regardless of the languages involved.

Glossary of Acronyms

BCS	Bosnian, Croatian, Serbian [languages]
CLSS	Conference and Language Services Section
ICC	International Criminal Court
ICTR	International Criminal Tribunal for Rwanda
ICTY	International Criminal Tribunal for the former Yugoslavia
IMT	International Military Tribunal
IMTFE	International Military Tribunal for the Far East
LSS	Language Services Section
SI	Simultaneous interpreting
TL	Target language

Notes

1. R. Morris (1989), 'Court Interpretation and the Record of Legal Proceedings: Eichmann v. Demjanjuk', *Parallèles, Cahiers de l'École de Traduction et d'Interpretation*, 11, pp. 9–28; R. Morris (1998), 'Justice in Jerusalem—Interpreting in Israeli Legal Proceedings', *Meta*, 43:1, pp. 110–18.
2. D. Fraser (2010), *Daviborshch's Cart. Narrating the Holocaust in Australian War Crimes Trials*. (Lincoln: University of Nebraska Press); L. Stern (1995), 'Non-English Speaking Witnesses in the Australian Legal Context: The War Crimes Prosecution as a Case Study', *Law/Text/Culture*, 2, pp. 6–31.
3. E. Elias-Bursać (2015), *Translating Evidence and Interpreting testimony at the War Crimes Tribunal. Working in a Tug-of-War* (Basingstoke: Palgrave Macmillan); C. S. Namakula (2014), *Language and the Right to Fair Hearing in International Criminal Trials* (New York: Springer); L. Stern (2001), 'At the Junction of Cultures: Interpreting at the International Criminal Tribunal for the Former Yugoslavia in the Light of Other International Interpreting Practices', *The Judicial Review*, 5:3, pp. 255–74; L. Stern (2011), 'Chapter 22. Courtroom Interpreting', in K. Malmkjaer and K. Windle (eds), *Oxford Handbook of Translation Studies* (Oxford: Oxford University Press), pp. 325–42; L. Stern (2018), 'Legal Interpreting in Domestic and International Courts:

Responsiveness in Action', in A. Creese and A. Blackledge (eds), *The Routledge Handbook of Language and Superdiversity* (Oxford: Routledge), pp. 396–410.
4. Stern, 'Non-English Speaking Witnesses in the Australian Legal Context'; Stern, 'At the Junction of Cultures'; L. Stern (2004), 'Interpreting Legal Language at the International Criminal Tribunal for the Former Yugoslavia: Overcoming the Lack of Lexical Equivalents', *The Journal of Specialised Translation* http://www.jostrans.org/index.htm, pp. 63–75; Stern, 'Chapter 22. Courtroom Interpreting'.
5. Elias-Bursać, *Translating Evidence and Interpreting Testimony at the War Crimes Tribunal.*
6. Stern, 'Interpreting Legal Language at the International Criminal Tribunal for the Former Yugoslavia'.
7. Stern, 'Non-English Speaking Witnesses in the Australian Legal Context'.
8. Fraser, *Daviborshch's Cart*; J. Karton (2008), 'Lost in Translation: International Criminal Tribunals and the Legal Implications of Interpreted Testimony', *Vanderbilt Journal of Transnational Law* 41:1; Namakula, *Language and the Right to Fair Hearing in International Criminal Trials.*
9. F. Gaiba (1998), *Origins of Simultaneous Interpretation: The Nuremberg Trial* (Ottawa: Ottawa University Press); J. Baigorri-Jalón (2014), *From Paris to Nuremberg. The Birth of Conference Interpreting*, trans. Holly Mikkelson and Barry Slaughter Olsen (Amsterdam: John Benjamins Publishing Company); D. Bowen and M. Bowen (1985), 'The Nuremberg Trials: Communication through Translation', *Meta* 30:1, pp. 74–77.
10. K. Takeda (2007), 'Sociopolitical Aspects of Interpreting at the International Military Tribunal for the Far East (1946–1948)', PhD thesis, Universitat Rovira i Vergili/Monterey Institute of International Studies.
11. Morris, 'Court Interpretation and the Record of Legal Proceedings: Eichmann v. Demjanjuk'; Morris, 'Justice in Jerusalem—Interpreting in Israeli Legal Proceedings'. On the Australian prosecutions, see Fraser, *Daviborshch's Cart*; Stern, 'Non-English Speaking Witnesses in the Australian Legal Context'; D. Bevin (1994), *A Case to Answer. The Story of Australia's First European War Crimes Prosecution* (Kent Town, SA: Wakefield Press).
12. Gaiba, *Origins of Simultaneous Interpretation: The Nuremberg Trial.*

13. An exception was made for a Russian judge who required interpretation (Arnold C. Brackman (1987), *The Other Nuremberg: The Untold Story of the Tokyo War Crimes Trials* (New York: William Morrow and Company), pp. 213–14).
14. L. Stern (2012), 'What Can Domestic Courts Learn from International Courts and Tribunals about Good Practice in Interpreting? From the Australian War Crimes Prosecutions to the International Criminal Court', *T & I Review*, 2, pp. 7–29.
15. Elias-Bursać, *Translating Evidence and Interpreting Testimony at the War Crimes Tribunal*, p. xii.
16. Gaiba, *Origins of Simultaneous Interpretation: The Nuremberg Trial*; Baigorri-Jalón, *From Paris to Nuremberg. The Birth of Conference Interpreting*; Takeda, 'Sociopolitical Aspects of Interpreting at the International Military Tribunal for the Far East (1946–1948)'; Elias-Bursać, *Translating Evidence and Interpreting Testimony at the War Crimes Tribunal*; Morris, 'Court Interpretation and the Record of Legal Proceedings: Eichmann v. Demjanjuk'; Morris, 'Justice in Jerusalem—Interpreting in Israeli Legal Proceedings'.
17. Stern, 'Non-English Speaking Witnesses in the Australian Legal Context'; Stern, 'Interpreting Legal Language at the International Criminal Tribunal for the Former Yugoslavia: Overcoming the Lack of Lexical Equivalents'.
18. Stern, 'Non-English Speaking Witnesses in the Australian Legal Context'; Xin Liu (2018), *Talking Like a Lawyer: Interpreting Cross-examination Questions into Chinese* (Chanchun: Jilin University Press).
19. Karton, 'Lost in Translation', p. 3.
20. S. Berk-Seligson (2002), *The Bilingual Courtroom. Court Interpreters in the Judicial Process*. (Chicago: The University of Chicago Press); S. Hale (2004), *The Discourse of Court Interpreting. Discourse Practices of the Law, the Witness and the Interpreter* (Amsterdam: John Benjamins); A. Hayes and S. Hale (2010), 'Appeals on Incompetent Interpreting', *Journal of Judicial Administration*, 20, pp. 119–30; S. Hale, N. Martschuk, U. Ozolins, and L. Stern (2017). 'The Effect of Interpreting Modes on Witness Credibility Assessments', *Interpreting*, 19:1, pp. 69–96.
21. Hale, *The Discourse of Court Interpreting*, pp. 213–14.
22. Hale, *The Discourse of Court Interpreting*, p. 214.

23. Stern, 'Interpreting Legal Language at the International Criminal Tribunal for the Former Yugoslavia: Overcoming the Lack of Lexical Equivalents'.
24. T. Watanabe (1998), 'Tokyo Saiban no Tsuyaku Kenkyu: Tojo Hideki Shogen o Tsujite', MA thesis, Daito Bunka University.
25. Takeda (2007), 'Sociopolitical Aspects of Interpreting at the International Military Tribunal for the Far East (1946–1948)', p. 16.
26. See Bevin, *A Case to Answer. The Story of Australia's First European War Crimes Prosecution*.
27. A. Martin and M. Ortega (2013), 'From Invisible Machines to Visible Experts: Views on Interpreter Roles and Performance during the Madrid Train Bomb Trial', in C. Schäffner, K. Kredens, and Y. Fowler (eds), *Interpreting in a Changing Landscape* (Amsterdam: John Benjamins), pp. 101–16.
28. E. N. S. Ng (2015), 'Judges' Intervention in Witness Examination as a Cause of Omissions in Interpretation in the Hong Kong Courtroom', *International Journal of Speech, Language, and the Law*, 22:2, pp. 203–27.
29. Gaiba, *Origins of Simultaneous Interpretation: The Nuremberg Trial*; Stern, 'At the Junction of Cultures'; Elias-Bursać, *Translating Evidence and Interpreting Testimony at the War Crimes Tribunal*.
30. R. Morris (1990), 'Interpretation at the Demjanjuk Trial', in David Bowen and Margareta Bowen (eds), *Interpreting: Yesterday, Today, and Tomorrow* (Amsterdam: John Benjamins), pp. 101–08; Morris, 'Justice in Jerusalem—Interpreting in Israeli Legal Proceedings'; Martin and Ortega, 'From Invisible Machines to Visible Experts'.
31. Stern, 'Legal Interpreting in Domestic and International Courts: Responsiveness in Action'.
32. Gaiba, *Origins of Simultaneous Interpretation: The Nuremberg Trial*; Takeda, 'Sociopolitical Aspects of Interpreting at the International Military Tribunal for the Far East (1946–1948)'; K. Takeda (2007), 'Making of an Interpreter User', *Forum*, 5:1, pp. 245–63; Ruth Morris, 'Interpretation at the Demjanjuk Trial'; Morris, 'Justice in Jerusalem—Interpreting in Israeli Legal System'; Baigorri-Jalón, *From Paris to Nuremberg. The Birth of Conference Interpreting*.
33. Director of Public Prosecutions of South Australia (1992), *Communication for Purposes of Litigation. Linguistic report in the War Crimes prosecution of Ivan Polyukhovich*, Report Commissioned by the

Director of Public Prosecutions of South Australia to be submitted in the *DPP v Polyukhovich* hearing at the Supreme Court of South Australia; Director of Public Prosecutions of South Australia (1992), *Communication for Purposes of Litigation. Linguistic report in the War Crimes prosecution of Heinrich Wagner*, Report Commissioned by the Director of Public Prosecutions of South Australia to be submitted in the *DPP v Wagner* hearing at the Supreme Court of South Australia; Stern, 'Non-English Speaking Witnesses in the Australian Legal Context'.

34. Gaiba, *Origins of Simultaneous Interpretation: The Nuremberg Trial*; Baigorri-Jalón, *From Paris to Nuremberg. The Birth of Conference Interpreting*.
35. Gaiba, *Origins of Simultaneous Interpretation: The Nuremberg Trial*; Baigorri-Jalón, *From Paris to Nuremberg. The Birth of Conference Interpreting*.
36. Gaiba, *Origins of Simultaneous Interpretation: The Nuremberg Trial*, p. 112.
37. Gaiba, *Origins of Simultaneous Interpretation: The Nuremberg Trial*, p. 129.
38. Gaiba, *Origins of Simultaneous Interpretation: The Nuremberg Trial*, p. 114.
39. Bowen and Bowen, 'The Nuremberg Trials: Communication through Translation'.
40. Bowen and Bowen, 'The Nuremberg Trials: Communication through Translation', pp. 75–76.
41. Bowen and Bowen, 'The Nuremberg Trials: Communication through Translation', p. 77.
42. Gaiba, *Origins of Simultaneous Interpretation: The Nuremberg Trial*, p. 110.
43. Gaiba, *Origins of Simultaneous Interpretation: The Nuremberg Trial*, p. 105.
44. Gaiba, *Origins of Simultaneous Interpretation: The Nuremberg* Trial, p. 108.
45. Morris, 'Justice in Jerusalem—Interpreting in Israeli Legal Proceedings'.
46. Morris, 'Court Interpretation and the Record of Legal Proceedings: Eichmann v. Demjanjuk'; Morris, 'Justice in Jerusalem—Interpreting in Israeli Legal Proceedings'.

47. Morris, 'Justice in Jerusalem—Interpreting in Israeli Legal Proceedings'.
48. Fraser, *Daviborshch's Cart*.
49. Stern, 'Non-English Speaking Witnesses in the Australian Legal Context'.
50. Stern, 'Non-English Speaking Witnesses in the Australian Legal Context'.
51. Stern, 'Non-English Speaking Witnesses in the Australian Legal Context'.
52. Fraser, *Daviborshch's Cart*; Stern, 'Non-English Speaking Witnesses in the Australian Legal Context'.
53. Bevin, *A Case to Answer. The Story of Australia's First European War Crimes Prosecution*, p. 185.
54. Director of Public Prosecutions of South Australia (1992), *Communication for Purposes of Litigation. Linguistic report in the War Crimes prosecution of Ivan Polyukhovich*, Report Commissioned by the Director of Public Prosecutions of South Australia to be submitted in the *DPP v Polyukhovich* hearing at the Supreme Court of South Australia; Director of Public Prosecutions of South Australia (1992), *Communication for Purposes of Litigation. Linguistic report in the War Crimes prosecution of Heinrich Wagner*, Report Commissioned by the Director of Public Prosecutions of South Australia to be submitted in the *DPP v Wagner* hearing at the Supreme Court of South Australia.
55. Stern, 'Non-English Speaking Witnesses in the Australian Legal Context'.
56. Morris, 'Justice in Jerusalem—Interpreting in Israeli Legal Proceedings', p. 6.
57. Stern, 'Non-English Speaking Witnesses in the Australian Legal Context'.
58. Watanabe, 'Tokyo Saiban no Tsuyaku Kenkyu: Tojo Hideki Shogen o Tsujite'.
59. Takeda, 'Sociopolitical Aspects of Interpreting at the International Military Tribunal for the Far East (1946–1948)', p. 15.
60. Ibid.
61. L. Culjak et al. (2010), 'Ethical Dilemmas in Court Interpreting: How Far Can Interpreters Go to Facilitate Communication?' (Master's for Advanced Studies in Interpreter Training, Seminar paper: École de traduction et d'interprétation, Université de Genève), p. 50.
62. Personal telephone interview with the Chief of Conference and Language Services Section of the ICTY (unpublished) 2013.

63. Stern, 'At the Junction of Cultures; Stern, 'Chapter 22. Courtroom Interpreting'.
64. ICTY Code of Ethics for Interpreters and Translators Employed at the International Criminal Tribunal for the Former Yugoslavia (1999), www.ictyorg/x/file/Legal%20Library/Miscellaneous/it144_codeofethicsinterpreters_en.pdf
65. Elias-Bursać, *Translating Evidence and Interpreting Testimony at the War Crimes Tribunal*, p. 58.
66. Elias-Bursać, *Translating Evidence and Interpreting Testimony at the War Crimes Tribunal*.
67. Elias-Bursać, *Translating Evidence and Interpreting Testimony at the War Crimes Tribunal*, p. 86.
68. Stern, 'At the Junction of Cultures'.
69. Stern, 'At the Junction of Cultures'.
70. Stern, 'Interpreting Legal Language at the International Criminal Tribunal for the Former Yugoslavia'.
71. Elias-Bursać, *Translating Evidence and Interpreting Testimony at the War Crimes Tribunal*, p. 90.
72. Elias-Bursać, *Translating Evidence and Interpreting Testimony at the War Crimes Tribunal*.
73. Elias-Bursać, *Translating Evidence and Interpreting Testimony at the War Crimes Tribunal*, pp. 182–93.
74. Stern, 'At the Junction of Cultures'; cf. Takeda, 'Sociopolitical Aspects of Interpreting at the International Military Tribunal for the Far East (1946–1948)', pp. 48–49, on the translation of 'Cabinet Councillor.'
75. Elias-Bursać, *Translating Evidence and Interpreting Testimony at the War Crimes Tribunal*, pp. 205–08.
76. Stern, 'At the Junction of Cultures'.
77. Elias-Bursać, *Translating Evidence and Interpreting Testimony at the War Crimes Tribunal*, pp. 214–17.
78. Stern, 'At the Junction of Cultures'.
79. Elias-Bursać, *Translating Evidence and Interpreting Testimony at the War Crimes Tribunal*, p. 145.
80. Culjak et al., 'Ethical Dilemmas in Court Interpreting: How Far Can Interpreters Go to Facilitate Communication?', p. 51.
81. Stern, 'What Can Domestic Courts Learn from International Courts and Tribunals about Good Practice in Interpreting?'. The author was one of the participants of the 2004 Round Table.

82. Stern, 'Non-English Speaking Witnesses in the Australian Legal Context'.
83. Interview with an ICC French interpreter (unpublished) 2013.
84. Interview with an ICC Sango interpreter (unpublished) 2013.
85. 'It is felt that the involvement of terminology specialists at the ICTY is long overdue': Stern, 'At the Junction of Cultures', p. 261.
86. Interview with an ICC terminologist (unpublished) 2013.
87. Interview with an ICC Sango interpreter (unpublished) 2013. Translation by author.
88. Stern, 'Chapter 22. Courtroom Interpreting', p. 333; Stern, 'Legal Interpreting in Domestic and International Courts: Responsiveness in Action'.
89. Stern, 'Legal Interpreting in Domestic and International Courts: Responsiveness in Action'.
90. Stern, 'Legal Interpreting in Domestic and International Courts: Responsiveness in Action', p. 405. Interviews with the ICC Sango interpreters (unpublished) 2013.
91. ICC trial observations (unpublished) 2013.
92. S. Angermeyer (2009), 'Translation Style and Participant Roles in Court Interpreting', *Journal of Sociolinguistics*, 13:1, pp. 3–28, cited in E. Ng (2013), 'Who Is Speaking?' in C. Schäffner, K. Kredens, and Y. Fowler (eds), *Interpreting in a Changing Landscape* (Amsterdam: John Benjamins), pp. 249–66, here p. 260.
93. K. Gustafsson, E. Norström, and I. Fioretos (2013), 'The Interpreter: A Cultural Broker?', in C. Schäffner, K. Kredens, and Y. Fowler (eds), *Interpreting in a Changing Landscape* (Amsterdam: John Benjamins), pp. 187–202.
94. Culjak et al., 'Ethical Dilemmas in Court Interpreting: How Far Can Interpreters Go to Facilitate Communication?', pp. 50–51.
95. Hale, *The Discourse of Court Interpreting*.
96. ICC trial observations and interviews with Sango interpreter (unpublished) 2013.
97. Interview with ICC Sango interpreters (unpublished) 2013. Translation by author.
98. N. Fletcher (2011), 'The Role of Euphemisation in Interpreting the Testimonies of the 1994 Tutsi Genocide in Rwanda', *Proceedings of the Synergise! Biennial National Conference of the Australian Institute of Interpreters and Translators: AUSIT*, pp. 218, in Stern, 'Legal Interpreting in Domestic and International Courts: Responsiveness in Action', p. 406.

99. Fletcher, 'The Role of Euphemisation in Interpreting the Testimonies of the 1994 Tutsi Genocide in Rwanda', p. 216–17.
100. Interview with ICC Sango interpreters (unpublished) 2013.
101. Demjanjuk trial 1989, Polyukhovich trial 1990–92.
102. Stern, 'Non-English Speaking Witnesses in the Australian Legal Context'.
103. Fraser, *Daviborshch's Cart.*

Working with Australian Defence Force Interpreters in Timor 1999 and Aceh 2005: Reflections Drawn from Personal Experience

Matt Grant

The realities of conflict, peacekeeping, and international humanitarian disaster reconstruction mean it is relatively rare for the military of any nation to deploy to offshore environments with language or cultural mastery, and for these reasons, good interpreters are critical to mission success. However, mission success relies on more than just good interpreters, as the experiences of the end user also have to be considered. Both language and cross-cultural communication skills are important for interpreter and end user alike, and the skills and experience of the interpreter have to be matched with the skills and experience of the military end user. This chapter presents a personal perspective on the Australian Defence Force experience of working with interpreters in two very different deployments: the 1999 International Force for East Timor (INTERFET) peacemaking mission and Operation Sumatra Assist, the humanitarian aid and disaster relief mission to the Indonesian province of Aceh following the 2004 Boxing Day tsunami. I personally experienced

---

M. Grant (✉)
University of Southern Queensland, Toowoomba, QLD, Australia
e-mail: Matt.Grant@usq.edu.au

© The Author(s) 2020
A. Laugesen, R. Gehrmann (eds.), *Communication, Interpreting and Language in Wartime*, Palgrave Studies in Languages at War,
https://doi.org/10.1007/978-3-030-27037-7_10

how the Australian Defence Force worked with interpreters on two atypical military operations overseas and observed how increased experience and the capacity to adapt led to increased rates of effectiveness.

While small numbers of Australians had served on peacekeeping operations in the 1980s and 1990s in deployments that never exceeded 1000 troops,[1] in the late 1990s, Australia's last large-scale military deployment was the Vietnam War. This left the Australian Defence Force with some collective knowledge, but only limited numbers of military personnel who actually had direct practical experience in working with interpreters while deployed on operations. The experiences of 1999 and 2004 would prove to be important steps in a steep learning curve.

Confronting 'Hiroshima'

As a young public affairs officer (PAO) serving in the post-Somalian deployment Army, I had heard stories of the experience of those who worked with interpreters in Somalia, Cambodia, and Rwanda, but the tales rarely matched the reality of relying on another person for everyday communication with a local populace, particularly when that other person was not vetted for security or their actual suitability to be an interpreter. For example, during the initial stages of the international response to the Boxing Day tsunami in Aceh, on the advice of our Civil Military Liaison team, I approached a stranger sitting on the hood of his four-wheel drive vehicle in the Banda Aceh Airport car park and asked if he would act as my driver/interpreter for a daily rate. Agreeing on the sum of 700,000 Rupiah per day[2] we set off on what would be several weeks of confused but workable communication; a map across my lap as I made hand gestures and grunted (the tone would be tenor for a positive response, baritone for a negative). Mistakes were made in our mixed English–Bahasa conversations. Often we would arrive at the wrong location, and it would take hours to cross the flooded and badly damaged city to arrive at what had originally been our intended destination.

Once we had reached where we needed to be, my driver, Agun, would step into interpreter mode, assisting me as I spoke with Indonesian Army members (TNI) or Banda Aceh residents. Woefully underprepared for this deployment to a totally unanticipated natural disaster at the furthest point northwest on the Indonesian Archipelago, I relied on my own previous experience with interpreters in East Timor, and on his ability firstly to understand my meaning, and then to communicate it faithfully, before translating the response from his native tongue into our shared 'dialect' in a way I could (hopefully) understand.

Over the next few weeks I regularly asked Agun to drive me to the portside residential area that Australian Defence personnel had taken to calling 'Hiroshima' because of the level of devastation caused by the tsunami. News crews were particularly fond of using this area as the location for their live television crosses as it offered a visceral representation of the destruction visited on the city. Dead bodies lay in unusual locations amongst debris. I have a clear memory of a man floating with the tide, his bloated corpse buoyant as he moved with the currents. Up and back he went for some hours, without dignity.

It was at this location that we had seen a corpse lying across the only access road leading out to the designated lodgement point for the Royal Australian Navy Landing Craft (LCM-8s) scheduled to link Royal Australian Navy Ship HMAS *Kanimbla* with the land-based efforts. Noting that the drivers of the trucks coming off the landing craft might mistake what appeared to be a collection of rags for rubbish and drive directly over—all in view of the world's news media who we had invited to film the arrival of more Australian troops—I moved the body off the road with the help of another Australian Army member. The body would be collected by the so-called *Hantu Laut* ('Ghosts of the Sea' or 'Sea Spirits')—the TNI detachment driving around the city in open-tray vehicles that they filled with corpses before delivering them to one of the mass graves pressed into service in an attempt to prevent an outbreak of cholera caused by the sheer scale of death and decay.

Almost daily we made the trip to 'Hiroshima' until one day, for no particular reason, I turned to Agun and asked how he had fared in the 'wave,' as the Acehnese referred to the tsunami. Wife and daughters gone, he told me. Here, he said, gesturing to the ground we stood on, at 'Hiroshima.' No words can describe how I felt at that moment. But with the hindsight of nearly a decade and a half, I can see that in an intense humanitarian crisis where tasks needed to be done at once, carrying on without respite day after day, I had been working like a machine, devoid of emotion. My interpreter had likewise become a machine, an extension of myself. Despite our good rapport, teamwork, and amicable relationship, I had lost the perspective of him as a person with his own agency, who was confronting his own traumas that he dealt with uncomplainingly, on a daily basis.

Ironically, empathy is an attribute that assists the public affairs role—an ability to understand some of what the local population is experiencing in order to craft communication campaigns that achieve the Commanders' Intent, the Holy Grail of military public affairs.[3] While the role of the public affairs officer (PAO) in the Australian military context is largely to provide information and advice to commanders on matters relating to public comment in order to shape domestic Australian and targeted foreign public understanding and awareness, the implication is that the PAO also draws information in through his or her dealings with independent news representatives and others they encounter as part of their day-to-day duties.

It stands to reason that in order to effectively operate in a foreign language environment, some language skills are essential. However, there is often not enough time to develop those skills prior to deployment. The response to the Indian Ocean tsunami, for example, was rapid and significantly altered as more information filtered through.[4] Because of rapidly changing military requirements, it is likely that local interpreters will continue to offer the solution to short-term military deployments.

It is also imperative that the PAO and interpreter are able to move within the Area of Operations semi-independently (i.e. to undertake a specific mission, dependent on security considerations and the projected outcomes of the activity). In East Timor in 1999, this meant obtaining a Transport Control Number and passing through various checkpoints around the country in vehicles equipped with short-wave radios meeting expected arrival times. In Aceh in 2005 the situation was much more fluid and I found myself, with the help of Agun, traversing the devastated city without any such restrictions.

The experience of having worked as a journalist prior to becoming an army officer had given me some knowledge of communicating with others of different backgrounds, although communicating extensively across language barriers had not been part of my previous skill set. By the time I deployed to Aceh in 2005 I had some prior experience with cross-cultural communication issues through serving as a member of the Peace Monitoring Group in Bougainville as part of a multinational, unarmed peacekeeping mission,[5] and on previous deployments through the Middle East and Timor. However, it was during my first deployment, to East Timor in 1999, that I experienced working with interpreters for the first time, and with mixed results.

East Timor Peacemaking Deployment 1999–2000

Following the departure of the colonial Portuguese, Australia watched as Indonesia annexed East Timor in 1975, essentially joining the small country with West Timor and the rest of the Indonesian archipelago. Over the coming decades Fretilin (the Revolutionary Front for an Independent East Timor) prosecuted its political case while the Falintil (The Armed Forces for the National Liberation of East Timor) waged guerrilla warfare against the Indonesians. In 1999 international political pressure saw Indonesian President B.J. Habibie push for a public vote within the East Timor province for autonomy. The ballot was held on 30 August 1999, and saw an overwhelming 78.5% vote for independence. As a result, pro-Indonesian integrationist militia groups rampaged through the capital Dili and through other key towns across the small country, forcing an estimated 300,000 people to flee across the border into West Timor to escape the violence.

Worldwide condemnation followed, and Australian Prime Minister John Howard sought United Nations agreement for Australia to lead a multinational military force to quell the violence and return the region to normality. Crucially, Howard specified that Indonesian approval was required before any force would mobilise, and on 15 September 1999, United Nations Security Council Resolution 1264 established INTERFET (the International Force for East Timor) under Australian leadership and commanded by Major General Peter Cosgrove. More than twenty sovereign nations combined to form INTERFET: Australia, Brazil, Canada, Denmark, Egypt, Fiji, France, Germany, Ireland, Italy, Jordan, Kenya, Malaysia, New Zealand, Norway, Philippines, Portugal, Singapore, South Korea, Thailand, United Kingdom, and the United States—with Major General Sonkitti Jaggabattra of Thailand identified as the deputy commander.

Through the early weeks of September, Australian military planners worked on the mission details that would culminate in the 20 September lodgement of the main Australian forces at Komoro Airfield in Dili, East Timor. Significantly, some Australian military had been in East Timor since June, initially on Operation Faber supporting the United Nations personnel overseeing the autonomy vote and later during Operation Spitfire evacuating Australian nationals.

The Australian Army official record states, 'By the end of the second day of deployment 3000 troops were on the ground and by the end of first week this had increased to 4300. In mid-November INTERFET peaked at nearly 11,500 personnel; 9300 were ground troops. Australia's commitment reached 5500.'[6] Chief of the Australian Defence Force Admiral Chris Barrie stated at the time that the INTERFET deployment was 'the most significant military undertaking we have had since World War II.'[7]

For the members of the initial INTERFET deployment the arrival in Dili was a shock. Some, who had served in Somalia or Rwanda, warned of 'Third World Syndrome' where a person becomes overwhelmed by the living conditions of those around them and focuses on the human suffering to the detriment of their situational awareness. My memory of Dili Airfield is that it was strewn with human faeces, toilet paper, discarded food containers, and other detritus—testament to the thousands of Timorese who had fled their homes and huddled at the airfield in the hope the United Nations aircraft that had carried the UN workers away would return to rescue them. The streets were unusually empty, with debris everywhere, while much of the urban landscape seemed to consist of burnt-out structures. For some days black smoke hung over the city as the pro-Indonesian militiamen continued to set fire to homes and commercial buildings.[8]

As the security situation improved over a few short weeks, local residents began to return to the city and to begin the process of rebuilding. At this point I was working out of the CPIC compound, the Combined Public Information Centre that housed the Civil Military Liaison team, our HQ INTERFET Public Affairs cell, and a small number of other teams from the United States and the United Kingdom. This group was joined by a Royal Australian Navy interpreter fluent in Bahasa, the official language of Indonesia.

While proficient in his core skill, the interpreter represented a shortcoming in Australian military planning. Where Bahasa was regarded internationally as the official language of East Timor while it was a province of Indonesia, following the autonomy vote, the subsequent violence and the arrival of INTERFET the feeling of many (if not all) Timorese was that Bahasa was the language of the occupier. Tetum, they felt, was their language, and after more than twenty-four years of Indonesia's rule, they were not about to abandon it when independence felt likely. More than once I engaged in conversation with local Timorese with the assistance of our Royal Australian Navy interpreter, who was becoming more and more frustrated with his inability to deliver communications support in his specialist-linguist role. On each occasion the exchange would be polite but ineffectual; simply put, without Indonesian provincial rules guiding their behaviour, there was no way a Timorese person was going to speak anything other than Tetum. Interestingly, from this miscalculation regarding local language, the Australian contribution to the INTERFET mission learnt early on about the necessity of Tetum language skills, and, possibly, a lesson in reserving immediate judgement over local customs or cultural requirements prior to having spent time in country.[9]

Although soldiers with rudimentary Tetum did arrive in my location, they had different operating priorities. A small team from the Australian Army's 4th Battalion (Commando) had deployed in the early weeks of the mission to provide close personal protection and some Tetum interpretation for the civilian news-media representatives attached to the 1st Media Support Unit based at the Turismo Hotel in Dili. Despite the presumption that this might provide further language support, their role was primarily to oversee the safe movement of news crews around the

Area of Operations, and not to perform any formal translator/interpreter role.[10] This experience shows that even when language support might notionally be present, it is not always available for all the end users who actually might need it.

Each member of the compound contributed a small amount of money to pay for the two Timorese cleaners who would sweep and wash the tiled floors of the buildings we occupied. I, like most, tried to be friendly and to engage in limited conversation with them. However, this arrangement soon changed from the usual pleasantries to an intensive Tetum language class in which the cleaners would instruct us on basic phrases and assess our delivery and inflection. We, in turn, would instruct them in basic English phrases. From this unconventional school we built our basic armoury of Tetum phrases such as *Diak ka lai?* or *Obrigado*.[11] This experience demonstrated a willingness of both locals and soldiers to make the most of the opportunity to engage in cross-cultural communication and to informally work together to resolve communication shortfalls.

Despite our best efforts the local engagements throughout this period were marked by partial understanding at best. This lack of cultural understanding and communication contributed, I feel, to the very Australian perspectives reported by civilian news media during the 1999 phase of Operation Stabilise, rather than the more obvious Timorese perspective of travelling the path to autonomy. In late 1999 it was impossible to see what awaited the world in just two years' time. However, for the Australian Defence Force at least, the journey towards understanding and valuing the input of language and cultural communication experts had progressed significantly. The East Timor operation revealed the challenge of providing language support for the mass deployment of large numbers of Australians at short notice. This was vastly different to the more manageable, small-scale peacekeeping of previous decades, where the limited size of deployments meant that the limited language resources of the Australian military had been able to adequately serve deployment needs. The lessons learnt from the INTERFET experience of large-scale military deployment would pay dividends during the years to come in the future conflict zones of Afghanistan and Iraq.

Indian Ocean Tsunami: Humanitarian Deployment in Aceh Province, Indonesia, 2005

A few minutes before 8.00 am on Sunday 26 December 2004, an earthquake measuring 9.4 on the Richter scale shook the ground of northern Sumatra, Indonesia for eight minutes. The wave created by the earthquake moved across the Indian Ocean at speeds approaching 500 miles per hour and reached the East African coast seven hours later. The devastation to the northern city of Banda Aceh was extreme, as it was across the western coastal areas of the Province. The United Nations estimated globally more than 225,000 people died as a result, with more than one million displaced.[12]

For the Acehnese the tsunami resulted in economic disruption on a grand scale. As a region that relied on oil and gas mining, agriculture, and fisheries for approximately 60% of its income, the effects of the wave were profound. Mining efforts ceased, fishing vessels lay strewn through the city streets, and even agricultural pursuits were affected by the penetration of saltwater far inland. Over 500 kilometres of coastline was destroyed by the waters and an estimated 130,000 killed with a further 500,000 displaced within the province.[13]

The eventual Australian military response of 560 troops on the ground with additional 400 offshore in a navy and air task group saw more than 1200 tonnes of humanitarian aid distributed via air, together with seventy aero-medical evacuations and more than 2500 people transported to hospital or further care. Another (estimated) 3700 people sought medical treatment from the military medical teams based at the Zainal Abidin hospital. Nearly five million litres of clean water were produced using the portable water-treatment plants and some 9000 cubic metres of debris cleared.[14] Such was the scale of the disaster, Chief Executive Officer of the Australian Red Cross, Robert Tickner said, that when considering the challenges the aid organisation had faced in its history, he would 'rank the First World War and the Second World War and then the tsunami. It is that big.'[15]

My role during the initial phases of this humanitarian aid and disaster relief operation was to head the public affairs effort in Banda Aceh, reporting to the operational headquarters situated in Medan 600 kilometres to the southeast. While initially I had two Army photographers with me they were redeployed after two days and I spent the next week working alone, liaising with the world's news media arriving in the region and moving about via my impromptu arrangement with Agun, my Acehnese driver. During this time, I was cautiously feeling my way around the situation, gaining insights from my interactions with news representatives from various organisations and countries and through my conversations with local people, foreign and Indonesian aid workers, and the TNI. Agun was, of course, front and centre in most of these discussions and through him I began to build an appreciation of the situation.

The initial phase was difficult for everyone. My handwritten notes scrawled into a field notebook from the passenger hold of a Royal Australian Air Force C-130 Hercules transport aircraft from when I first flew over the area read:

> First impressions from the back of a C-130 is principally one of how similar it looks to Dili in Sep 99—although on an impossibly larger scale … (flying) low level up the West coast, moving from untouched Sumatran fishing village to the point where the wave began—village, village, paddy field, rocky headland, sand, pushed over trees, debris stretching kilometres inland, nothing moving. The sea still muddy grey with long lines of silt running from river mouths deep into the ocean.[16]

The streets of Aceh were blocked with trapped seawater and debris, the structural integrity of buildings that had borne the force of the wave was suspect[17] and potentially dangerous, and it seemed that everywhere we looked, there was evidence of death, whether human or animal. At the end of each day Agun would drive me to the airfield where I would hand over his daily payment and make arrangements for the following morning, before walking alongside a flooded canal to the Australian Army tent lines where I had my temporary home. Hard tropical rain had turned the area into a mud pit and keeping dry was impossible. Add mosquitoes, cobras, and humidity and the full picture becomes more apparent.[18] From here I would work by lamplight, answer news-media enquiries by SMS,[19] and make my evening situation report to Medan.

As the humanitarian relief operation settled into 'steady state,'[20] I was joined by a Deployable Field Team from the 1st Joint Public Affairs Unit out of Canberra and an interpreter from the Australian Embassy in Jakarta. A Javanese man, Mubarak, brought with him the necessary language skills but also insights into the culture of the people we were there to help. Within days of his arrival (to live with and work alongside the wider team based out of the quagmire beside the Banda Aceh airfield), Mubarak had begun to exert a subtle influence over how we approached our tasks. While continuing to provide standard language interpreting services, Mubarak also provided cross-cultural communication services and, more importantly, independently began to take actions to build rapport between locals and foreigners in order to promote positive outcomes in the ongoing humanitarian relief effort.

Given the nature of the deployment it was unsurprising that we were supplied with hard rations (*rats*) to eat—canned food prepared with preservatives designed to keep the meal fresh for a number of years and across a wide range of climates. While I (like everyone else in the Australian Defence Force (ADF)) had eaten ration packs in the heat and the cold, most would decline to identify the cuisine as a meal of preference. Indeed, I would expect most, if not all, people who have lived off 'hard rats' for a period of time to share a similar ambition—to eat fresh fruit and vegetables. As it happened, approximately three weeks after the tsunami wreaked destruction across the region, a local food market opened its stalls and Mubarak insisted that he and I go there. Having enjoyed the same preservative-laden fare for a few weeks I did not require a great deal of persuasion and so Mubarak, Agun, and I set off for the markets intent on returning with enough greens for all of our team.

A proud and distinct region of Indonesia and a formerly independent Sultanate, Aceh defines itself through religion and local Acehnese culture. To find itself overrun with Australians, Germans, British, Americans, and Turks (and so many more) must have been confronting to Acehnese sensibility. (One student activist, Daudy, was quoted as saying the military aid in particular concerned local people who felt that aid was a 'second colonisation.'[21]) Yet, as we left Agun's Kijang Bensin SUV and made our way into the markets, I was to experience a particularly humbling and emotional shopping trip among people who were themselves enacting one of the first acts of normalcy in their community for weeks.

A small group of people had gathered at the market and Mubarak informed me that they were actually there because they wanted to express their gratitude for the efforts of the Australians. They placed various food items in a large cardboard box that they thrust into my arms. I stood there for thirty minutes shaking hands, being slapped endlessly on the back, refusing more food until Mubarak whispered in my ear that it would cause offence to decline. The mood was one of celebration—of a society triumphing despite the enormous losses. When we left the market, I struggled to hold the overflowing box of fresh food, given by people who had lost almost all they owned before the disaster. It had been an opportunity for some of the Acehnese community to say 'thank you' to a representative of one of the international groups that had responded to the tragic events of 26 December and I have never felt more humbled by the resilience of the human spirit. We drove back to our accommodation past the broken houses and the children playing in the swollen creeks and I pondered the cultural communication aspects of that afternoon's excursion. Without language support, I could not have entered that market with any real ambition for success. With Mubarak, however, we had made a meaningful connection in a public place, albeit in a way usually reserved for senior officers or politicians rather than just another field officer hoping for a preservative-free meal in a land unbowed by possibly the greatest disaster of the twenty-first century.

We had, in effect, closed the loop between the military logistics, medical, and engineering efforts and the Acehnese community. By refusing payment for their produce, and by being given an opportunity to express their gratitude, these people had done everything they could to complete the transaction between Indonesians and Australians. I think Mubarak knew this even before we set off to the market.

Conclusion

There are various dimensions to consider when evaluating experience of military communicating and interpreting, with a significant consideration being the experiences of those who rely on the skills of interpreters to do their job. Studies can understandably focus on the very challenging experience of interpreters themselves, but the experience of the end user also needs to be considered to provide a nuanced understanding of the complexities implicit in communicating and interpreting. Peacekeeping and humanitarian relief operations offer their own unique challenges to military personnel deployed in the field, and the experience of working with interpreters who provide both direct language translation and cross-cultural understanding has been invaluable. My personal experience provides examples of how the Australian military quickly adapted to the requirement to rapidly deploy troops into crisis zones with language support, of how adaptation to local conditions occurs, and how practice and familiarity was to enhance the experience for end users of interpreter services.

Notes

1. For more on these deployments see Peter Londey (2004), *Other People's Wars: A History of Australian Peacekeeping* (Sydney: Allen & Unwin).
2. Author's notes. According to a field notebook stub written by the author and signed by Agun.
3. 'Commanders' Intent' is the military term used to neatly summarise the preferred mission outcomes intended by any number of simultaneous activities at the direction of the person in command, the Commander. Meeting the Commanders' Intent in a public affairs sense may mean to communicate—through words and pictures transmitted by multiple news-media channels—those outcomes.
4. Originally the author was instructed to pack civilian clothes and fly to Phuket, Thailand as part of the Disaster Victim Identification operation. Between boarding a domestic flight from Townsville and arriving at the mounting headquarters in Brisbane, Australia, that mission had changed from Thailand to Indonesia and required field kit for what was expected to be several weeks of living in harsh conditions.
5. Richard Gehrmann, Matt Grant, and Samantha Rose (2015), 'Australian Unarmed Peacekeepers on Bougainville, 1997–2003', *Peace Review*, 27:1, pp. 52–60.
6. https://www.army.gov.au/our-stories/operations/east-timortimor-leste

7. Defence Public Affairs Press Release 277/99 released by Defence Public Affairs Organisation 16 September 1999 https://reliefweb.int/report/timor-leste/east-timor-media-conference-chief-defence-force-admiral-chris-barrie-darwin
8. In the early days of the deployment, smoke began streaming from a neighbouring building to Headquarters INTERFET. The Force Regimental Sergeant Major, Dale Sales, stuck his head out of a second-floor window and enquired loudly of nobody in particular: 'Is anyone going to do something about that?' Together with a few others the author jumped the fence and entered the building to find a number of fuel-soaked mattresses burning fiercely and emitting pungent, choking black smoke. This was an example of a diversion, or distraction, as well as a message that the militia were still among us and could still cause us concern.
9. In the early stages of the deployment it was not unusual for older Timorese men to come to a rigid halt when they encountered uniformed Australia troops and offer a salute—a hangover from colonial days, perhaps, or from Indonesian rule.
10. The Australian Commando Association makes brief mention of the commandos attached to 1MSU; however, the author's recollections are of the professional service provided by those members during escorted media convoys around Timor in the early months of the operation. https://www.commando.org.au/Commando%20History/2%20Cdo%20Regiment%20History/
11. 'How are you?' and 'Thank you.' *Diak Kai Lai* was usually accompanied by a thumbs up/thumbs down gesture, literally meaning 'good or bad?'
12. *Tsunami Recovery: Taking Stock after 12 months,* Report from the UN Secretary-General's Office of the Special Envoy for Tsunami Recovery.
13. While there are many available reference materials attesting to these figures they remain an estimate. The UN figures point towards 116,000 homes destroyed in Aceh as a result of the tsunami and approximately 12% of the population displaced.
14. https://web.archive.org/web/20121104225220/http://www.defence.gov.au/optsunamiassist/default.htm
15. Joint Standing Committee on Foreign Affairs, Defence, and Trade (2006), 'Australia's response to the Indian Ocean Tsunami'.
16. Author's notes. Personal field notes from deployment as member of Combined Joint Task Force 629 on Operation Sumatra Assist, 3 January 2005.

17. On my first night in Banda Aceh on 3 January 2005 a loud crash woke us. It was a shopping centre collapsing approximately one kilometre away from our location as a result of the water damage.
18. Well, almost. According to my field diary notes, some days into the mission, an Australian Army health officer conducted tests of the mud we lived in and found (unsurprisingly, given we were surrounded by paddy fields being worked with beasts) that the 'mud' was more bovine excrement than soil.
19. In the early days of the deployment the local mobile towers didn't have the capacity to carry voice calls but could sustain SMS messages, which became the preferred means of communication between news-media representatives.
20. An Australian military term referring to rate of effort. For example, there is the 'high tempo' environment of the lodgement phase and once the desired long-term routine has been established, it is considered to be 'steady state.'
21. A. Ride and D. Bretherton (2011), *Community Resilience in Natural Disasters*, (Basingstoke: Palgrave Macmillan), p. 43.

Risk Perception and Its Management: Lessons from Iraqi Linguistic Mediators for the Australian Defence Force in the Iraq War (2003–2009)

Ali Albakaa

War is one of the most destructive events for any nation.[1] It takes lives, destroys homes, and displaces people from their homelands.[2] War's objectives can include 'peace-enforcement, state-building, counter-insurgency,

---

This chapter draws on my current doctoral research in Linguistics and Applied Linguistics at the School of Languages, Literatures, Cultures and Linguistics, Faculty of Arts, Monash University, Australia, titled *Iraqi local interpreters for the Australian Defence Force in the war zone: From linguistic competence to cultural mediation*. The thesis examines the oral history of role, status, and positionality of Iraqi Arabic-English interpreters who worked for the Australian Defence Force (ADF) to make recommendations for future ADF operational language planning. In particular I would like to thank Major General Paul McLachlan, Dr Howard Manns, Professor Alistair Thomson, and Brigadier Ian Langford for their assistance.

Disclaimer: Under the terms of research ethics approval from the Department of Defence and Veterans' Affairs Human Research Ethics Committee, the designated Defence sponsor from the Australian Defence Force has read this chapter and approved publication. Approval of publication does not in any way suggest that the ADF endorses the contents or conclusions of this chapter. The chapter includes quotes from interviews conducted by the author with ADF military personnel and with local Iraqi interpreters. The analysis and conclusions are solely the work of the author.

A. Albakaa (✉)
Monash University, Melbourne, VIC, Australia
e-mail: ali.albakaa@monash.edu

© The Author(s) 2020
A. Laugesen, R. Gehrmann (eds.), *Communication, Interpreting and Language in Wartime*, Palgrave Studies in Languages at War,
https://doi.org/10.1007/978-3-030-27037-7_11

humanitarian aid, and not least, counter-terrorism.'[3] In the case of the Iraq war (also known as the Second Gulf War, 2003–11), the international coalition forces deployed their personnel to achieve several strategic objectives. The first was the US goal to neutralise the alleged threat of Iraq's weapons of mass destruction and long-range missile programs.[4] This was considered a major threat to international security, mainly by the US, UK, Australia, France, and Middle Eastern countries. An anti-terrorism campaign was the second strategic objective, whereby US President George W. Bush alleged that Iraq aid[ed] and protect[ed]' the Al Qaeda terrorist organisation by providing technical assistance to construct chemical weapons.[5] The Australian Defence Force (ADF) was among the international coalition forces that deployed military personnel to support these objectives.

Since war is dangerous, the ADF train their military personnel mentally and physically. Periodic risk-management training is one of the most important types of training that the ADF provides to their deployed forces.[6] This pre-programmed approach plays an important part in preparing personnel before, during, and after any deployment.[7] Personnel typically have access to different types of support and guidance from their employer in terms of risk management. In 2002, for example, the secretary of Defence and the Chief of the Defence Force endorsed a top-down systematic approach to risk-management in Defence.[8] As a result, a risk-management framework was established which requires all Defence personnel to complete risk-management training for possible overseas deployment.[9] The Australian bush (natural environment) has been used in such training efforts and is used as a simulated battle space to help ADF military personnel to learn how to respond to numerous, unpredicted threats. This training includes building clearances, room clearances, escorting convoys through ambushes, and other soldier skills.[10] The Australian Defence Directorate of Mental Health also operates a number of mitigation strategies to support the health and safety of their deployed military personnel in Iraq and Afghanistan. Self-Management and Resilience Training (SMART) is one such program which aims to train ADF military personnel to be more resilient under pressure.[11] These training programs are not limited to those who serve in war zones, but also provided to those who might be deployed in disaster relief environments.[12]

Linguistic support is an element of planning that is crucial to the success of military operations in foreign nations.[13] For this reason, military organisations of different nations recruit different types of linguists to support the interests of their deployed forces. According to the US counterinsurgency field manual, the US forces split the linguistic-support personnel into three categories[14]: Category I: local nationals with security screening but no clearance, Category II: US citizens with a secret level clearance, and Category III: US citizens with top-secret clearance.[15] Category I linguists are usually hired locally and require security vetting.[16] They engage with the US forces to provide their soldiers with 'basic interpretation to activities such as patrols, entrance coverage, open-source intelligence collection, and civil military operations.'[17] Category II linguists are US citizens with a security clearance from the US military-intelligence agency. They possess good attributes in terms of oral and written communication which qualify these types of linguists for military communication with high level commanders. Category III linguists are also US citizens but with top-secret clearance.[18] Unlike Category I, Category III linguists have excellent oral and written communication skills and are restricted to work at divisions and high ranks commanders. Only Category II and III linguists are authorised to work on sensitive and classified information within the counterinsurgency operations.[19]

Like the US forces, the ADF also has a military personnel policy manual (MILPERSMAN) that guides commanders and supervisors to administer and manage Defence personnel.[20] The MILPERSMAN distinguishes between uniformed and non-uniformed Defence personnel in counterinsurgency operations. However, ADF linguists' support categories are not clear and are not as detailed as those of the US forces. The MILPERSMAN categorises the Defence personnel into three types: Contractor (3–6), Defence Civilian (3–7), and Defence locally engaged employee (3–7).[21] A contractor (3–6) is identified as a person who is recruited by the ADF to perform certain skills for ADF military operations on a temporary or short-term basis. The contractor works under the supervision of an Australian Public Service employee or ADF member.[22] The staff classification scale used by the ADF forces also includes a Defence civilian, who is a person other than a Defence member who performs duties with the authority of an authorised officer and must consent to subject him/herself to ADF discipline during their missions.[23] The locally engaged employee (LEEs), the ADF's third category, is identified as a person who is recruited from overseas by a contract or under *Section 74 of the Public Service Act 1999*.[24]

The last category of employee is my specific focus in this chapter. These LEEs were employed by many coalition nations during the wars in Iraq, and while their experience had elements in common with the experience of those working for Australians, the issue of Iraqi linguistic mediators (ILMs) working specifically for the ADF has thus far rarely been explored. LEEs were recruited and worked with ADF troops but as such were unlikely to have access to risk-management training in the Iraqi armed conflict as was experienced by ADF members trained in Australia.

The chapter examines the experiences of Defence linguists in times of war with specific reference to the conflict in Iraq. 'Defence linguists' are LEEs recruited by the Australian Defence Force (ADF) under a fixed contract of employment to mediate between ADF combat units and Iraqis. These LEEs, and this comes from my own experience as a war zone interpreter and translator in Iraq, were known by the ADF as 'Terps' [an abbreviation for interpreters] and by other allied forces as 'Terps' and also 'translators'. This chapter pays specific attention to the ADF's Operation Catalyst between 2003 and 2009 as part of the US-led coalition forces post the Second Gulf War. Using oral history as a research method and drawing on ILMs' experiences and understandings, I examine risk as perceived and experienced and ADF and ILMs' approaches to risk management, and consider the outcomes and lessons learnt. This examination is vital because it will enable us to understand how ILMs interpreted risk and chose to take actions as responses to the risks they experienced. As Abrams puts it: 'oral history is a practice, a method of research. It is the act of recording the speech of people with something interesting to say and then analysing their memories of the past.'[25] One effective use of this method in interpreting studies is the work of Torikai which examined the diplomatic interpreters' habitus in post-Second World War Japan.[26] This chapter also presents the views of ADF personnel regarding risks to ILMs and the management of these risks, along with an account of the availability of policy applying specifically to ILMs.

Before proceeding, several terms used in this chapter need to be defined. Risk relates to 'a decision of an individual or a collective to act in such a way that outcomes of this decision' either harm or cause possible damage to lives and reputations.[27] In other words, risk refers to 'a process by which military personnel/linguists provide (one-way) or (exchange two-ways) responses to certain risks.'[28] To avoid redundancy, 'linguistic mediators' (LMs) is used in this chapter 'as an umbrella term including both written rendition and oral interpretation that transfers linguistic and cultural knowledge across different languages.'[29] Beyond this, 'linguistic mediation' can be defined as an oral interlineal exchange form of 'human mediations,' which distinguishes itself from other non-linguistic forms of mediation (Coste and Cavalli 2015).[30]

A Proposed Model

To analyse the nature of risks in the theatre of war in Iraq, I use a model of the ILMs' risk and risk-management (see Fig. 1). This model is based on the categories of risks developed by Pah Petru, a colonel in the Romanian army, and is used as a starting point to trace the nature of risks in the Iraqi geosocial and political arena.[31] I have chosen this model because life-story interviews allow an approach to the issue of risk through these LMs' own narratives. As Tălpaș puts it: 'Such risks, which are various and complex, can manifest themselves at any time and in any place.'[32] This study is an attempt to develop a framework to support a consideration of risk-management training as an important part of a proactive policy for both individuals and collectives. Such a framework broadly follows the notion that dealing with risks in war is a process that is continuously occurring, given that new risks arise even when others have been successfully managed. Thus it uses the idea of a 'risk cycle,' which represents different ways in which risk can occur, or be ameliorated, or otherwise responded to, via different possible trajectories in different kinds of armed organisations. The themes that emerge from this model are not only of interest to translation and interpreting scholars who are focused on military linguistic meditation

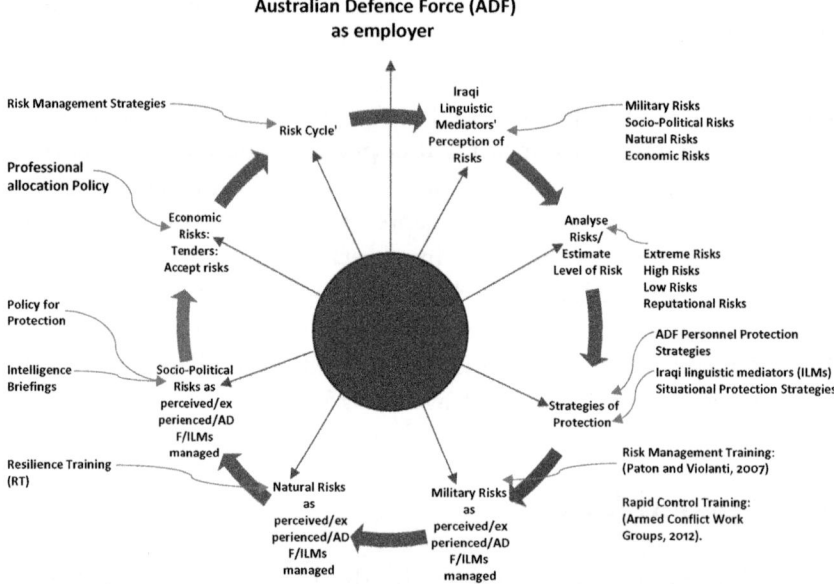

Fig. 1 Iraqi linguistic mediator's (ILM's) risk cycle and risk management in conflict zones or armed conflict

as practice in conflict zones or armed conflicts, but also historians of Australian combat and non-combat military operations abroad.

The model used here considers:

(a) Risk as perceived and experienced by ILMs. Within this stage of the model, I look at the nature of risks and the circumstances which influenced the work of military linguistic mediation in the theatre of war in Iraq.
(b) In the next stage of the model, the ADF responds to each type of risk. Here, I seek to trace the ADF risk-management options which were implemented by the ADF to protect LEEs from each type of risk.
(c) In the final stage of the model, the situational risk-management strategy is shown. Here I explore the strategies as managed by ILMs to deal with each type of risk. These particular considerations are explored through the eyes of ADF military personnel and ILMs who mediated between the ADF troops and local protagonists from Iraq.

Perceptions of 'Risk,' 'Threat,' or 'Hazard' for Iraqi Linguistic Mediators

Armed attacks affect everyone they involve, not only the ADF personnel, but also their ILMs.[33] In the Iraq conflict, the collective threat of armed attack was manifested in clashes between two opposing religious groups or political ideologies. Operating as insurgents, terrorist groups primarily perceived themselves as the representative agents of all Muslims and characterised their opponents from the West as infidels who deserved to be killed for occupying Muslim lands. Other insurgents with varied political motivations also include Saddam Hussein Ba'thists, Iraqi nationalists, and elements from neighbouring countries and their allies. Insurgents from neighbouring countries in particular were a significant collective threat to coalition forces and their ILMs, as well as Iraqi nationals. This threat arose through the financing and training of terrorists and sending them to fight in Iraq. Conventional military forces, on the other hand, operate in opposition to the political elements who aim to disrupt their own military operations in the nations they occupy.[34] These political ideologies placed ILMs in a difficult position. They occupied a contested space between opposing forces because they worked with foreign military organisations and were perceived as not being loyal to their own people and society. The following sections present the cycle of risk as perceived and experienced, how the ADF and linguists managed each risk, strategies of ILMs to deal with each type of risk, and considers what lessons were learnt. Explanation of each of these issues will contribute to creating a better understanding of what constitutes risk for ILMs and how foreign military organisations can incorporate these factors into the planning and execution of future military operations.

Military Risks

Military risks pose significantly potent threats to the role, status, and positionality of LMs in armed conflict, and are also life-threatening. In Iraq, exposure to weapons operated by terrorist groups, foreign fighters, and militia placed LMs at risk of suffering significant physical and mental injury. Examining a comparable insurgency, Tálpas has analysed risk management during the conflict in Afghanistan and has revealed that the threats or risks to the occupying military represented by insurgent forces focused on two specific groups: the international coalition forces personnel themselves and LMs who were often seen as collaborators with international coalition forces.[35] This military risk emerged because LMs accompanied the international coalition forces in many of their military missions.

Scholars have argued that, in combat, a professional's reactions are likely to be different from the reactions of those who are untrained.[36] These differences are considerable and should be linked to policy on risk management.[37] During a sudden attack, trained professionals know what to do.[38] Their training and experience are more likely to enable them to remain calm and effective in the face of violence or react based on drills and standard operating procedures that have been rehearsed.[39] By contrast, untrained participants are more hyper-alert and bewildered when confronted with an unexpected, violent assault. Their response to the cycle of violence is likely to be a reflection of their own inexperience with high-pressure, threatening scenarios.[40]

In the Iraqi armed conflict, deployed ADF troops recruited Iraqi civilians to act as LMs between their forces (and related personnel) and other local protagonists from Iraq. These LMs were required to practise their linguistic-mediator duties in remote and often dangerous areas:

> I also had to fly to Bessmaya training camp with the Australian training team to interpret for Iraqi soldiers … the camp [Bessmaya] was also very big like Tallil … its location, I think, was 40 or 50 kilometres from Baghdad. We had to travel to Baghdad to interpret for the ADF and help them with their training of the Iraqi soldiers. Of course Baghdad was the most dangerous province not like Samawa or even Nasiriyah. (ILM, Omar, Dhi Qar, 2018)

Working with the ADF in the Iraqi armed conflict also required ILMs to travel with ADF combat units on missions to meet key local leaders:

> It was 10 years ago but from my memory we had a whole range of experiences. We actively met with Sheiks in the area—the key leader engagement—and what we were trying to do was to meet with all the key leaders of the area we could. And you know ask them what they thought were the biggest issues for them and try to help them. Of course we have done this through the local interpreters. (ADF Company Commander, John Hickey, 2018)

Others were required to provide task-force linguistic support to train the New Iraqi Army who had been recruited after the 2003 war. These military linguistic-mediation practices frequently exposed ILMs to the collective risk of injury or death.

ADF troops used their 'rules of engagement' as a force to protect their ILMs in Iraq armed conflict. Rules of engagement informed the prevention of any types of risk or danger for those who provided the linguistic support for their troops. The ADF refers to the 'rules of engagement' as 'rules that are specifically designed to avoid civilian casualties and damage to civilian infrastructure but also to provide the maximum level of protection for their troops.'[41] As one high-ranking officer observes:

> Certainly, we had the capacity within our rules of engagement to protect Iraqi nationals or interpreters in this particular who we perceived to be under threat when we were around them. (ADF Major General, Paul McLachlan, Commander of 1st Division and the Deployable Joint Force Headquarters, 2017)

ILMs were given a level of protection equal to that provided to ADF troops on the ground. John Hickey, who worked for the ADF as company commander, expressed his view of the ADF's non-discriminatory behaviour towards protection in this way:

> From what I saw people [local linguistic mediators] were provided with body armour. They go with us with the same vehicles as us. When we leave Tallil Camp, local interpreters have [the] same level of protection as what I had and others from my combat team units. (ADF Company Commander, John Hickey, 2018)

A maximum level of protection was also acknowledged by some of the front-line military personnel. Risk and danger to ILMs were managed based on the 'rules of engagement.' ADF military personnel were required to include the ILMs in any safety briefing. As one of the front-line soldiers who served in the south of Iraq narrates his experiences: 'As ADF personnel we were required to include the interpreters in any safety brief conducted prior to any form of movement' (ADF front-line military personnel, Thomas Rowland, 2017). The key finding is that the ADF troops used the 'rules of engagement' to protect themselves and their ILMs. Any response to risk or danger must not exclude ILMs.

Nevertheless, as shown in Fig. 1, ILMs perceived and rated the military risk as the primary and most extreme risk which war exposed them to. This risk occurred during and after their daily assignments with the ADF combat units on the ground. Majeed, who was a patrol's LM with combat units, explains this in detail:

> You travel with the ADF and you do not know when your moment will be … I mean when you will die. In most of my patrols with the ADF, they never tell me about the location they visit. You have to expect two things, either you will be hit by RPG7 [rocket-propelled grenade] or roadside bombs which could finish your life easily … I remember in 2007 we were attacked by an RPG in Al-Shatrah, but no one died in that attack. I told the soldier who was next to me that I won't work anymore. Yes, they support us with helmet and body armour. (ILM, Majeed, Dhi Qar, 2017)

This account of military linguistic mediation demonstrates that the ILM's immediate response was one of concern for self-preservation. One of the ADF responses to this type of risk was to issue Majeed with protective clothing, such as body armour and a helmet to protect him from military assault. This approach to protection was also acknowledged by an ADF training-team instructor who noted:

> Local interpreters were supplied with ballistic vests, helmets, and the same vehicular protection as ADF personnel; when travelling to and from Iraqi barracks and Camp Tallil. (ADF Training Team Instructor, Sam Hooker, 2017)

These protection measures were necessary to protect the ILMs from the attacks of terrorist organisations. However, the unexpected assault left Majeed anxious in the face of close-proximity violence. Majeed's reaction in telling ADF personnel that he was not willing to work anymore suggests a panicked mental state. Such a response was likely to aggravate ADF personnel's anxiety during such attacks, despite the training that they had received prior to their deployment. Similarly, Sam, who worked with ADF patrolling units, acknowledged that his assignment with ADF combat units exposed him to several types of risk:

> We had been hit by an IED (Improvised Explosive Device) and I remember this was during our visit to Al-Gharraf. It was a really terrifying attack. We were lucky that no one died during that attack. I remember the car [Bushmaster] was damaged … of course, I was very confused and worried … I did not know what to do and even the soldier who I was with could not help. All he said was 'stay here, do not move' and he went inside the tank [Bushmaster] talking to someone else. After that I had to wait with him. (ILM, Sam, Dhi Qar, 2017)

These unpredictable and deadly assaults impacted on Sam who had been assigned to provide linguistic support to ADF combat units. Sam's immediate reactions and response escalated rapidly into panic and fear during the attack and in his interactions with the ADF military personnel. This type of panic and fear, and being 'confused and worried,' are characteristic of untrained people responding to violence in armed-conflict scenarios.[42] After experiencing the assault, Sam used his personal situational risk-management in becoming highly dependent on the ADF military personnel to help him to manage that particular risk. This is simply because neither Majeed or Sam were physically or mentally prepared or trained to respond to these attacks, unlike the highly trained ADF personnel.

Paton and Violanti have argued for the importance of risk assessment and management to strengthen the resilience of personnel to unexpected armed attacks.[43] This includes training all professionals, such as law-enforcement officers, firefighters, military personnel, and *linguistic mediators in armed conflicts* [my emphasis].[44] Such professionals need to understand how to respond to panic, fear, and unexpected attacks as well as how to control irrational responses. ILMs needed explicit training to help them survive, for example, prior training on how to effectively embark and disembark from an armoured vehicle during combat.

Other ILMs felt that some ADF military personnel were favouring their own 'personal protection' over 'collective protection.' An example of this is narrated by an ILM:

> We had a military visit around Al-Nasiriyah city and we stopped near a house, which was built of mud. When all the patrols stopped, the ADF captain who was in charge of the patrol instructed his soldiers to send me to check the house for them to see if someone was inside ... but I refused, and I told them 'let your Captain go and check that house because you are the soldiers.' After that they went inside that house and they found inside that house some photos which belonged to some local militias. (ILM, Rahman, Dhi Qar, 2017)

The ADF combat units' personnel were hyper-alert that the 'mud house' was likely to be an ambush set up by their enemies. As a consequence, the patrol officer in charge on that mission had instructed members of his team to ask the ILM to go and check that house. Perhaps the ADF captain or his crew members wanted Rahman to check the house because Rahman could speak with the occupants in a less confronting manner than those occupiers could. Rahman had a similar sense to the ADF personnel that the 'mud house' was likely to be an 'enemy trap' for him, and he used his own situational risk management to avoid being the victim in a possible enemy ambush.

I argue here that this interaction between the ADF military personnel and the ILM presents serious problems. Firstly, the decisions of these ADF combat units placed Rahman at risk of being harmed or killed. Secondly, instructing Rahman to check the house is considered under the Iraqi culture as *Dosat beit* [invasion of the house's privacy]. If Rahman entered the house and saw some women inside with no veil, the owner of the house could subject Rahman to a tribal law to seek *fasel* [reparation]. Rahman also engaged in unwise action when he suggested the ADF Captain go to check the house by himself. Rahman was supposed to educate the ADF Captain about his role as an ILM and remind him that he was a civilian not a combatant. However, Rahman could not be expected to act in accordance with the ADF professional standard because he had not been trained or given guidance about his role within the military context. The Captain's action was not necessarily typical, and it should be noted that in 2009 in Afghanistan, an Australian soldier, Mark Donaldson, was awarded the Victoria Cross for bravery after rescuing his wounded Afghan linguistic mediator (ALM).[45] Donaldson exposed himself to heavy enemy fire to draw attention from the ALM who had been wounded. The issue here is not limited to inappropriate tasks being given to Rahman; the Captain himself had treated and positioned the ILM as if he were an integral part of the ADF combat unit. It is likely that, had the LM undertaken this reconnaissance-style task, this would have adversely affected the status of the ILM as a civilian.

The lessons to be learnt here are, first, the understanding by both parties of the exact role of the LM, and second, an acknowledgement that once trust and a level of professional familiarity is established, the ILM may offer advice on atmospherics (which may be considered as part of contributing to the group's situational awareness). Apart from that, the ideal action would have been for the Captain and Rahman to have gone together towards the house to avoid these unnecessary risks.

Natural Risks

Injuries from exposure to heat, cold, and other environmental factors were among other serious threats to ILMs. Foreign military organisations hired ILMs based on their skills and knowledge of their own culture, but they often did not know that linguistic mediation, like all practice professions, requires experience and knowledge beyond technical linguistic skills.[46] Occupational health and safety studies reveal that individuals may be trained to act as LMs, but they may never have been trained in how to protect themselves from environmental hazards.[47] Analysis of environmental risk during the conflict in Afghanistan, for example, has revealed that ALMs were recruited to perform the linguistic-mediation task but they were never given resilience training to help them cope with the challenging and hazardous situations they were exposed to.[48] With this lack of training, wartime LMs have run risks and exposed themselves to situations which were likely to have an impact on their health. For example, exposure to extreme temperatures that could reach up to 45°C constituted the most serious environmental threat to ALMs.[49]

During the Iraq conflict, working with ADF troops required ILMs from Iraq to travel with them in remote areas across the southern regions of Iraq. This required ILMs to cope with bad weather conditions in these remote areas. Such areas were likely to be foreign terrain to urbanised, tertiary-educated Iraqis whose skill set included high levels of English competence and capacity to engage with foreigners, rather than survival skills for remote or rural areas. This natural environmental risk was identified and rated by ILMs as high level, and contributed to their anxiety and stress. This stress would also have applied equally to the linguists and the Australian forces, and if anything, high temperatures would have had a greater impact on the Australian troops because of the equipment and clothing they wore. However, the ADF were at least trained to resist natural risks, unlike ILMs who came from civilian universities, and other professions. Hassan recalled his experience as a patrol ILM:

> Every time they take me and [we] stay in the desert for more than three nights. I was required to sleep and eat as if I was a military officer not as a civilian person. Well, sometimes they provide food and sleeping bags. Yes, that is all. (ILM, Gazwan, Dhi Qar, 2017)

Camping across Iraqi southern deserts with ADF combat units was considered a hazardous assignment by ILMs. The southern deserts are home to a large variety of insects, scorpions, and snakes, such as the Sayyed Dakhil snake which is considered by Iraqis to be one of the deadliest in the world. Omar, a local patrolling LM, explains:

> Yes, they used to travel and stay in the desert because they were required to travel to different districts and sleeping in areas next to these places was to save their time for the next day's travelling. To be honest, I could not sleep in most of my work because you are likely to be bitten by a snake or scorpions. The type of soil was mostly with cracks which are usually homes for

these animals. To them [ADF military personnel] it was very normal to sleep on the ground. (ILM, Omar, Dhi Qar, 2018)

ADF logistical support to protect their ILMs from this kind of natural hazard was limited. For example, access to sleeping bags was regulated and restricted to ADF military personnel because sleeping bags had been issued to their military personnel prior to deployment into Iraq, meaning an extra supply of sleeping bags was not available for ILMs. As one ILM recalls:

> I remember the liaison officer talked to me over the phone and all my friends that we need to bring our blankets or sleeping bags. I told him can you provide us with sleeping bags, he said no these things are only [provided] to the ADF. (ILM, Nadir, Dhi Qar, 2017)

These shortages in logistical support, such as the supply of sleeping bags, were also a concern for other ILMs who anticipated being issued appropriate equipment when deployed in the field overnight. For example, Abbas, who had worked for ADF patrol teams until they withdrew from Nasiriyah, detailed his dissatisfaction with the contractual conditions to which he had agreed:

> I used to accept most of the patrol's jobs, but they did not provide me with [a] blanket or sleeping bags like the ones they used. If you look to our contract it says: Article 10 'You are financially responsible for all items of clothing and equipment issued to you by the employer. Any losses of or damage to equipment or clothing may be deducted from your salary.' (ILM, Abbas, Dhi Qar, 2017)

To respond to this type of environmental risk, ILMs took the matter of protective clothing into their own hands by purchasing sleeping bags from the American PX store on base, while others had the opportunity to receive them from the ADF but were required to return them after completing specified tasks. There were only limited sleeping bags available for sale at the American supermarket inside the US military base. Sameer recounts this:

> In most of the patrols, I had to sleep on the 'camp bed replacement canvas' and the weather was very cold. They do not have even blankets. I could not sleep the whole night and I used to wait for the driver to run his car engine [Bushmaster] and ask him to put the heating system on because it was very cold. I asked one of my friends who work with the US army to buy me a sleeping bag from the American market inside Tallil, but he said they had run out of them. (ILM, Sameer, Al Muthanna, 2017)

These experiences of Nadir, Sameer, and others were similar to my own experience on ADF patrol missions. On a very cold day, I was required to camp with the ADF combat units in the desert because my commanding officer had to make many visits to key local political leaders in southern Iraq. When it came time to sleep, I found out that ADF combat units had no spare sleeping bag for me. To resolve this, one Captain from the civil military cooperation (CIMIC) offered me his personal sleeping bag. Offering his personal sleeping bag to me meant that the CIMIC officer had to sleep all night using only his bag's cover. A similar lack of logistic support to an ILM who was hired locally was discussed in the history of operational support in Bosnia-Herzegovina. In that conflict, the lack of a social welfare system even resulted in these LMs deciding to purchase their own health insurance to mitigate the risks of workplace injury.[50]

These environmental workplace hazards which ILMs faced provide a clear sense that we had not been given access to the same pre-deployment resilience assessment, training, and post-working debriefs as our ADF military personnel companions. Resilience training should be undertaken collectively because if one party is trained while the other is not, the latter's lack of knowledge is likely to impact on the performances of those who have been trained.

Socio-Political Risks

The socio-political risks faced by LMs came up for debate as early as 2003, particularly in the context of such work in Iraq and Afghanistan. Scholars such as Mihaela Tălpaş explain attacks on LMs as a result of the significant role they play in accessing confidential information.[51] Others, such as Joseph Lo Bianco, suggest that terrorist organisations' opposition to LMs stems from their own belief that translating and interpreting for occupying forces is behaviour that conflicts with the interests of the occupied community.[52] Insurgents perceive that the work LMs do in interpreting for foreign military organisations means they are helping the 'occupiers' to understand their communities' realities.[53] Providing linguistic support to train the newly recruited Iraqi armed forces in the post-war period was also considered against their interests. These political ideologies positioned war-zone language mediators as those who had sided with 'occupying' military troops.[54]

In the Iraqi armed conflict, the socio-political risk was rated by ILMs as high and possibly an extreme risk compared to potential natural or environmental risks. ILMs perceived the presence of insurgent militia as a threat to them because militia and other political segments considered them to be an integral part of the ADF. Mohammed, an ILM with the ADF training team deployed to train the Iraqi Armed Forces, explains this in detail:

> One day, I had been followed by a car which belonged to local militia from my home till I reached the military base and when I told the Captain (who was responsible for the military training), he told me 'Well, we cannot do anything' and it would be better if I took a few days off till things got better. (ILM, Mohammed, Dhi Qar, 2017)

A conflict field guide for translators/interpreters (T/Is) and users of their services was produced in 2012 by the international association of conference interpreters (AIIC) and Red T which is a 501(c)(3) non-profit organisation advocating for the protection of translators and interpreters in high-risk settings. It recommends a number of basic rights and responsibilities for parties involved in armed conflict. Interpreters and translators 'have a right to protection both during and after the assignment.'[55] However, the ADF were not able to provide protection to those ILMs outside of ADF combat situations. Alternatively, if the ADF *had* provided protection to some ILMs who they believed to be at risk, would the ILM be happy to be permanently accommodated on a base away from his family or friends? Would the ILM accept US or ADF military discipline inside the base? Moreover, if the ADF offered urgent protection to some ILMs who they believed to be at risk and gave them the opportunity to travel to Australia, would other ILMs then accept remaining in Iraq and continuing to practise military linguistic mediation? And if the ADF offered all ILMs protection and sent them to Australia, who would then be LMs for these troops? The answer to these questions was gathered from the interviews of ILMs. They acknowledge that it would be very hard for them to stay inside military bases for many reasons. The first reason was associated with security, while the others were associated with cultural differences and status. In terms of security, ILMs found that staying inside military bases was likely to put their life at risk because the ADF and other troops are also targets. As one of the ILMs narrated:

> Of course it would be difficult because the ADF are also targeted by militia and terrorist[s]. If I accept this I may die in one of [these] attacks. I think it would be easy for single people but not for us as married people with kids. (ILM, Mohammed, 2019)

Other ILMs Iraqi stated that it would be very hard to bring their families and stay with military personnel who have different cultural norms:

> If I were there and I have been threatened. I will ask to protect me and take me either to Australia or other safe place. If they [The ADF] said not I will stop completing and change my place. (ILM, Saad, Dhi Qar, 2019)

The right to protection after the assignment or outside business hours was remembered with sadness by Major General Paul McLachlan:

> The difficulty of course is when an ADF element is not present which at the time of the early phase, the interpreters were living locally and going home and we were not necessary on the base for the whole period of time. So, there were times when interpreters who have been utilised were not protected by the Australian Forces. (ADF Major General, Paul McLachlan, 2017)

This situation highlights that the ADF 'rules of engagement' were limited to protecting ILMs during their work but not afterwards. Like journalists in armed conflict situations, ILMs who travelled with US patrols were seen as a constituent part of the international coalition forces. This ideological affiliation was mentioned by another ILM Iraqi who stated that some militia members used to wait at the taxi-car garages to see who went to the military base at Tallil, and then list them as 'traitors' or 'supporters to the occupiers':

> I went to hire a taxi because I did not have a personal car at that time and when I arrived there I found many of those militia were waiting to see who picked up the taxi into the US military base … by the way even the taxi driver was worried and changed his use of terms from announcing he was taking passengers to 'qaedat al Emam Ali' which literally means 'to Ali airbase' into taking them to 'Um Elshwag' [which is the name of a village near the US military base]. (ILM, Ameer, Dhi Qar, 2017)

In the absence of a risk-management strategy, ILMs had to rely on their own initiative to protect themselves from both social and political threats. One ILM stated that he had to hire a private taxi driver to take him and other ILMs to work. As noted by one of the ILMs, Mohammed:

> I then said to my friends, it will be better for us if we hire a taxi driver whom we know we trust; at least this will help us to avoid being killed like sheep and since that time we never used the public taxi garages. (ILM, Mohammed, Al Dhi Qar, 2017)

Distrust among ILMs in their interaction with a variety of local protagonists and the fear of being targeted in the future made them use other strategies to protect their identity. Moyameer noted that when he travelled with the ADF to militia-affiliated villages, he used to change his dialect of Arabic from an Iraqi dialect into an Egyptian one to avoid being questioned about the place he lived:

> Many of our locals are quite sympathetic to the militia or the others. So, to protect myself I had to change my dialect and talk to some locals in an Egyptian dialect. But this dialect put me in trouble with my community. I was interpreting, and everything was okay but what happened is that when the Australian officer was talking to the locals, he referred to the word of

'bag' in his speech and you know in Iraq we call it 'Jantah' but in the Egyptian dialect it is different and Egyptians call it 'Shantah' and when I could not remember the particular dialect, I said it in the Iraqi way. This made the locals laugh at me and they found out that I am Iraqi … no way, I did not tell the Australian officer that I changed my dialect. (ILM, Moyameer, Dhi Qar, 2017)

These innovative risk-management strategies show that although ILMs used their own strategies in off-base threat environments, they were not always successful. I also personally undertook the strategy of avoiding being recognised by the local militia. During one of my linguistic-mediation assignments, I was sent as a LM with the ADF security patrols to visit a village in the north of Nasiriyah Province. The nature of the work was to provide security support to other ADF combat units which were supposed to visit the same location in the future. An ADF Lieutenant was in charge of that patrol and I was required to help him with his translation needs. When I arrived at the village, I was asked to disembark from the armoured vehicle and to walk towards some of the local villagers. I sought to use one of my risk-management strategies to protect myself from any future risk consequences: I hid my identity because those local villagers were not known to me and they were likely to question me about my identity. After I engaged with those villagers, I was asked by them about my identity prior to interpreting. To protect my identity, I told them that I was from Canberra and my family were still in Australia where they had moved a long time ago. However, my strategy failed because one of the ADF soldiers revealed my identity as one of the ILMs. The ADF soldiers were not adequately aware of the potential precariousness of our situation.

Economic Risks

Along with the economic reform of Iraq, during the war, international projects were implemented to rebuild water infrastructure, hospitals, schools, and other significant projects. Many of these projects were funded by the deployed international coalition forces. However, the way these funds were handled placed ILMs in life-threatening positions within their community. The majority of these foreign military organisations gave construction tenders directly to some ILMs. Sameer, an ILM who worked at the Iraqi Police Station in Nasiriyah, explained what he regarded as mishandling:

> Most of [the] military forces used to give construction tenders to interpreters and asked them to bring local contractors. I know one interpreter who worked with us used to bring tenders and give them to contractors that he knows. He becomes very rich and did not come to Australia because he preferred to stay there. Some interpreters used to take 50% of each project that they gave to the Iraqi contractors. This case was not only with the Australians but also with the US and Italians. This put our life in danger just like the threat of militia and terrorists. Well, this caused a conflict between the Iraqi contractors and these interpreters. Well, you cannot tell the troops that asking or giving tenders is something wrong and they must not do that because you and I will be jobless. (ILM, Sameer, Dhi Qar, 2017)

This tender-allocation policy influenced the role, status, and positionality of ILMs. It increased the risk to these ILMs. Saad, an ILM at the Iraqi local police station, saw this as a crisis:

> The contracting issue is a big story in Iraq. One interpreter [non-ADF linguistic mediator] has been shot because he used to decide which project a certain contractor should take and not the others. Of course, he could do this because he knows the rate of each tender and he interprets that for them. I know one interpreter who worked with the Italians opened a construction company as a result of the money he used to receive from his own contractors, and while he worked with them as an interpreter. (ILM, Saad, Dhi Qar, 2017)

A similar perception was also expressed by another ILM:

> Many military officers used to have friendship with interpreters and they ask them to bring contractors. They give direct contracts to the Sheikh they visit and these Sheikh used to give these contract to sub-contractors. (ILM, Khaleel, Dhi Qar, 2017)

Having the status of LM with the military forces meant all ILMs were seen to have the power to receive and allocate tenders to local contractors. This economic risk generated two types of risks on the ground. The first risk was that local contractors and other individuals began to hassle ILMs, since they continually asked them to give them construction tenders. Ahmmed, an ILM working with the patrolling combat units stated:

> Everyone started asking: You are working as an interpreter with the ADF, so why can't you get some tenders and we will give some money. Our people had a belief that we all have this type of capacity to bring tenders and when I told them that this was not my job, they did not believe this and accused me of being a liar. (ILM, Ahmmed, Dhi Qar, 2017)

This led to an increased risk of kidnapping for ILMs. The risk of kidnapping as a common threat occurred because the majority of locals saw them as being part of the wealthiest layer of the Iraqi society. This type of risk is mentioned in the story of an Iraqi police-station LM as follows:

> After the war many people have been kidnapped and most of the time kidnappers ask for money. Kidnappers see who is rich and as soon as they have this kind of information, they send someone to kidnap him or a member of his family. We as interpreters we are in the same situation; because these forces gave projects to interpreters, people have an idea that we are all very rich. (ILM, Rowan, Dhi Qar, 2017)

Such risks influenced the normal everyday life of these ILMs. The involvement of some ILMs in allocating the tenders resulted in putting others in danger of being taken hostage by those seeking money from their families.

Most of these ILMs had to accept this risk caused by economic factors and were unable to respond with their own strategies, in contrast to their use of previously mentioned strategies applied to mitigate other risks. This is because ILMs were worried that informing or educating foreign military organisations about the tender-allocation policy would be likely to put their 'linguistic mediation status' at risk, and result in them losing their jobs.

Conclusion

This chapter has examined the nature of the risks faced by ILMs who worked with the ADF during the Iraq War. It has highlighted key issues for both translation and interpreting scholars and military historians to take into account in future research, and suggests further research questions. Why did this (level of) risk management occur, particularly in ADF non-combat operations in Iraq? What was its effect on the Australian mission, and what does an understanding of a LM's risk management have to offer to the future of combat and non-combat military tasks around the world? Answering these questions comprehensively is beyond the scope of this chapter, the purpose of which was to highlight and detail the risks faced by ILMs through the lens of the cyclical war risk-management model. This section of the chapter is, therefore, a summary of the findings with some recommendations offered to the ADF for their future military operations.

One of the overarching lessons is an imperative for the ADF to prepare serving soldiers better to understand the role, status, and positionality of ILMs in such difficult circumstances. However, there are other subsidiary lessons which I detail below:

Lesson 1 The ADF recruited locally engaged civilians as contractors but they did not provide them with adequate risk-management strategies to address different parts of the cycle of risks. This occurred on the ground because they had no obvious, written, protection policy related to locally engaged contractors, and this left ILMs in a difficult, stressful, and potentially deadly position. As a result, ILMs faced different types of risks in practising military linguistic mediation for the ADF. These risks came in different forms and encompassed military, natural, socio-political, and economic risks. Some of these risks involved short-term effects, while others had long-term effects for ILMs. The military risk was the first-hand risk which influenced their immediate reactions to the attacks they experienced when under fire during their work with the ADF. Lack of periodic risk-management training left ILMs facing different challenges. ILMs were sometimes forced into an ambiguous role between their academic training and the demands of the military environment which were not met by their skills. To protect these language specialists from this type of risk, it is recommended that ADF should train their staff and LMs to prevent the latter from feeling they are being treated as 'hung out to dry' for their enemies. One of these programs is the risk-management paradigm proposed by Paton and Violanti to manage risks associated with terrorist or local militia attacks.[56]

Lesson 2 Factors associated with environmental hazards also contributed towards exposing ILMs to significant personal risks. ILMs were recruited to assist ADF combat units, but they were not trained in how to deal with environmental hazards. This left them under ongoing pressure. Despite these challenges they provided excellent contributions to the ADF. It is recommended that the ADF policy and language-planning personnel consider implementing resilience-training programs for their current and future LMs.

Lesson 3 Conflict between the foreign military organisations and certain political segments left ILMs in an invidious situation at times: seemingly caught between the work they were doing for the ADF in Australia's contribution to rebuilding Iraq and at ideological odds with the insurgents. Pro-insurgent political elements targeted these ILMs during the armed conflict. The ADF should consider providing 'intelligence briefings' and other training to help their ILMs to face the risk which comes from exposure to opposing political and military elements in the fluid and complex sphere that characterises modern counterinsurgency.

Lesson 4 The tender-allocation practices used by foreign military organisations have increased the risks associated with perceived affluence and political allegiance for all language mediators. In the absence of clear guidelines for the role, status, and positionality of LMs, ILMs participated in creating risks for other ILMs. The foreign military organisations also participated in adding risk by giving ILMs tenders for contracting projects. It is recommended that the ADF needs to develop policy to avoid using LMs or prohibit them from participating in tender negotiation. This should remain the remit of trained personnel who work with the ADF contracting staff at the appropriate headquarters. One way would be to announce projects through the media rather than through LMs. This would prevent LMs from bringing their own local contractors and engaging in what became a clear conflict of interest.

Overall, the biggest issue was that the ADF protection of ILMs was based on the knowledge of 'rules of engagement' rather than on a broader policy. ILMs seemed to be largely unaware of these rules because the rules were considered to be classified under the ADF directions and sharing these rules was considered a security breach. Revealing these rules to the public or anyone outside the military might mean the information could be used by enemy intelligence as a useful resource against the ADF. If we propose that ILMs were aware of their protection as part of the ADF 'rules of engagement' they could in theory have been engaged in shooting against the enemy. If this had taken place and ILMs had caused civilian casualties, this would have gone against the ADF claims which were made by the former Chief of Defence Force, Air Chief Marshal Angus Houston: 'Our members operate under strict Rules of Engagement which are specifically designed to avoid civilian casualties and damage to civilian infrastructure.'[57] The point here in the case of the ADF is that the ADF rules of engagement were something belonging to the ADF as combatants under the international law. However, ILMs were civilians who needed a written policy to guide their interaction with the military personnel they worked for. In the absence of specific policy, everyone acted in accordance with what they believed to be right based on their own experience.

In conclusion, this chapter has assessed the lessons learnt (or identified) from the experience of ILMs who worked for the ADF as Defence LEEs. It aims to promote effective risk-management action for future ADF military operations. Current and future planners can learn from these lessons to avoid the repetition of past errors, and also to sustain those effective processes that were adopted, in any future military operations. However, one distinctive contribution of this study is that it has drawn on the experiences and perceptions of ILMs themselves. Any LM faces professional trials in performing their primary linguistic role, but all of the risks identified in this chapter emphasise the varied challenges that had to be overcome by LMs in the complex and challenging experience that was the Iraq War. This study is an urgent call for policy-makers and language-planning leaders like those in the ADF to write a policy for interpreters, translators, and linguists in conflict and non-conflict zones whose risks are not clearly considered in policy aimed at military personnel. Given the different types of physical and psychological risks the ILMs faced, governments need to optimise their protection. If—as I suspect— military linguistic mediation through LMs provides important operational advantages, it needs to be included in national security operational planning.

Interviews

I recorded all the following interviews for an oral history project that was not funded by any organisation or institutions. These audio recordings are not available to the public due to the security circumstances that these ADF military personnel or their ILMs might face if they were identified by others. However, some samples of transcripts will be available to the public in my thesis. The names given below are pseudonyms with one exception, but the times and dates represent faithfully the interviews. I hold a record matching the real names with the pseudonyms.

All the following interviews were conducted by Ali Albakaa.

A. **ADF military personnel**
Paul McLachlan (real name), Interview 1, 14 December 2017
John Hickey, Interview 1, 17 November 2017
Steven Mcleod, Interview 1, 12 December 2017
Interview 2, 14 December 2018
Sam Hooker, Interview 1, 13 December 2017
Thomas Rowland, Interview 1, 15 December 2017
B. **Iraqi linguistic mediators (ILMs)**
Omar, Alsaleem, Interview 1, 30 March 2018
Interview 2, 6 April 2017
Majeed, Al-Alawi, Interview 1, 19 July 2017
Interview 2, 30 July 2017
Sam, Alezerjawi, Interview 1, 10 March 2017
Interview 2, 15 March 2017

Rahman, Almusawi, Interview 1, 16 March 2017
Interview 2, 18 March 2017
Mohammed, Alsultani, Interview 1, 27 April 2017
Gazwan, Al Sadiq, Interview 1, 22 March 2017
Interview 2, 28 March 2017
Nadir, Al Yaseen, Interview 1, 13 April 2017
Interview 2, 14 April 2017
Abbas, Al Kadhimi, Interview 1, 19 April 2017
Interview 2, 20 April 2017
Sameer, Al Abbas, Interview 1, 17 April 2017
Interview 2, 18 April 2017
Ameer, Al Yaqoupi, Interview 1, 28 April 2017
Mohammed, Al Habeeb, Interview 1, 11 May 2017
Interview 2, 15 May 2017
Moyameer, Al Nawas, Interview 1, 17 May 2017
Interview 2, 18 May 2017
Sameer, Al Husseini, Interview 1, 8 September 2017
Interview 2, 10 October 2017
Saad, Al Karimi, Interview 1, 20 October 2017
Interview 2, 22 October 2017
Khaleel, Al Abdei, Interview 1, 8 November 2017
Ahmmed, Al Obaide, Interview 1, 1 November 2017
Rowan, Al Qasimi, Interview 1, 8 November 2017
Interview 2, 22 November 2017

Notes

1. Jan Angstrom and Isabelle Duyvesteyn (2010), *Modern War and the Utility of Force: Challenges, Method and strategy* (USA: Routledge).
2. Angstrom and Duyvesteyn, *Modern War and the Utility of Force*.
3. Angstrom and Duyvesteyn, *Modern War and the Utility of Force*, p. 1.
4. Amir Al Qarelleh (2012), 'Weapons of Mass Destruction and the Problematic Role of the Mass Media in the Invasion of Iraq', PhD thesis, University of Western Sydney, p. 76, http://researchdirect.uws.edu.au/islandora/object/uws%3A14294/datastream/PDF/view

5. Al Qarelleh, 'Weapons of Mass Destruction', p. 28.
6. Svetoslan Gaidow and Seng Boey (2005), *Australian Defence Risk Management Framework: A Comparative Study* (Edinburgh, South Australia: Australian Government Department of Defence, Commonwealth of Australia), p. 2.
7. Gaidow and Boey (2005), *Australian Defence Risk Management Framework*.
8. Gaidow and Boey, *Australian Defence Risk Management Framework*.
9. Gaidow and Boey, *Australian Defence Risk Management Framework*.
10. Andrew O'Connor, 'Australian Army Reservists Preparing to Be "Battle Ready" for Possible Overseas Deployment', ABC News, 26 May 2017, https://www.abc.net.au/news/2017-05-26/army-reservists-more-than-weekend-warriors/8557588
11. Andrew Cohn and Australian Psychological Society, 'Resilience Training in the Australian Defence Force', *InPsych*, 2010. https://www.psychology.org.au/publications/inpsych/2010/april/cohn
12. Cohn and Australian Psychological Society, 'Resilience Training'.
13. Ian P Jones and Louise Askew (2014), *Meeting the Language Challenges of NATO Operations: Policy, Practise and Professionalization* (Basingstoke: Palgrave Macmillan), p. 230.
14. A. Nagi John (2008), *The U.S. Army/Marine Corps Counterinsurgency Field Manual* (London: The University of Chicago Press), pp. 336–346.
15. John, *The U.S. Army/Marine Corps Counterinsurgency Field Manual*, pp. 345–46.
16. John, *The U.S. Army/Marine Corps Counterinsurgency Field Manual*, pp. 345–46.
17. John, *The U.S. Army/Marine Corps Counterinsurgency Field Manual*, pp. 345–46.
18. John, *The U.S. Army/Marine Corps Counterinsurgency Field Manual*, pp. 345–46.
19. John, *The U.S. Army/Marine Corps Counterinsurgency Field Manual*, pp. 345–46.
20. Roxanne Kelly (2017), *Military Personnel Policy Manual* (Canberra: Australian Government/Department of Defence), http://www.defence.gov.au/PayAndConditions/ADF/Resources/MILPERSMAN.pdf
21. Kelly, *Military Personnel Policy Manual*.
22. Kelly, *Military Personnel Policy Manual*.

23. Kelly, *Military Personnel Policy Manual.*
24. Kelly, *Military Personnel Policy Manual.*
25. Lynn Abrams (2010), *Oral History Theory* (London: Taylor & Francis Ltd), p. 1.
26. Kumiko Torikai (2009), *Voices of the Invisible Presence: Diplomatic Interpreters in Post-World War II Japan* (Amsterdam: John Benjamins), p. 197.
27. Jörn Birkmann (2013), 'Risk', *Encyclopedia of Natural Hazards* (Dordrecht: Springer), p. 856.
28. Michael K. Lindell (2013), 'Risk perception and communication', *Encyclopedia of Natural Hazards* (Dordrecht: Springer), p. 870.
29. Tian Luo (2016), 'Augmenting Combat Power: Military Translation in China-Burma-India Theatre', *Linguistica Antverpiensia, New Series: Themes in Translation Studies*, 15, pp. 143–61.
30. Daniel Coste and Marisa Cavalli (2015), *Education, Mobility, Otherness: The Mediation Functions of Schools* (Language Policy Unit, DGII – Directorate General of Democracy, Council of Europe).
31. Mihaela Tălpas (2016), 'Words Cut Two Ways: An Overview of the Situation of Afghan Interpreters at the Beginning of the 21st Century', *Linguistica Antverpiensia, New Series: Themes in Translation Studies*, 15, pp. 241–59.
32. Tălpas, 'Words Cut Two Ways', p. 247.
33. Tălpas, 'Words Cut Two Ways'.
34. Stian Kjeksrud et al. (2016), *Protection of Civilians* (Oxford: Oxford University Press), p. 116.
35. Tălpas, 'Words Cut Two Ways'.
36. Armed Conflict Work Group of the International Work Group on Death, Dying, and Bereavement (2013), 'Armed Conflict: A Model for Understanding and Intervention', *Death Studies*, 37:1, pp. 61–88, DOI https://doi.org/10.1080/07487.2012.655647
37. Armed Conflict Work Group, *Armed Conflict*, pp. 61–88.
38. Armed Conflict Work Group, *Armed Conflict*, pp. 61–88.
39. Armed Conflict Work Group, *Armed Conflict*, pp. 61–88.
40. Armed Conflict Work Group, *Armed Conflict*, pp. 61–88.
41. Nautilus Institute (2014), 'Rules of Engagement – Afghanistan and Iraq', accessed May 20, 2014 https://nautilus.org/publications/books/australian-forces-abroad/afghanistan/rules-of-engagement-afghanistan-and-iraq/

42. Armed Conflict Work Group, *Armed Conflict*.
43. Douglas Paton et al., 'Terrorism Stress Risk Assessment and Management', p. 225.
44. Douglas Paton et al., 'Terrorism Stress Risk Assessment and Management', p. 225.
45. Emma Rodgers (2009), 'Soldier Awarded VC for Afghanistan Bravery', *ABC News*, 16 January 2009, https://www.abc.net.au/news/2009-01-16/soldier-awarded-vc-for-afghanistan-bravery/268276
46. Robyn K. Dean and Robert Q. Pollard, Jr. (2013), *The Demand Control Schema: Interpreting as a Practice Profession* (North Charleston, SC: CreateSpace Independent Publishing Platform), p. 154.
47. Ali Darwish (2010), *Translation Applied: An Introduction to Applied Translation Studies* (Melbourne: Writescope Publishers), p. 340.
48. Tălpas, 'Words Cut Two Ways'.
49. Tălpas, 'Words Cut Two Ways'.
50. Michael Kelly and Catherine Baker (2012), *Interpreting the Peace: Peace Operations, Conflict and Language in Bosnia-Herzegovina* (UK: Palgrave Macmillan), p. 116.
51. Tălpas, 'Words Cut Two Ways', p. 249.
52. Joseph Lo Bianco (2008), 'Tense Times and Language Planning', *Current Issues in Language Planning*, 9:5, pp. 155–78.
53. Lo Bianco, 'Tense Times and Language Planning'.
54. Lo Bianco, 'Tense Times and Language Planning', p. 155.
55. FIT-IFT, AIIC and Red T. (2012), 'Conflict Zone Field Guide for Translators/Interpreters and Users of Their Services' Version 3. https://www.fit-ift.org/wp-content/uploads/2013/03/T-I_Field_Guide_2012.pdf
56. Douglas Paton et al., 'Terrorism Stress Risk Assessment and Management', p. 225.
57. Nautilus Institute, 'Rules of Engagement – Afghanistan and Iraq'.

Section V

Conclusion

Section V

Conclusion: Cross-Cultural Communication and Language in Wartime: Reflections and Future Directions

Richard Gehrmann and Amanda Laugesen

Soldiers at war do not spend most of their time fighting and killing, contrary to Hollywood depictions of conflict. To fully understand war, we need to move beyond the immediacy of combat to examine other dimensions of the military experience, for to reconstruct 'the world beyond combat is to reconstruct a central part of the social and cultural experience of soldiers in wartime.'[1] Such a task is required both of the military researcher focusing on social issues and, equally importantly, of the military researcher focusing on strategic, operational, or tactical issues. Both need to accept the immediacy and significance of the world beyond combat.

R. Gehrmann
School of Humanities and Communication, University of Southern Queensland, Toowoomba, QLD, Australia
e-mail: Richard.Gehrmann@usq.edu.au

A. Laugesen (✉)
Australian National Dictionary Centre, Australian National University, Canberra, ACT, Australia
e-mail: amanda.laugesen@anu.edu.au

© The Author(s) 2020
A. Laugesen, R. Gehrmann (eds.), *Communication, Interpreting and Language in Wartime*, Palgrave Studies in Languages at War,
https://doi.org/10.1007/978-3-030-27037-7_12

This collection has shown that language is a critical component of the wartime cross-cultural experience, but cross-cultural communication in war is about more than just using an interpreter to convey information between two parties. Those communicating need to be aware of the nuances of the interpreter's role and also of how they project their own ideas, values, and assumptions into any cross-cultural engagement. This remains critical whether cross-cultural engagement occurs during the training of military linguists, during war itself, or in the highly complex war-crimes trials that sometimes follow a conflict. As Kitzen and Vogelsang have noted from the experience of the Dutch in Afghanistan, there is always a two-way component to communication. Any situation involving verbal contact between the military and others is one in which 'interviewer and interviewee are exchanging words, phrases and gestures, and on both sides these are always understood, or not, on the basis of a much broader perception.'[2] Understanding the complexity of this communication has been a primary aim of this collection.

Experiences of Cross-Cultural Communication

In reflecting upon his experiences after serving several months as a soldier during the Vietnam War, Terry Burstall noted:

> My perceptions had narrowed so much by this time that there were for me only two kinds of people in Vietnam: those in the villages, who hated us and showed it; and those in the towns, who hated us and didn't show it too openly because they were making a dollar and waiting to rip us off. The only way we ever met Vietnamese was when we went on leave and there they were the pimps, the bar girls, the bar owners and black market racketeers. It was a very lopsided view of the Vietnamese that we developed.[3]

For a combatant to hold such a distorted and negative view is of course not uncommon, and both language skills and the capacity to engage in genuine cross-cultural communication helps to bridge such gaps.

Some military organisations have placed great emphasis on the significance of cross-cultural communication as well as language skills. This has been the case for the Dutch military, which between 2008 and 2011 employed Dr Willem Vogelsang, a senior academic from the University of Leiden, as cultural adviser to their forces deployed to Uruzgan province in southern Afghanistan. Vogelsang had spent much of his academic life studying Afghan history and culture, and was the author of one of the standard academic texts on the country's history as well as numerous specialist works on ancient and modern Afghanistan and on the wider Middle East.[4] The engagement of highly trained regional and cultural advisers such as Vogelsang offers a positive example of how military organisations can focus on the benefits of understanding and communication in wartime. But focus on cross-cultural communication does not only need to exist at the level of command, as ordinary soldiers trying to communicate with others of different backgrounds also need guidance. With effective cross-cultural communication, ordinary soldiers can both perform their task better and benefit from feeling and perhaps becoming more cosmopolitan and engaged with the society in which they are operating. Research should perhaps focus not just on policy to achieve utilitarian military goals but also on the potentially transformative effects that can be engendered by effective human communication during war.

Despite the positive Dutch example mentioned above, even in the wealthiest and most powerful armies there can be a disconnect between the intention to provide soldiers with requisite cultural knowledge and the reality of doing so. Rhodes Scholar and United States Marine Craig Mullaney experienced a suite of briefings when he deployed to Afghanistan in 2003, with some presentations leaving him less than prepared. He recounts:

'How do we know who's a bad guy?' I asked.
'They speak Arabic.'
'How do we know whether they're speaking Arabic or Pashto?'
The briefer didn't have a response and my level of confidence shrank.[5]

Fortunately for the Oxford-educated Mullaney, he was comfortable with other cultures. His fiancée was a Hindi speaker and having learnt Hindi to impress her, he found that similarities between Hindi and the Urdu spoken by some Afghans gave him an occasional chance to communicate directly with local people. Clearly not the average soldier, he could use his personal cultural skills to understand Afghans as people, while utilising his military skills to perform his professional role.

Life in a war zone means soldiers come into contact with those that are different to them. War means culture shock, viewing an exotic 'other,' and having the chance to reflect on the identity of others and the identity of themselves as part of a transformational experience, as Amanda Laugesen points out in her account of Australians in the First World War in this volume. Her chapter shows that the exposure to allies such as the British and New Zealanders brought home to Australians significant essential differences between themselves and their allies, despite apparent commonalities of the English language and cultural links. Knowledge of difference can be linked to the borrowing of selected language terms and the development of a sense of being culturally distinct, or even of being racially superior. Similar understandings of difference between allies are noted by Richard Gehrmann in his chapter on Australian soldiers in Iraq and Afghanistan.

Linguistic borrowings have long been a component of cross-cultural communication in wartime, and these demonstrate both the veteran status of those who use such words as well as a form of cosmopolitanism. Everyday use of military terms as well as local languages becomes a conscious act of borrowing during wartime. Creation of explicit glossaries serves to exclude the novice and include the warrior, marking the identity of each. Here the use of language marks a cross-cultural decision by individuals and groups to denote their own cultural distinctiveness, and even their cultural superiority over non-soldiers, a further theme identified by both Laugesen and Gehrmann in their examinations of cross-cultural communication and language in wartime.

Strategies of Communication and Language Teaching

This collection has also reflected on strategies of communication and language teaching, and the way linguistic communications are developed prior to conflict remains fundamental to studying the role of languages in wartime. Language training is often expensive and time-consuming. States make a considered decision to have their military personnel learn foreign languages, and these might be the languages of either potential allies or potential enemies.

Teaching another language can have significant cross-cultural impacts on the host society. The language teachers themselves perform the function of cultural broker, whether they are native speakers or not. They serve to communicate ideas about both the culture(s) and language(s) they teach, whether in the more culturally cosmopolitan environment of twenty-first-century Melbourne as described by Yavar Dehghani, or in Jennifer Joan Baldwin's more restricted and circumscribed White Australia of the 1930s. In both cases, language teachers can be understood as cultural brokers serving a national need. There can be an uneasy tension between prosaic or utilitarian military requirements and the perspective of a language teacher passionate about the culture of their birthplace or that of a place they have learnt of and become enamoured with.

Military language policy can also be understood as having a far wider framework that relates, at least in part, to their own distinct national culture of military communication,[6] a point that connects to Jasmin Gabel's chapter in this volume. National ideologies or discourses can play an important role in the way wars are justified and communicated, and finding ways of making sense of how these frameworks shape communication is one task that was taken up in this volume.

Experiences of Interpreters

The experience of interpreters and those who use their skills is perhaps the raison d'être of almost any analysis of the historical and contemporary experience of language in wartime. Studies of interpreters show they are often positioned in the margins. If members of the military, they at least have the benefit of a uniform and identity that places them clearly on one side in a war, although they might also feel culturally conflicted, as the experience of Kayla Williams in Iraq shows (discussed in the Introduction).[7] Yet others wearing military uniform, such as the White Russians who served in the German army during the Second World War in Oleg Beyda's case study, might be positioned in a liminal space, identifying as both partly German but also partly Russian. This was particularly the case for the ethnically German emigrés from the Baltic States whose Russian, German, and Baltic identity was very much situational. They could perform the role of cultural mediators to mitigate the excesses of the Nazi occupation while still serving their own anti-Communist agenda, existing in an uncomfortable, even dangerous, liminal zone.

This positionality of being in the margins is further demonstrated by interpreters recruited in-country who lack the authenticity of being full members of the military. As Catherine Baker identifies in her study of interpreters in Bosnia-Herzegovina, civilian interpreters stand out from soldiers in four specific ways: their lack of weapons, their lack of specific training for the task of war zone interpreting, their different level of resilience, and even if given a uniform, their inability to wear this correctly in a manner that enables them to seamlessly merge into the military environment that surrounds them.[8] These individuals may feel under pressure from all sides as seen in some of the examples of some Iraqi civilian interpreters discussed by Ali Albakaa. In the case of the Indonesians who interpreted for Matt Grant, their separation from the soldier can occur at a deeper level. The interpreters in Grant's encounters were locals who lived in a world defined by mass deaths, unlike the foreign soldier who could return home when a task was completed. To local interpreters, the task of cultural mediation and linguistic translation is paramount, but they are also required to identify with both the people of the homeland and the people of the foreign army that employs them.

Exploring the world of judicial engagement requires quite different skills to those of the soldier-interpreter. Military interpreters in a combat zone might be required to translate and interpret short, sharp, immediate statements, while military document translators usually have the luxury of being removed from the battleline and having a degree of relative leisure to consider the meaning of an immutable piece of written text. Signals intelligence analysts listening to transmissions may have the benefit of recording equipment that allows them to correct translations of recorded speech. But there is a different imperative for those interpreting in war-crimes trials. There may be transcription recordings, but there is a present and immediate impact from mistranslating, or from creating a false nuance or false understanding. Any error of communications can be problematic in wartime, but miscommunication leading to conviction of war crimes and the quiet tension of the court room can provide their own levels of stress as both Georgina Fitzpatrick and Ludmila Stern discuss in their chapters. In the case of the Japanese war-crimes trials, the fact that the Japanese defendants had Japanese interpreters with excellent English meant that less skilled Allied military translators could be employed to monitor Japanese translators rather than to actually translate.

In wartime, accurate interpretation was a military necessity, whereas in war-crimes trials accurate interpretation is critical for judicial fairness. Stern notes that during the Nuremberg war-crimes trials, the German expression *Ja* 'yes' could be regarded as an admission of guilt whereas when used at the start of a sentence it actually equates with 'well …' and functions as a discourse marker, a difference which can have significant implications. Similar court-room implications can emerge when investigating acts of sexual violence, as shown with the tribunal examining the 1994 Rwandan genocide. It faced the challenge of interpreters using euphemisms rather than vulgar, offensive, or taboo terms for genitals or violent sexual assault, in keeping with what was considered culturally appropriate by the witness and counsel.

The varied accounts of the interpreting experience in many of the chapters in this book cannot hope to be comprehensive, but they aim to provide the reader with significant insights into the changing historical experience of these important cultural and linguistic mediators.

Directions for Future Research and Some Challenges

Much remains to be done in researching languages in war, the very least being that research needs to move languages from the margins: if not to a more central position, to a place where they cease to be regarded as ephemeral. Footitt and Kelly make the point that there is a wide gap between those who study translation and thus emphasise the role of languages in war, and the vast majority of historical work on warfare that suggests 'the total absence of languages, their occlusion.'[9] Military history and studies of war have become an increasingly crowded space with different disciplines jostling for inclusion, and different marginalised perspectives demanding recognition. The call to expand research into the role of languages at war is not a request for special consideration of a neglected minor area of study, but for the recognition of what is undeniably that most elemental of human interactions, communication between individuals.

Multinational deployments, whether as peacekeeping operations or NATO-style war fighting operations, are clearly a feature of twenty-first-century warfare, emphasising the significance of this as an area of future research. The primary significance of language in such coalition operations has been explored, but the contributions in this book by Gabel and Gehrmann emphasise that there is scope to undertake research that considers differences in the underlying cultural structures that encompass the national style of a given military, as well as cross-cultural communication.

A positive and exciting aspect of contemporary research is the adoption of technologies and their adaptation to scholarship and learning, and this is as apparent in the study of language in war as it is in a wide range of other fields. Increasing digitisation and the capacity to interrogate research data computationally allows scholars around the world to access raw materials and primary data in a manner unparalleled by their predecessors. The boundaries of future directions of research on language and wartime are potentially far greater than we perhaps imagine—albeit with the caveat that open scholarship on contemporary conflicts may be less possible in an age where official secrecy continues to place constraints on what can be said. For example, in June 2019, the Australian Federal Police gained worldwide attention when they conducted a raid of the Australian broadcaster ABC's offices, ostensibly on the grounds of verifying the source of a leak of information in relation to possible ADF war crimes in Afghanistan.[10]

Technologies provide greater opportunities to undertake research on contemporary wars, although this will potentially clash with the security requirements of increasingly cautious, nationally-based intelligence structures. The global information age is one where much open-source data is freely accessible, so we will be able to hear the stories of interpreters and those who have worked with them, and to interrogate such sources of information. However, what is positive for academic researchers can be a negative for military practitioners. The legitimate declassification of language-related material is at odds with a world where organisations such as WikiLeaks have the capacity to bring about massive data leaks, and such experiences will make governments increasingly careful about the release of military-related material.

It is also worth remembering that the free and open research which occurs after a conflict takes place with the presumption that future conflict is not imminent, and that the information released about recent conflicts will not create security challenges or compromise existing security and intelligence structures. Lessons were learnt after the First World War when a range of individuals, including the former First Lord of the Admiralty Winston Churchill, openly published about the activities of Room 40, the British cryptographic unit. Despite the presumption that sharing information would not be problematic following the conclusion of the war to end all wars, the exposure of British wartime military intelligence capability was seen as a security breach impacting upon national defence.[11] It is almost certain that the lesson of being too open has been learned, and academic researchers of the future may have to wait decades before gaining access to some aspects of the history of language and communication at war. For example, the nature of intelligence analysis and collection suggests that study of the use of language in signals intelligence will continue to remain relatively closed to scholars.

The immediate post-Cold War era was a time of relative openness during which previously antipathetic or antagonistic governments openly released information about past military practices to each other and to the scholarly community. An emergence of a more globalised culture with greater levels of cross-cultural communication will arguably lead to increasing levels of cosmopolitanism and openness. This process has had economic and social dimensions, and what Kenichi Ohmae called the borderless world[12] has become a reality that shapes academic research. However, the second decade of the twenty-first century may become one where borders and scholarship become closed rather than open. If predictions of a new Cold War between liberal democracies on the one hand and the increasingly authoritarian Russian and Chinese states eventuate, this will further restrict scholars who seek to access the history of recent conflicts.

And what of the future of the interpreter? Increasing technological developments might lead to the replacement of the interpreter, nullifying the role of what has been a constant in human warfare for as long as speakers of different languages have come into conflict. Automatic language translation devices and text-based language conversion have become more widespread, and speech-to-speech translation devices have helped to overcome language barriers. Research has progressed on the use of automatic translation systems in war.[13] Technology is already having an impact on the role of interpreters in a variety of fields.[14] Deployed troops now have the capacity to record speech and transmit this to a home station for analysis.

While it might appear that automatic devices have the capacity to supersede the traditional role of the interpreter in terms of formal conveyance of ideas and statements, as well as interpretation of responses, the critical role of the human being as a language advisor and cultural broker remains. With future conflicts undoubtedly involving some level of continued cross-cultural interaction, it seems more than likely that the traditional role of the interpreter will be adapted; troops may find greater use for pocket translation devices, but language mediators will continue to find a place for themselves in the battle space of the future.

Notes

1. Amanda Laugesen (2012), *'Boredom is the Enemy': The Intellectual and Imaginative Lives of Australian Soldiers in the Great War and Beyond* (Farnham: Ashgate), pp. 2–3. See also Tristan Moss and Tom Richardson (eds) (2018), *Beyond Combat: Australian Military Activity Away from the Battlefield* (Sydney: University of New South Wales Press).
2. Martijn Kitzen and Willem Vogelsang (2016), 'Obtaining Population Centric Intelligence: Experiences of the Netherlands Military Presence

in South Afghanistan', Gerard Lucius and Sebastiaan Rietjens (eds), *Effective Civil-Military Interaction in Peace Operations* (Cham: Springer), pp. 77–88, here p. 86.
3. Terry Burstall (1990), *A Soldier Returns* (St Lucia: University of Queensland Press), p. 7.
4. See for example Willem Vogelsang (1992), *The Rise and Organisation of the Achaemenid Empire: The Eastern Iranian Evidence* (Leiden: Brill); Willem Vogelsang (2002), *The Afghans* (Oxford: Blackwell); Gillian Vogelsang-Eastwood and Willem J. Vogelsang (2008), *Covering the Moon: An Introduction to Middle Eastern Face Veils* (Leuven: Peeters).
5. Craig Mullaney (2009), *The Unforgiving Minute: A Soldier's Education* (New York: The Penguin Press), p. 225.
6. Franziska Heimburger (2013), 'Imagining Coalition Warfare: French and British Military Language Policy before 1914', *Francia*, 40, pp. 397–408, here p. 402.
7. Kayla Williams (2005), *Love My Rifle More Than You: Young and Female in the US Army* (London: W. W. Norton & Company).
8. Catherine Baker (2010), 'It's Not Their Job to Soldier: Distinguishing Civilian and Military in Soldiers' and Interpreters' Accounts of Peacekeeping in 1990s Bosnia-Herzegovina', *Journal of War & Culture Studies*, 3:1, pp. 137–50.
9. Hilary Footitt and Michael Kelly (2012), 'Introduction', in Hilary Footitt and Michael Kelly (eds), *Languages at War: Policies and Practices of Language Contacts in Conflict* (Houndmills: Palgrave Macmillan), pp. 1–15, here p. 2.
10. The leak had already been identified as coming from David McBride, a former military lawyer. He is currently charged with several offences, including breaching the Defence Act and theft of Commonwealth property. See 'Afghan Files Leak Accused David McBride Faces ACT Supreme Court for First Time', *ABC News*, 14 June 2019, https://www.abc.net.au/news/2019-06-13/abc-raids-afghan-files-leak-accused-court-canberra/11206682
11. Rhodri Jeffreys-Jones (2018), 'The Sensitivity of SIGINT: Sir Alfred Ewing's Lecture on Room 40 in 1927', *Journal of Intelligence History*, 17:1, pp. 18–29, here pp. 22, 27.
12. Kenichi Ohmae (1995), *The End of the Nation State: The Rise of Regional Economies* (New York: Simon and Schuster).

13. Vincent Rafael (2012), 'Targeting Translation: Counterinsurgency and the Weaponization of Language', *Social Text*, 30:4, pp. 55–80.
14. See for example Henry Liu (2018), 'Help or Hinder? The Impact of Technology on the Role of Interpreters', *FITISPos International Journal*, 5:1, pp. 13–32.

Index[1]

A

Aceh, 207–219
ADF, *see* Australian Defence Force
Afghanistan, war in, 45, 46, 50, 64
American military language, 52, 55–56
Arabic, 7, 13, 14, 29–31, 33, 36–38, 47–49, 56, 61, 98, 192, 241
Australian Defence Force (ADF), 15, 16, 48, 49, 59, 60, 103, 207–219, 223–249, 262
Australian English, 36, 38, 39

C

Cross-cultural communication, 4, 13, 14, 17–19, 25–39, 45–64, 183, 207, 211, 214, 217, 255–264
Cultural knowledge, 13, 131, 227, 257

D

Dari, 49, 106
Dutch army, 47, 57–60, 62, 256
Dutch military culture, 58–60

---

[1] Note: Page numbers followed by 'n' refer to notes.

E

East Timor, 15, 49, 55, 209–214

F

First AIF, 15, 27, 31
First World War, 6, 7, 15–17, 25–39, 45, 55, 74, 75, 77, 79, 83, 84, 215, 258, 263
French language, 7, 38

G

German language, 31, 32, 136, 179
German Wehrmacht, 145

I

International Criminal Court (ICC), 171, 173, 174, 178, 186, 187, 189–191, 193, 194, 196
International Security Assistance Force (ISAF), 56, 61, 62, 109–124
Interpreting, 3–19, 32, 47, 95, 98–103, 107, 119, 154–163, 171–197, 217–219, 226, 227, 239, 241, 242, 245, 260, 261
Iraqi (language), 223–249
ISAF, *see* International Security Assistance Force

J

Japanese language, 10, 11, 16, 73–85, 154, 156, 176, 185

L

Language learning, 7, 27–30, 39, 76, 98, 108
Language teaching, 16, 18, 73, 74, 76, 78, 84, 85, 98, 258–259

M

Military jargon, 178

P

Pashtun, 47, 49, 56
Prisoners of war, 6, 30, 31, 141, 142, 154, 155, 169n53
Profanity, 53

R

Russian emigrés, 132, 134, 135, 140–142
Russian language, 134

S

Second Iraq War, 15, 17
Second World War, 7–10, 15, 16, 31, 38, 50, 57, 74, 75, 78, 79, 82–85, 109, 116, 117, 144, 153, 173–174, 177–185, 215, 259
Simultaneous interpreting (SI), 173, 174, 178, 179, 186, 189, 190

T

Translating, 7, 10, 13, 14, 32, 37, 77, 95, 99, 156, 157, 176, 188, 209, 239

U

US army, 12, 158, 238

W

War crimes, 153, 155, 163, 173, 174, 177, 181, 186, 187, 196, 261, 262

War-crimes trials, 4, 11, 16, 19, 153–163, 171–196, 256, 260, 261

War on Terror, 17, 45–64, 109

Women, 30, 34, 54, 75, 77, 104, 105, 141, 143, 155, 165n11, 234

Printed by Printforce, the Netherlands